IMAGES
of America

SAN FRANCISCO'S AQUATIC PARK

IMAGES
of America

SAN FRANCISCO'S AQUATIC PARK

Bill Pickelhaupt

ARCADIA
PUBLISHING

ISBN 978-0-7385-3084-0

Published by Arcadia Publishing
Charleston, South Carolina

Printed in the United States of America

Library of Congress Control Number: 2005933424

For all general information, please contact Arcadia Publishing:
Telephone 843-853-2070
Fax 843-853-0044
E-mail sales@arcadiapublishing.com
For customer service and orders:
Toll-Free 1-888-313-2665

Visit us on the Internet at www.arcadiapublishing.com

This book is dedicated to my mother, Joyce Pickelhaupt.

Contents

ACKNOWLEDGMENTS

I would like to give a warm acknowledgment to Bill Kooiman and David Hull of the San Francisco Maritime Museum for their help over the years with my various projects. My work started with them.

Special recognition goes to Nancy Olmsted, a woman of unparalleled intelligence who taught me how to pull a mass of material together.

Shirley Coleman gave me a collection of her family photographs that show how her father and his friends played in Black Point Cove nearly 100 years ago. That treasure greatly enriches this book.

Susan Goldstein, Pat Akre, Susie Taylor, Andrea Grimes, and Tom Carey (also known as the gang at the San Francisco History Room of the Main Library) have become my family over the last decade. Thanks for the generosity with your time.

INTRODUCTION

San Francisco's Aquatic Park is unique in San Francisco as one of the city's very few underappreciated spots of great beauty. Located just to the west of the hustle and bustle of Fisherman's Wharf, Aquatic Park's daytime serenity is surpassed only by the thrilling glitter of Tiburon and Belvedere's lights, reflected in San Francisco Bay as one stands on the Promenade of the park at night. An even better view of the bay from Marin and Contra Costa counties can be gained from Muni Pier. The people of San Francisco and the Bay Area in general were almost robbed of this wonderful park, as the conflict between development and recreation raged for more than a century in the little cove.

Known as Black Point Cove because of the dark shade of the trees in Fort Mason (the cove's westerly boundary), the location was isolated from the settlement of Yerba Buena and Mission Dolores during the gold rush. Even as these settlements became San Francisco in the 1850s and 1860s, Black Point Cove was considered remote enough to allow establishment of the Pioneer Woolen Mills and the Selby Smelter, and far enough away from the reach of the law to host several highly illegal bare-knuckle boxing matches in post–Civil War San Francisco. Yet the commercial interests shared the cove with a hearty breed: swimmers flocked to the shores of Black Point Cove, and many small swim houses catered to the needs of these men and women, boys and girls.

The San Francisco *Daily Alta* noted in 1869 that a man named William Lenz had drowned while swimming from "Charley's" swim house in the cove and that the cove had been a popular beach for those fond of saltwater swimming "for a long time." Around 1867, Carleton Watkins took a stereoview of a group of four young boys, naked as the day they were born, letting the surf break over their feet, as the boldest among them moves hesitantly into the chilly water (even after a long warm spell in summer, the temperature of the bay usually does not exceed 65 degrees Fahrenheit). The most famous victim of the waters of Black Point Cove was banker William C. Ralston, who perished in the cove on a line with Tonquin Street the day he lost control of and was booted out of the Bank of California.

The little swim houses and woolen mill fell into decline as the 1880s came to an end, but the decision of the Dolphin Swimming and Boat Club to move from the foot of Montgomery Street (now known as Columbus Avenue) to build a new boathouse at the foot of Van Ness Avenue held enormous importance for Black Point Cove. Even though the contemporary Sanborn Insurance Map described Van Ness Avenue as "impassible by (horse) teams," visionaries at the club saw a water park for the recreation of the citizens of San Francisco. In 1908, the Dolphins were joined by the South End Rowing Club and the Ariel Rowing Club, both driven from a short stay in Central Basin (near Mission Rock at the foot of Sixteenth Street) by the State Board of Harbor Commissioners. San Francisco's development interests, particularly along the waterfront, saw the catastrophe of the 1906 earthquake and fire as a great opportunity to fill in shallow parts of the waterfront. After Long Bridge and Mission Bay (the north side of which would be where

Pac Bell Park is now situated) were filled in and disappeared forever, the northern waterfront next fell in the sights of developers.

The State Belt Line Railroad was built across the cove in 1913, and the clubs had to continually fight to prevent the Harbor Commissioners from dumping the borings from the Fort Mason Tunnel in front of the docks of the clubs. If the clubs' access to the water were cut off, that would be the death knell of the clubs and public access to the cove. The harbor commissioners went so far as to remove part of the South End dock at one juncture.

Ed Scully, a South End member since the early 1890s, led a fight to protect the site as a park and to get the San Francisco Board of Supervisors to commit the city to conversion of the cove to an aquatic park. Scully and others forged an alliance with organizations interested in public health, welfare, and recreation. Old-time South Ender John L. Herget, a member of the board of supervisors and well-known as "Young Mitchell" from his days as a championship boxer, helped on the political front. Beginning in 1909, the clubs held a series of Aquatic Park Days to publicize successive ballot propositions to finance park construction. (Several striking photographs survive from these events). Although all ballot measures fell short of the two-thirds approval needed for passage, the board of supervisors, in 1918, went on record in favor of an aquatic park for the citizens of San Francisco. The city spent the next decade acquiring the property necessary for the park. Then the Great Depression hit.

The city was able to build Municipal Pier (known as Muni Pier) in 1931, but funds ran out. The State of California did some work in 1932 and 1933, but also lacked the funds to carry the project through to completion. The federal government took on the construction of Aquatic Park as a Works Progress Administration (WPA) project in late 1935. We not only have the park, but posterity also benefits from the fact that the WPA had a photographer come through the park nearly every month from 1936 to 1938 to provide a graphic record of progress on construction.

What is now the Maritime Museum Building was intended to be the home of the Dolphin, South End, and Ariel clubs. The South Enders did not like the building, because there were no handball courts; Dolphin Club members wanted their own clubhouse. The streamline Moderne building, with its Benny Bufano murals, basically sat empty until Karl Kortum, a chicken farmer from Petaluma, approached the board of supervisors with the notion of a Maritime Museum for San Francisco, and the Aquatic Park building as the museum. Alma Spreckels was Kortum's financial backer.

Kortum brought several vessels into the park, but the situation came to a head in 1953, when the *Fort Sutter,* an old riverboat that had made the run from Sacramento to San Francisco, was brought into the cove by Kortum associate Barney Gould. The intent of Kortum and Gould was to turn the decrepit hulk into a "high-tone" restaurant, bar, and gambling casino. The hulk was run up on the beach right next to the eastern comfort station. The rowing clubs, just next door and dwarfed by the decayed vessel, complained on numerous counts, and the old tub was moved to the western side of the park in late 1953. It sat there and decayed even further over the next six years. Finally, a group of four young men, rumored to be South End Rowing Club members, doused the deck with gasoline and set the tub ablaze. It is said the flames could be seen from Berkeley.

One

Black Point Cove
Woolen Mills and Swim Houses

Black Point Cove was indeed far from the village of Yerba Buena and Mission Dolores. Yet early settlers built small houses and businesses on the sandy beach of the cove by 1850 or earlier. In the 1850s, waters of San Francisco Bay lapped the shore of Black Point Cove near the present North Point Street. The Pioneer Woolen Mills was constructed in 1858 in the cove to supply the needs of San Francisco's burgeoning population.

A dire necessity for the growth of San Francisco—for any city—is fresh water. Fresh water had been transported from Sausalito for use by city residents or came from Mountain Lake in the earliest days, but by the mid-1850s, a redwood flume ran from Lobos Creek around the base of Fort Mason, to a pumping station at the foot of Van Ness Avenue. Operated by the Spring Valley Water Company, the station pumped water to a reservoir part way up Hyde Street Hill.

From the 1850s, swim houses shared the cove with these industrial establishments. In the late-1860s, much of the sand that formed the lower portion of what is now Hyde Street was carried off to form fill around the city. The newly flattened area became home to the Selby Smelter, a venture of a San Francisco mayor.

As the 1800s wore on, the Pioneer Woolen Mills closed, unable to compete with more efficient Eastern mills. The transcontinental railroad drastically dropped freight prices, and even though the Pioneer Woolen Mills utilized underpaid Chinese labor, they could not survive. In 1895, the Dolphin Club moved from the area east of Hyde Street, known as "Bilge Water Cove," to a newly built boathouse. Swimming, with the addition of boating, was about to be reborn in Black Point Cove.

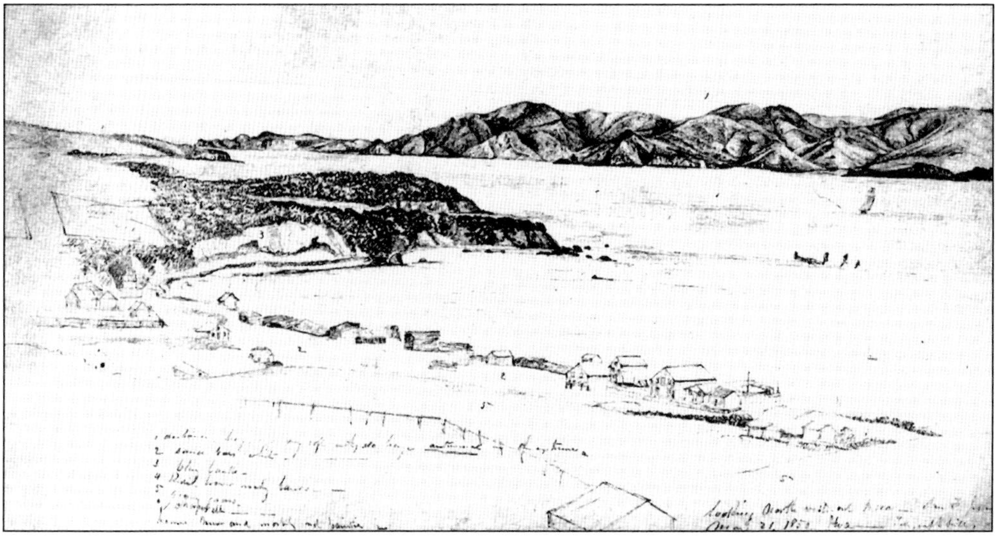

Three months before California became a state, on May 21, 1850, James Audubon completed this amazing sketch of Black Point Cove. Twenty-four buildings, some no more than huts, lined the shore, which Audubon notes is "sand bar white." It appears the redwood flume runs along the shore of Fort Mason, which is described as having blue banks. Another remarkable feature is the wreck of the ship *Tonquin*. The *Tonquin* ran aground on a sand spit off Black Point Cove, and the tops of its three masts are clearly visible in the center right of this drawing. The *Tonquin* gave its name to Tonquin Street, which runs on a line off the stern of the *Thayer* at Hyde Street Pier. That point is about where William C. Ralston drowned in August 1875.

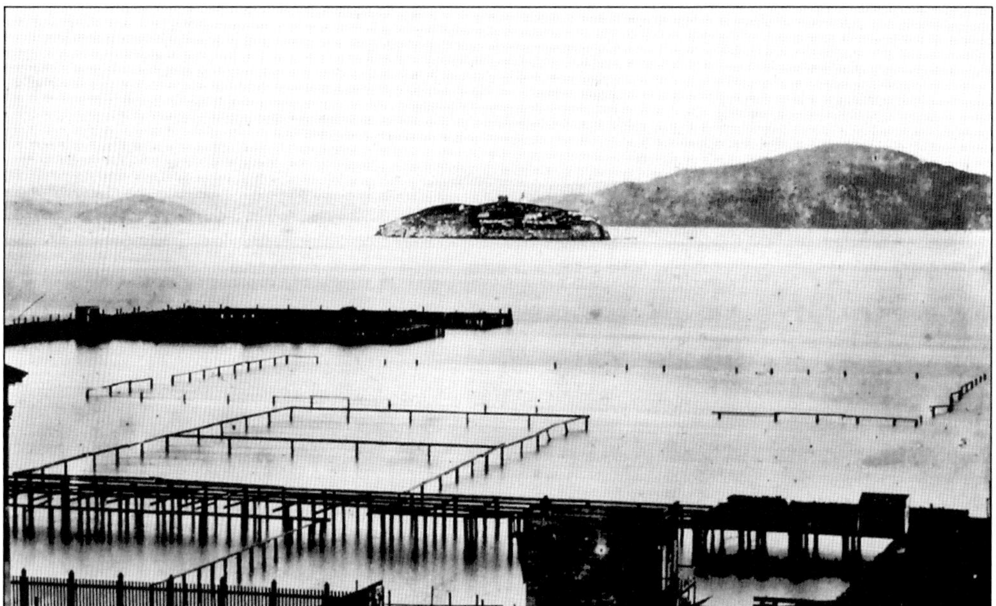

Water lots, staked out at Meiggs Wharf (Pier 39), were sold throughout the 19th century to be developed for use as piers, warehouses, businesses, or residences. Near Black Point Cove, the area from North Point and Bay Streets, has been filled in down to Jefferson.

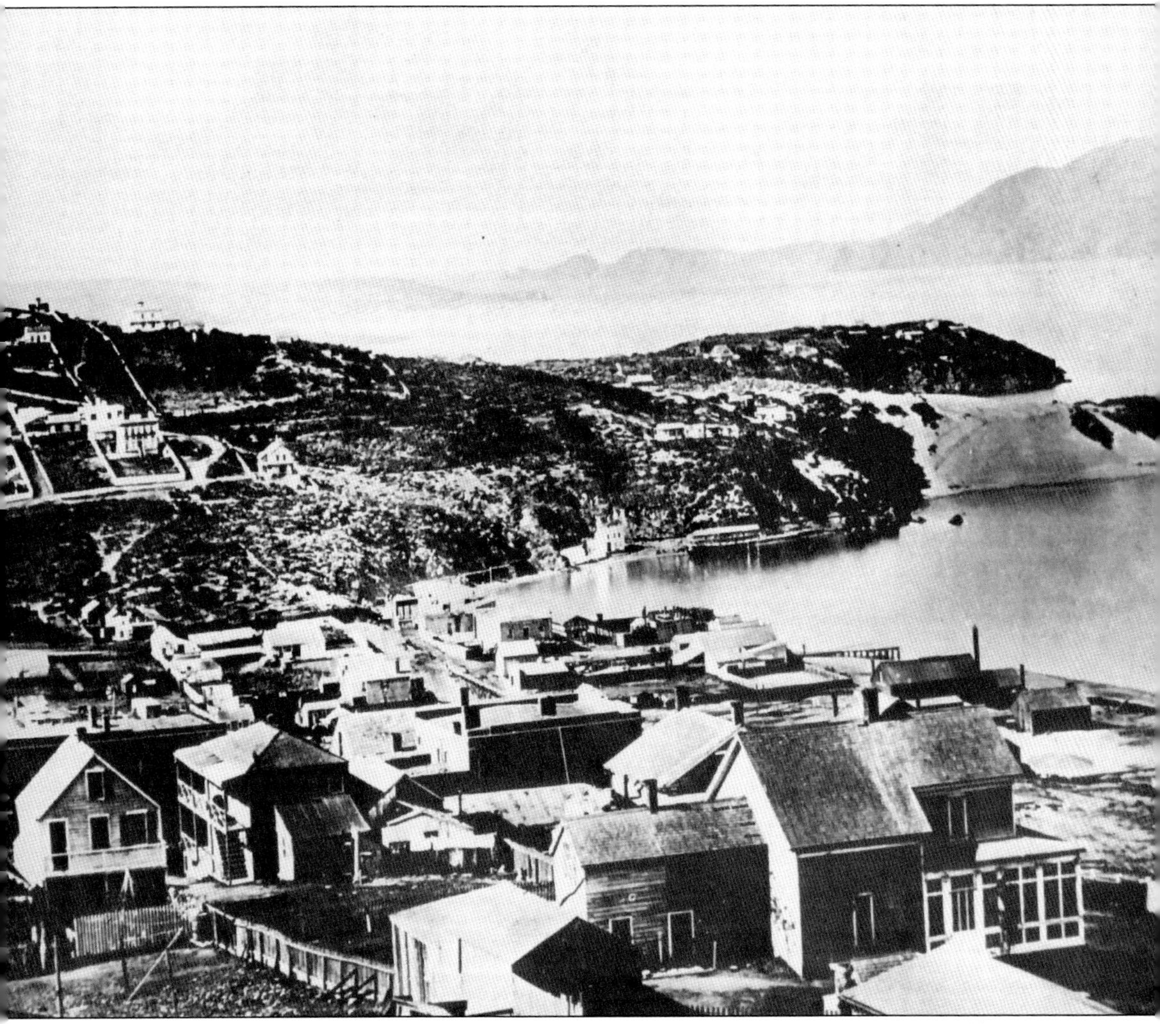

This 1850s view was taken looking from Telegraph Hill to Black Point Cove, the Golden Gate, and Marin County. The large, sandy hill in the center right of the picture is Hyde Street Hill, with Black Point just beyond. The prison ship *Euphemia* is pictured here on the near side of Hyde Street Hill, on shore just right of center. San Francisco had difficulties raising the funds to get a secure jail built in the 1850s, so escapes were fairly common. The *Euphemia* provided a bit more security.

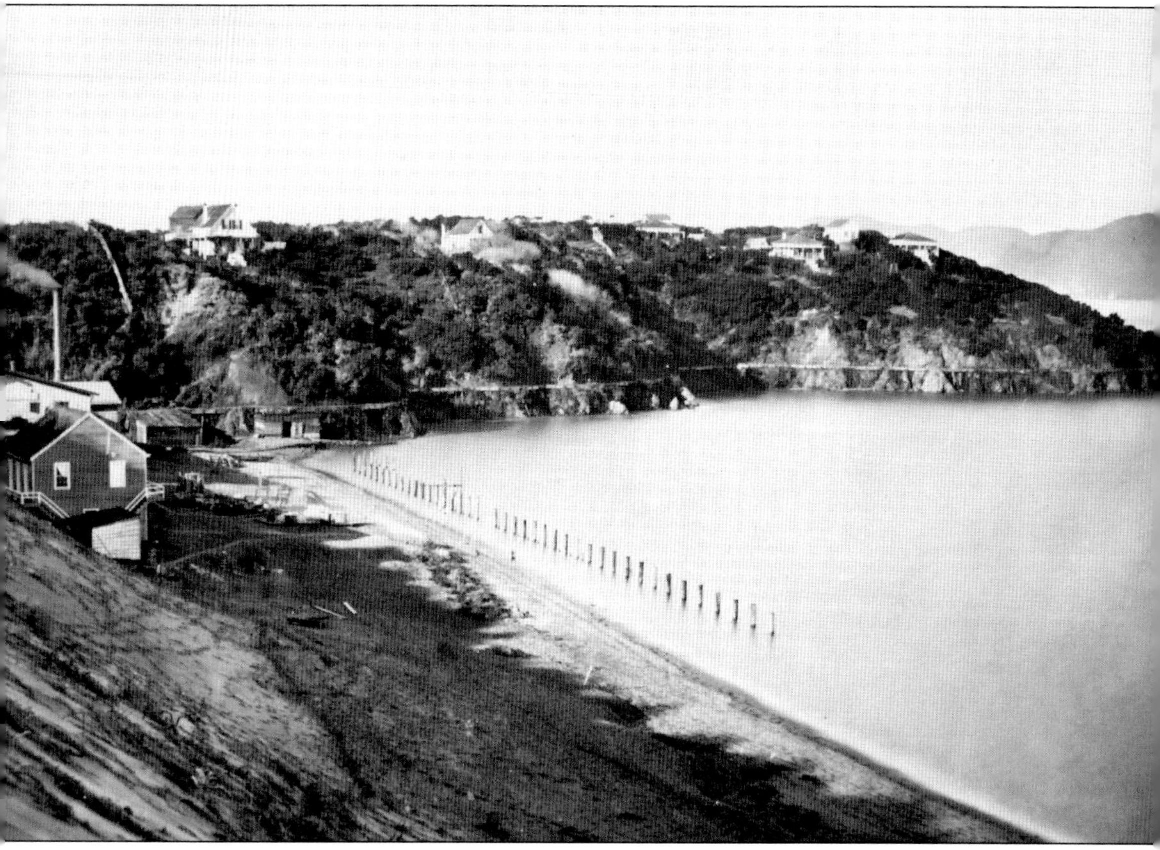

In this photograph of Black Point Cove in 1858, the redwood flume along the base of Black Point is clearly visible. Pilings run the length of the woolen mills to prevent ships and lighters from running aground as they loaded, unloaded, or tied up.

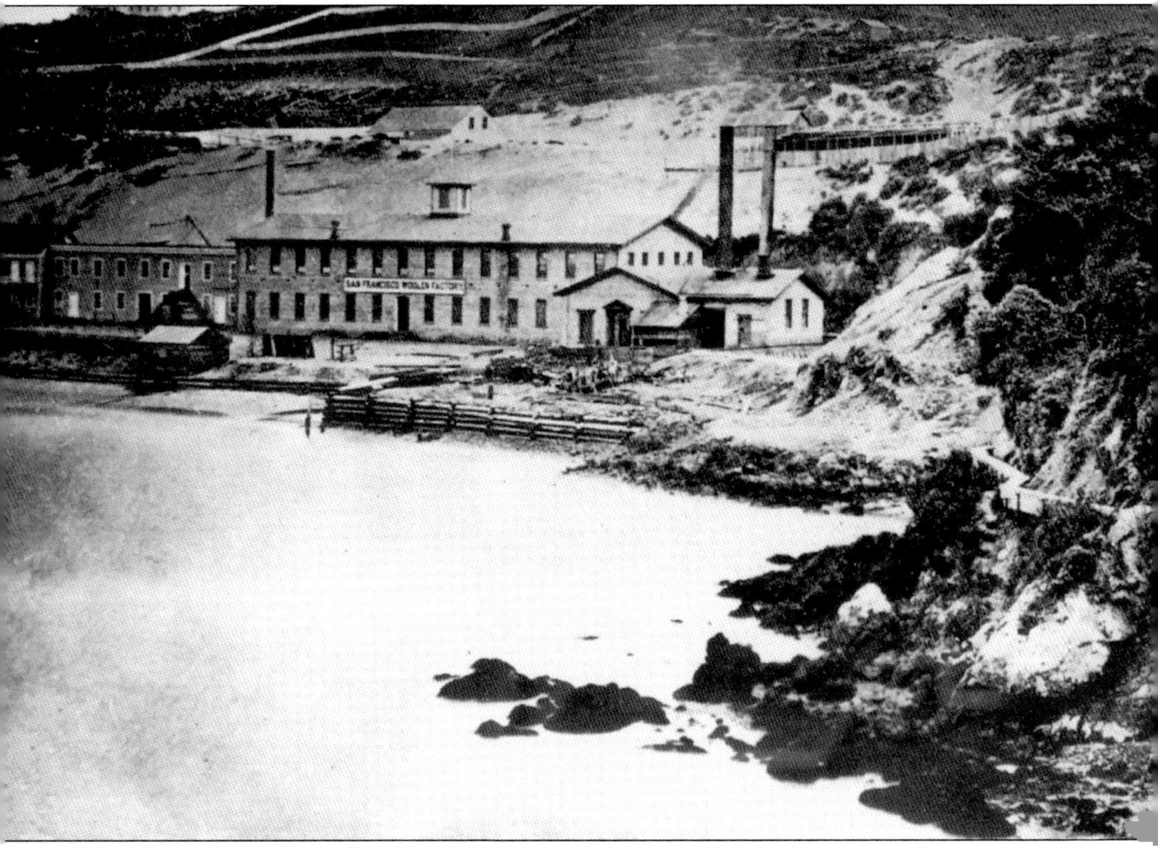

This photograph taken a few years later shows a little more development along the west end of the cove. A retaining wall has been built, and the area looks more groomed.

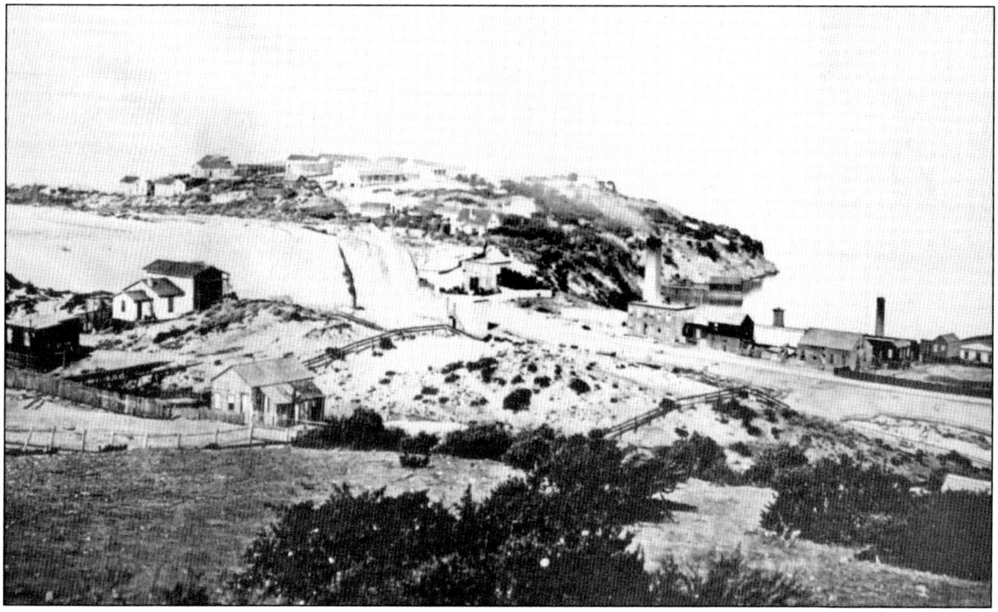

In 1862, Bay Street makes its way to Fort Mason. The Pioneer Woolen Mills has a more permanent look, and there is a government wharf with a covered building visible just to the right of the larger smokestack.

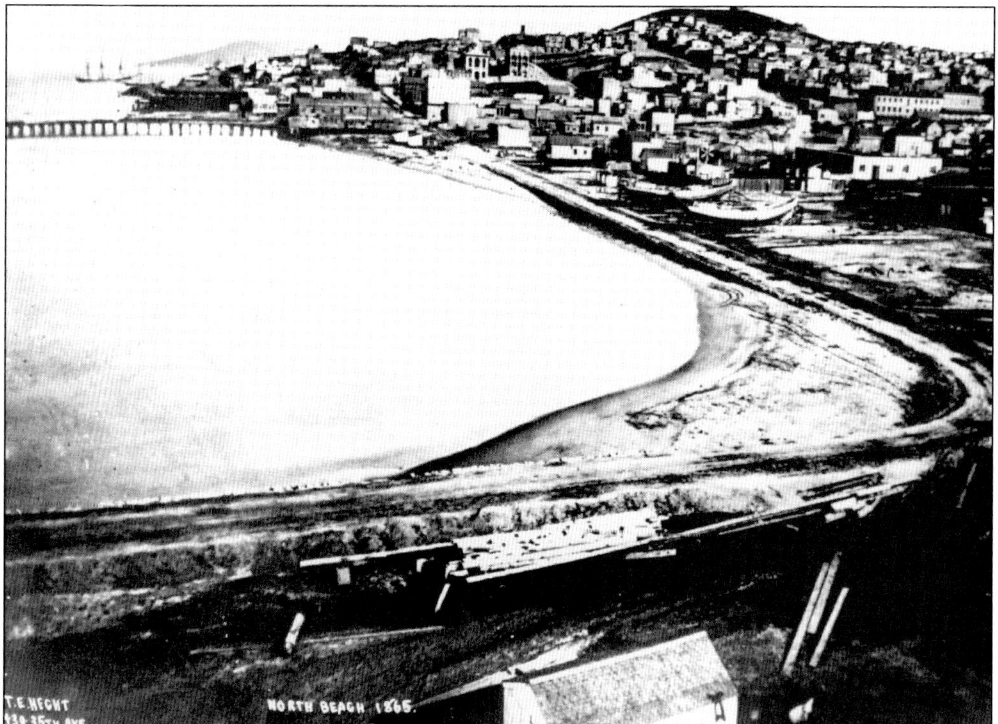

A toll road ran along the shore east of Black Point in what was then referred to as North Beach. In this 1865 photograph, large vessels are under construction in the foreground in what was considered a remote area of the city. Meiggs Wharf is in the background.

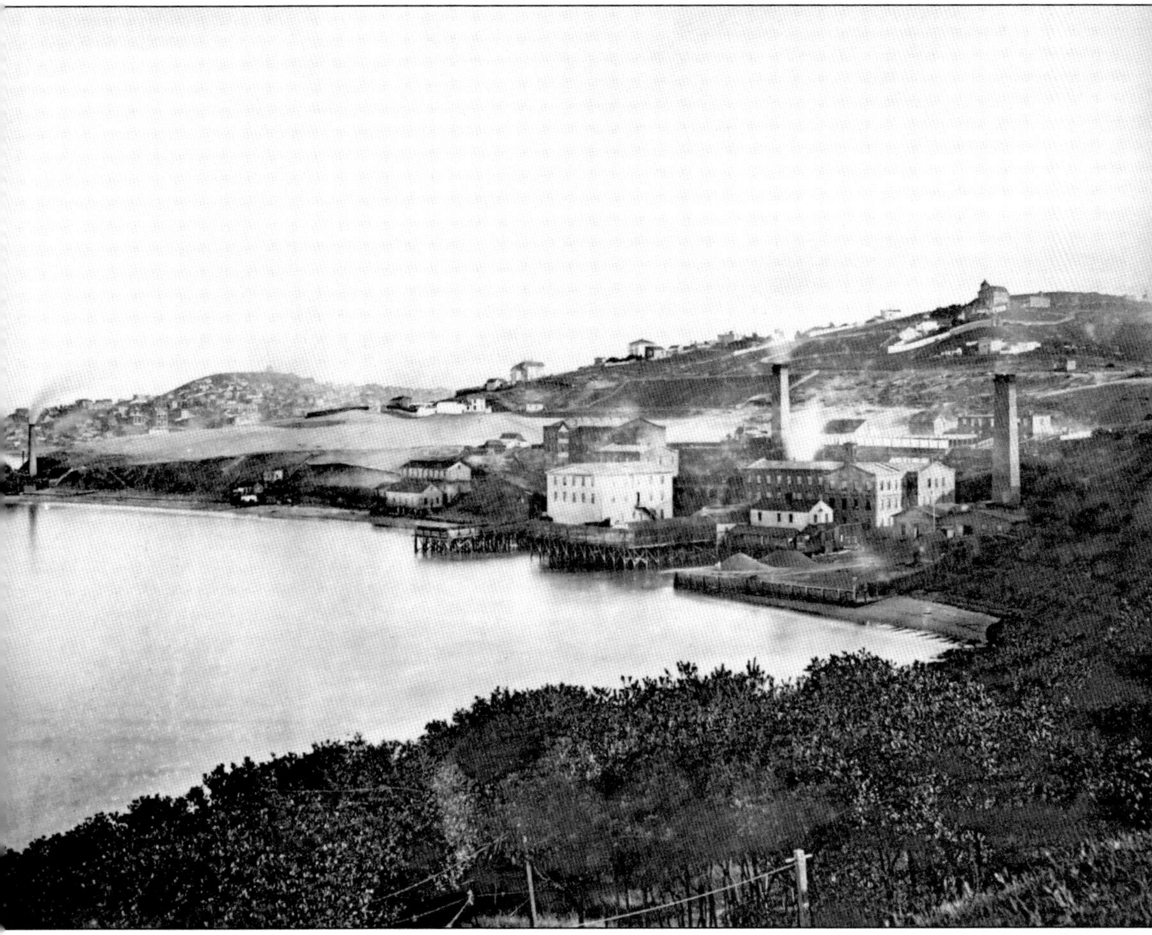

In the 1870s, Hyde Street Hill had been largely carted off near the cove. On the left side, Selby's Smelter belches smoke, while the Pioneer Woolen Mills are to the right. The Neptune Baths are to the left of the woolen mills in the foreground.

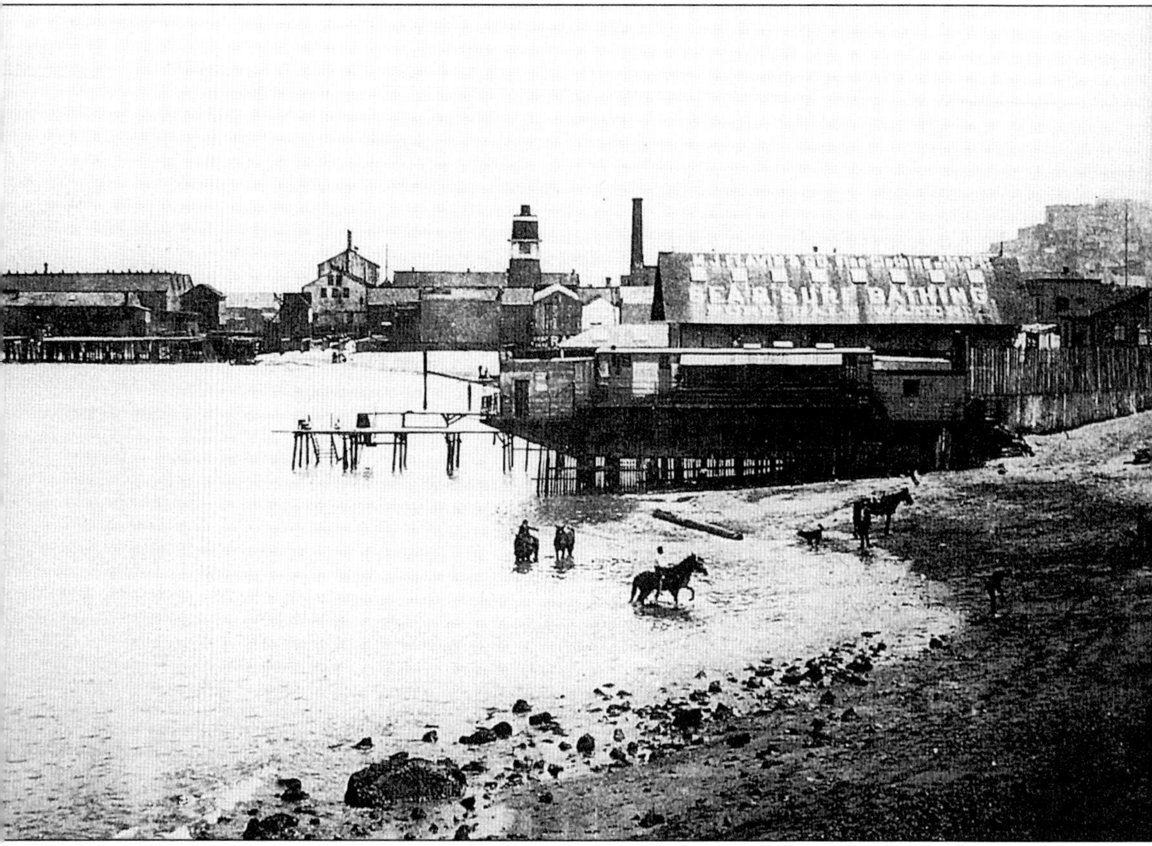

In this rare close-up of a swim house, M. J. Flaven's Fine Clothing shares billing with the Sea and Surf Bathing house in the rooftop advertisement. The stairs from the changing area and dock to the water are clearly visible, while men, horses, and a dog play on the shore.

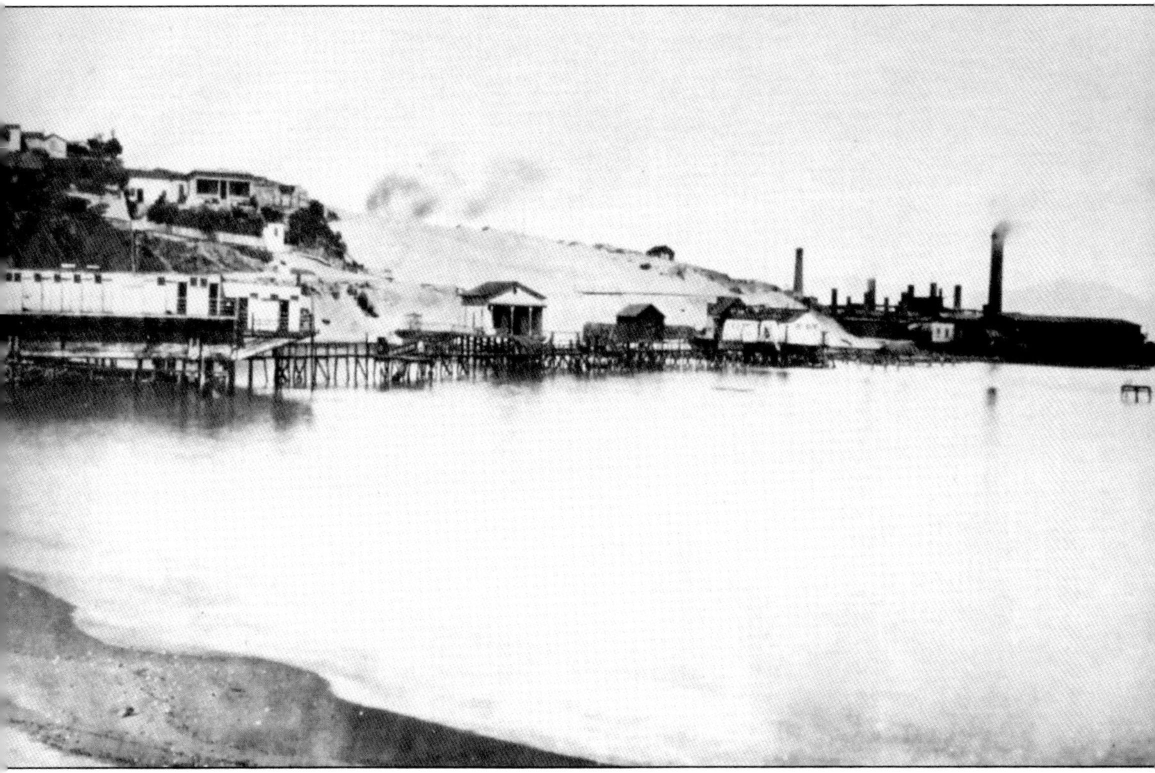

Flanked by swim houses on either side and with the Selby Smelter in the background, the Dolphin Club (with columns at the entrance) sits at the foot of what is now Columbus Avenue. Founded in 1877 by 25 men, mainly of German extraction, the Dolphin Club was more noted for its swimmers than its rowers.

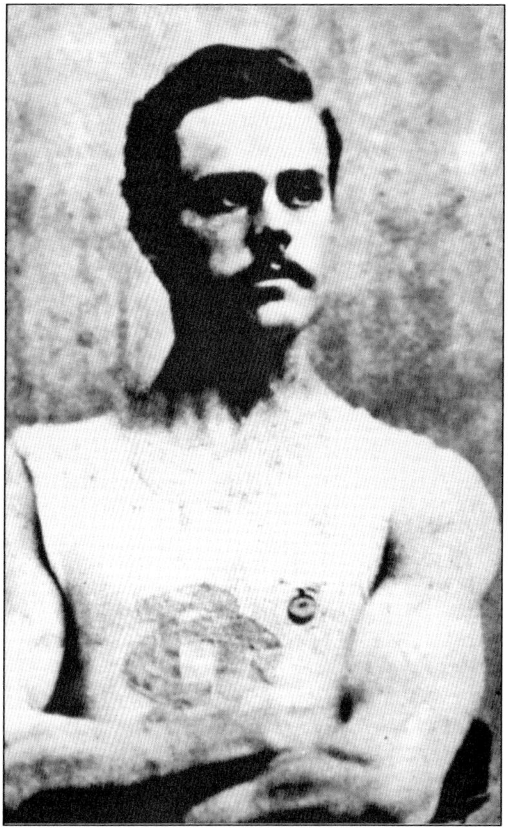

Emil Kehrlein is pictured after a Dolphin Club rowing victory in 1879. Emil and his brother Valentin Jr. were founding members of the Dolphin Club. Emil became involved in various forms of the entertainment scene in San Francisco: he had an opera house built and ran a string of movie houses during World War I. He was reportedly the first to accompany silent movies with music. He is most well-known for his interest in the Hotel Nymphia, the largest brothel in San Francisco at the beginning of the 20th century. He and his partners wanted to call the business the Hotel Nymphomania and populate it with females of that persuasion, but even the very liberal San Francisco Police Commission could not approve that name, so it was shortened to the Nymphia.

David Crowley Sr. "hooks on" to the British ship *Marlborough Hill.* A boatman used a 10- or 12-foot hook to allow him to climb up the side of the ship, while a boat boy kept the small boat upright and kept it from being smashed to pieces by the sides of the large ship.

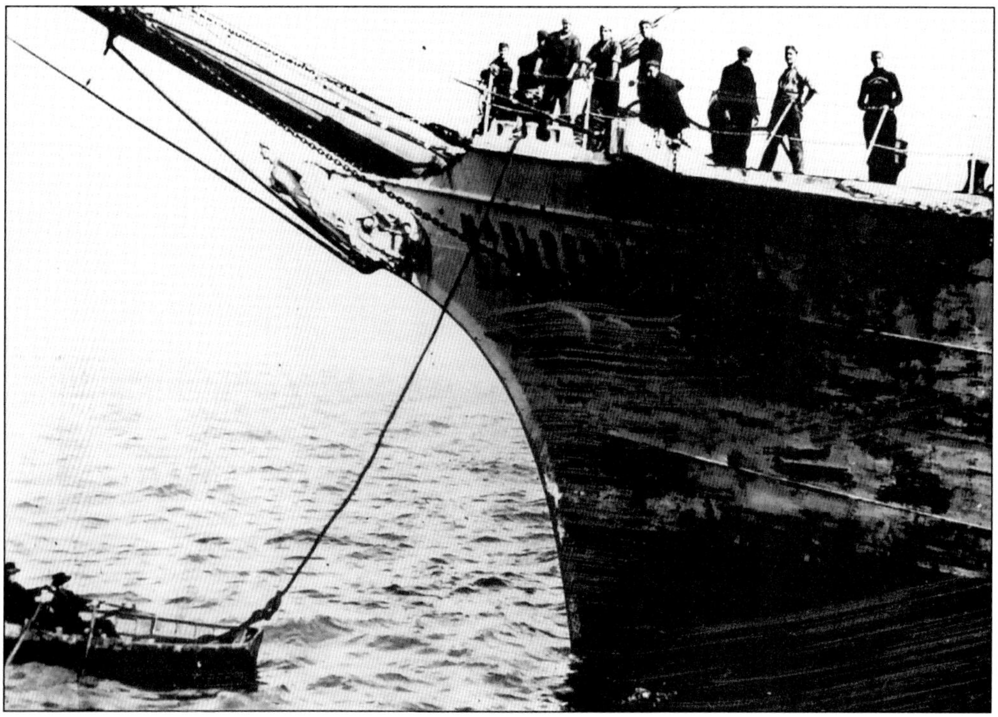

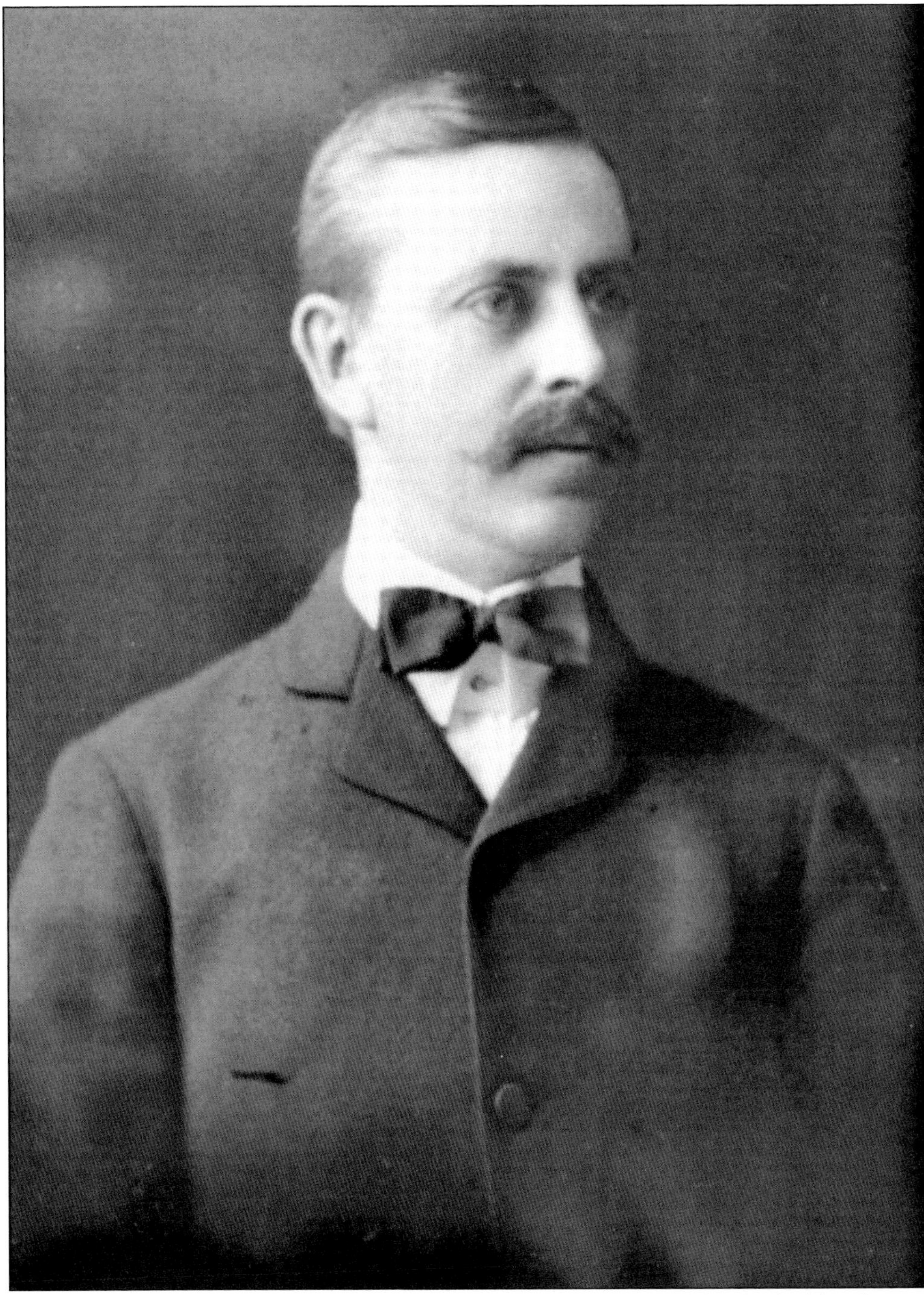

Valentin Kehrlein Jr. did not suffer the bad press his brother Emil did, but he had his share of problems. In the late 1890s, the Dolphin Club expelled the brothers due to their affiliation with Hotel Nymphia and various infractions, so they started the Triton Rowing Club. Located in the small triangle of land formed by the intersection of Columbus, Beach, and Leavenworth, the city had its revenge for the Nymphia when it filled in the water around the Triton Club in 1903 and denied them access to the bay.

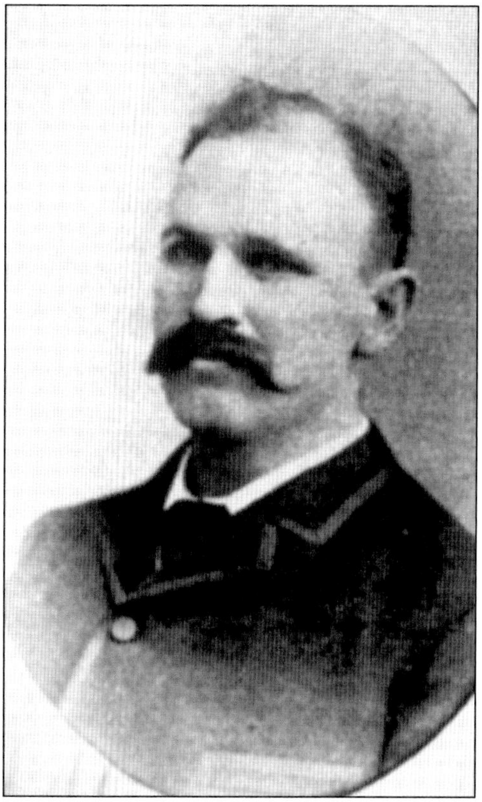

John T. Sullivan was an active member of the Pioneer Rowing Club and owned a shoe store near Powell and Market Streets. The business of Caucasian shoe and cigar makers suffered as lower-paid Chinese dominated the businesses in the 1870s. Sullivan became involved in politics and was part of Chris "Blind Boss" Buckley's board of supervisors in the early 1880s. The board was notorious for its corruption, and Buckley fled to Canada to avoid prosecution.

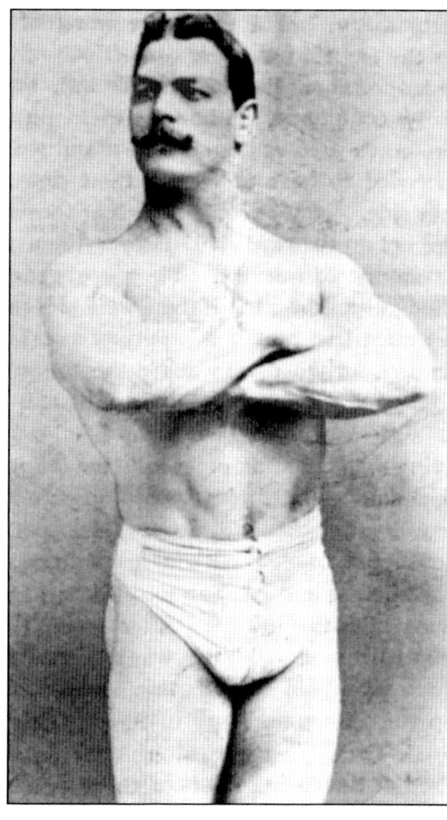

Prof. George Miehling was a Dolphin Club swimmer and gained fame as a wrestler. The title "professor" was frequently taken on by managers of boxers or wrestlers, or men who wanted to train those interested in such occupations, to convey the superior knowledge the manager possessed. Miehling's talent was highly enough regarded that he was employed by the Olympic Club as a trainer.

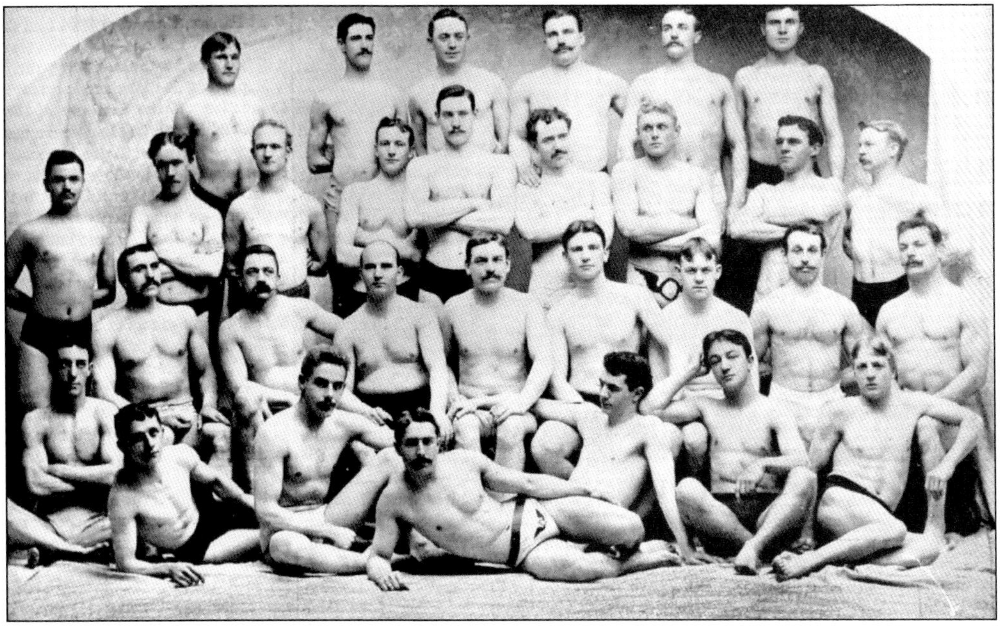

Members of the Olympic Club swim team are pictured in 1893. George Miehling is in the second row, last person to the right. The most famous Dolphin Club rower of the 1890s, Alex Pape, is in the third row, third man from the right, with a distinctive winged "O" on his swim trunks.

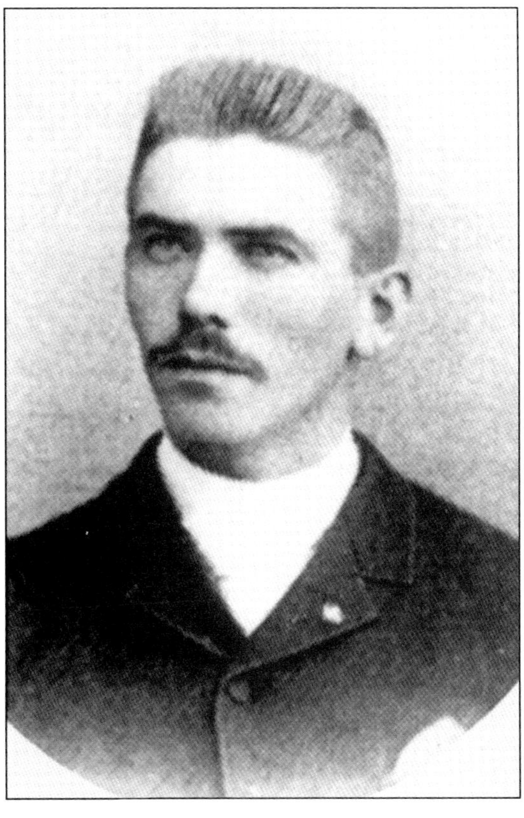

C. C. Stutz, a Dolphin Club member, ran a butcher shop in the midst of the sailors' boardinghouses. His runner was John "Jack the Ripper" Barr.

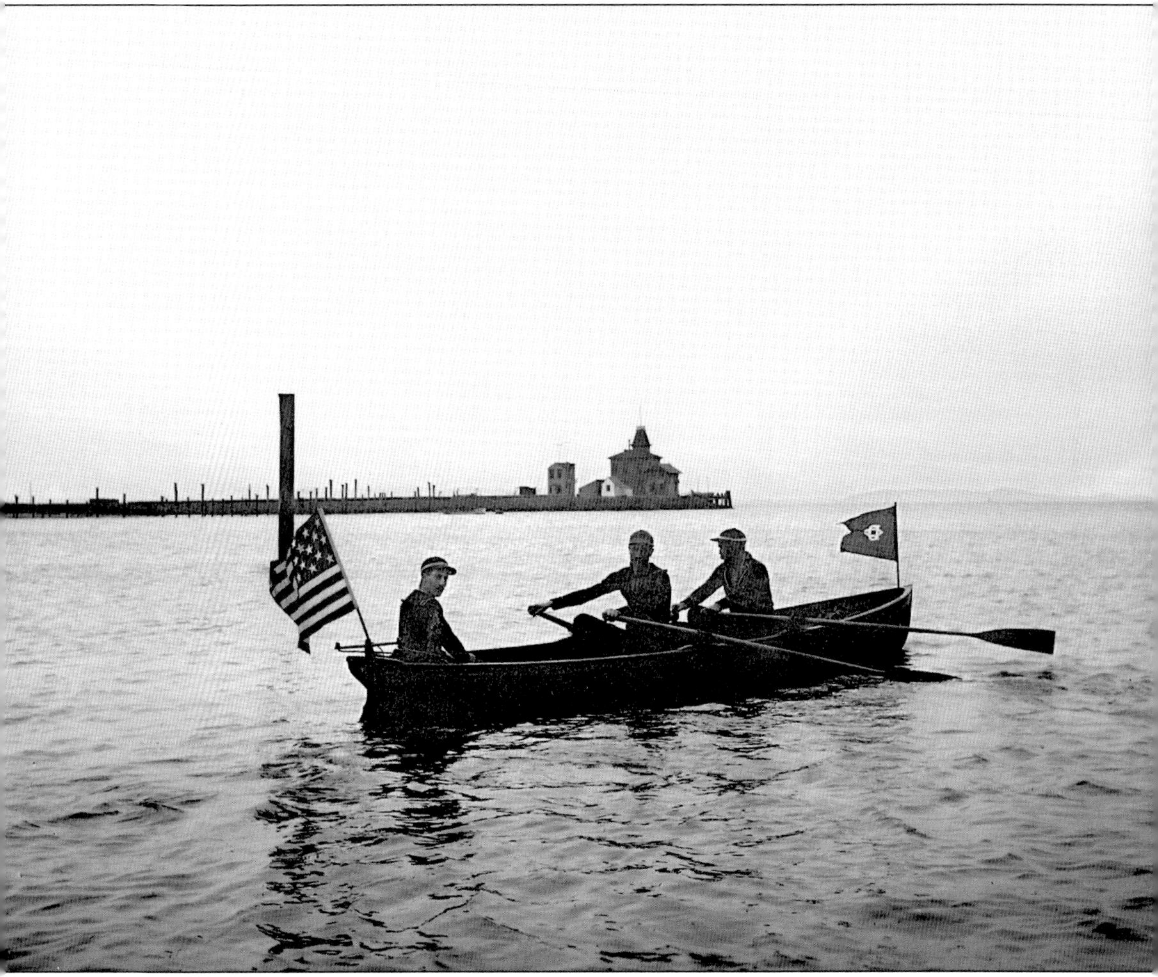

Three Dolphin Club rowers take a club Whitehall for a spin around Meiggs Wharf in 1894. The man on the left does not row, but he is not just along for the ride. He is the coxswain, responsible for control of the rudder, which steers the boat.

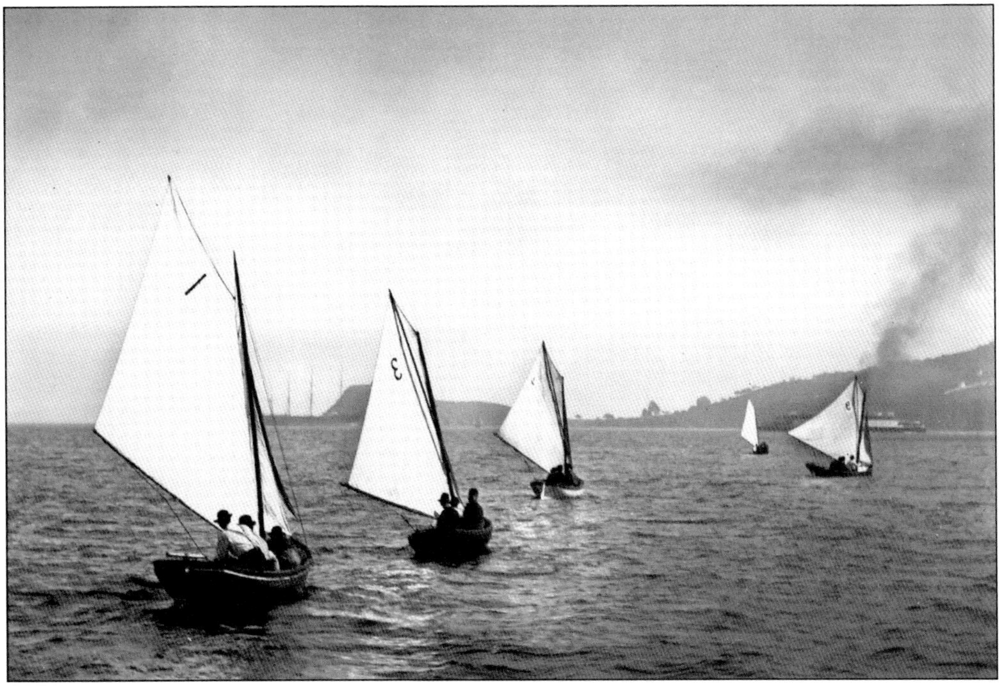

A Whitehall sailing race in the 1880s was an extremely competitive affair. The city of San Francisco sponsored Whitehall races during the 1880s and 1890s on the Fourth of July, and the participants were drawn from the ranks of the shanghaiers of the city's waterfront and their runners. The boats carried names of Irish politicians or figures from Celtic or Nordic mythology.

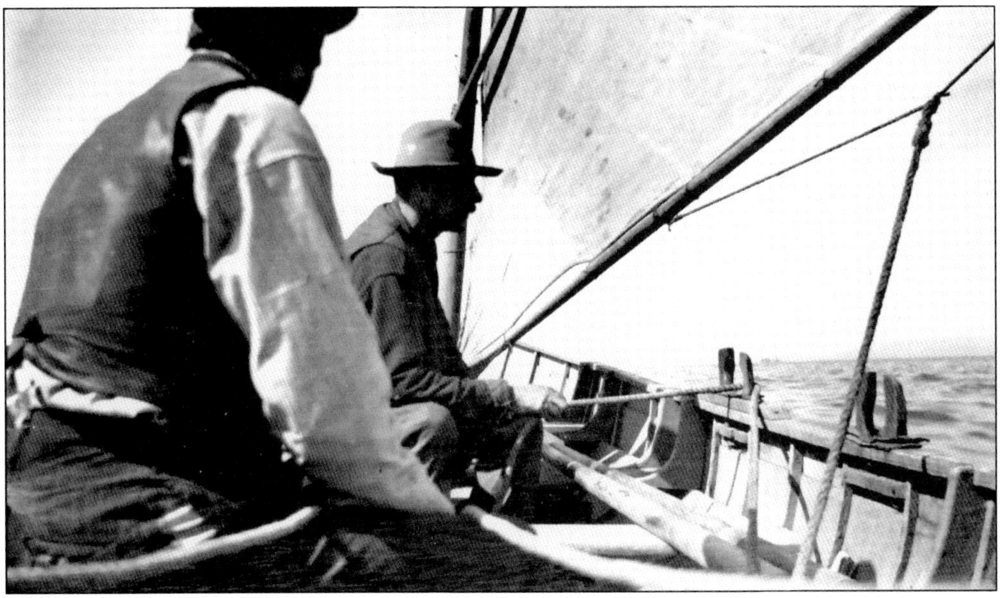

In the 1890s, the Desmond brothers sail their Whitehall east of Meiggs Wharf. The thole pins on the gunwale of the boat usually served to position the oars, but today the oars are stowed and a line is run through a set of the tholes to control the sail. A sail saved a tremendous amount of effort for boatmen, if the wind was adequate, and the boat faced a struggle against a strong flood tide and west wind coming up to Meiggs Wharf (now Pier 39).

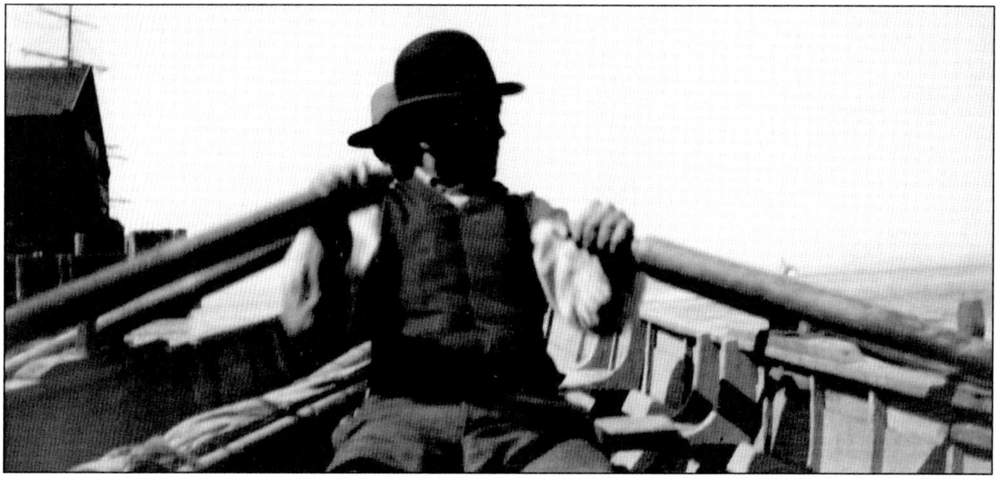

With sail down and oars back in position, the Desmonds go about their business. At one time, they were boatmen for a Chinese laundry.

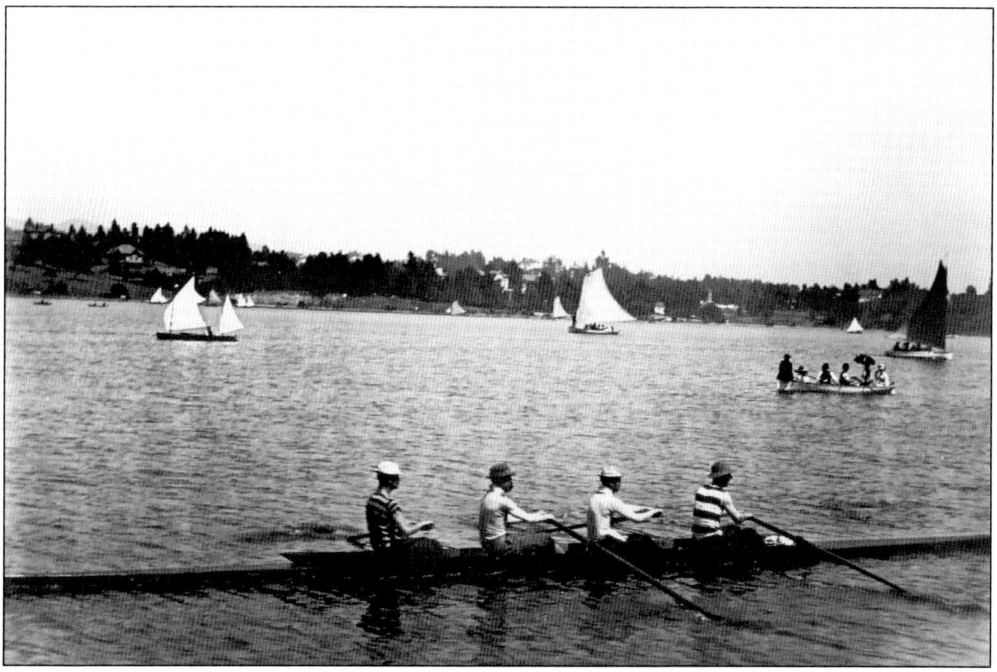

Another hotbed of rowing and sailing was Lake Merritt in Oakland. The ladies and gentlemen in this photograph are purely out for recreational purposes and enjoyment of the lake.

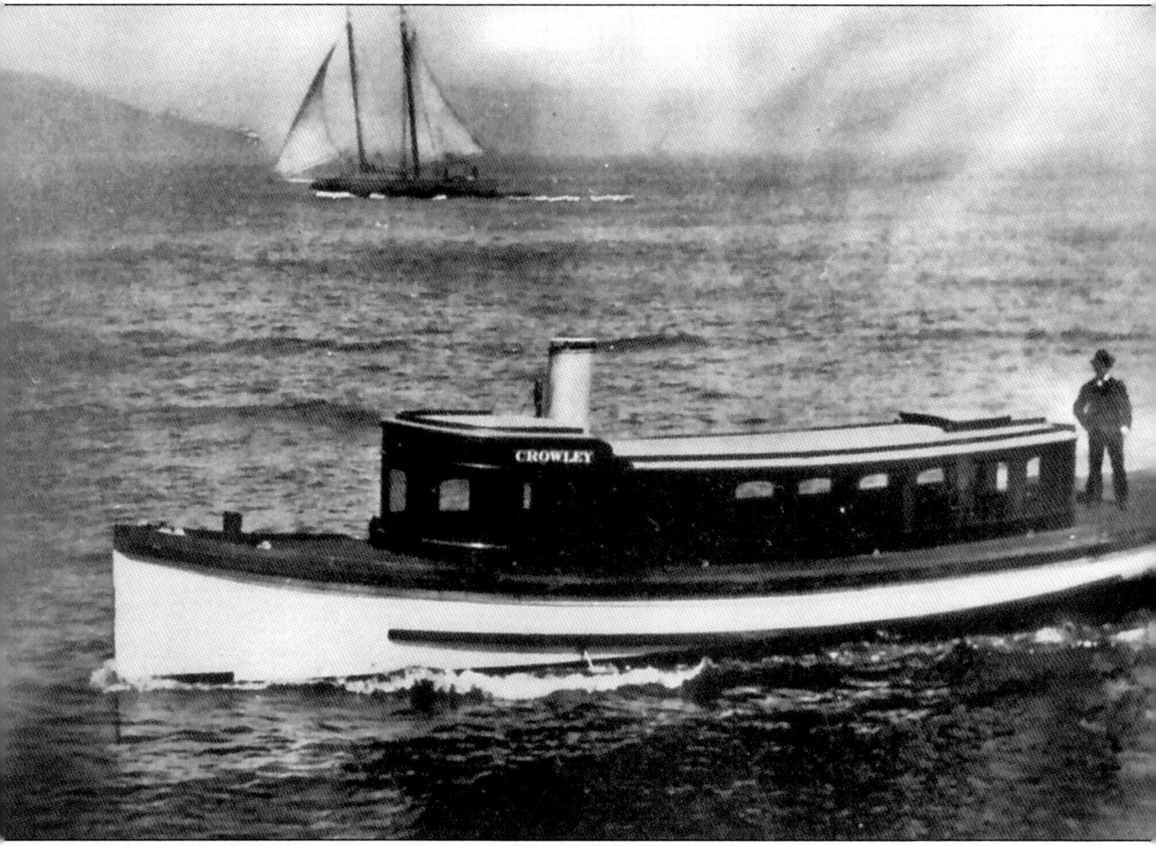

Around 1900, Tom Crowley stands on the deck of his gasoline launch *Crowley*. This was one of several gasoline launches that Crowley had South End member John Twigg build for him before the 1906 earthquake. Not one for sentiment, Crowley sold them for scrap when they had served out their useful lives.

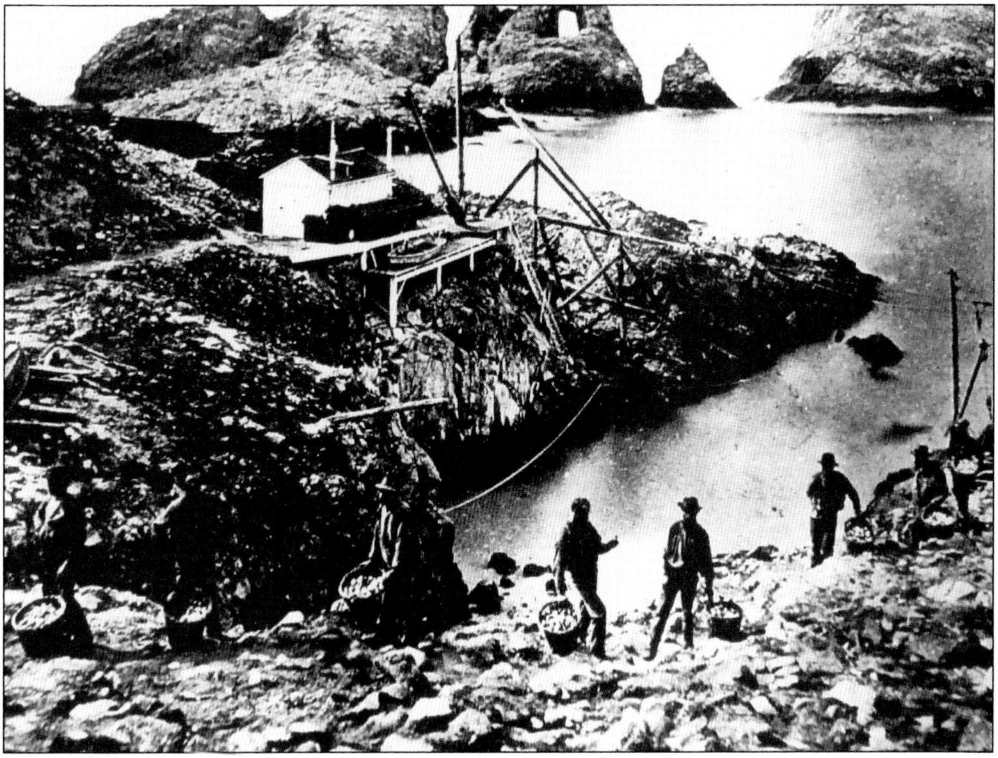

Whitehall boatmen gather murre eggs on the Farallone Islands in the 1870s. It was easier to raid murre nests than to establish chicken farms in early San Francisco.

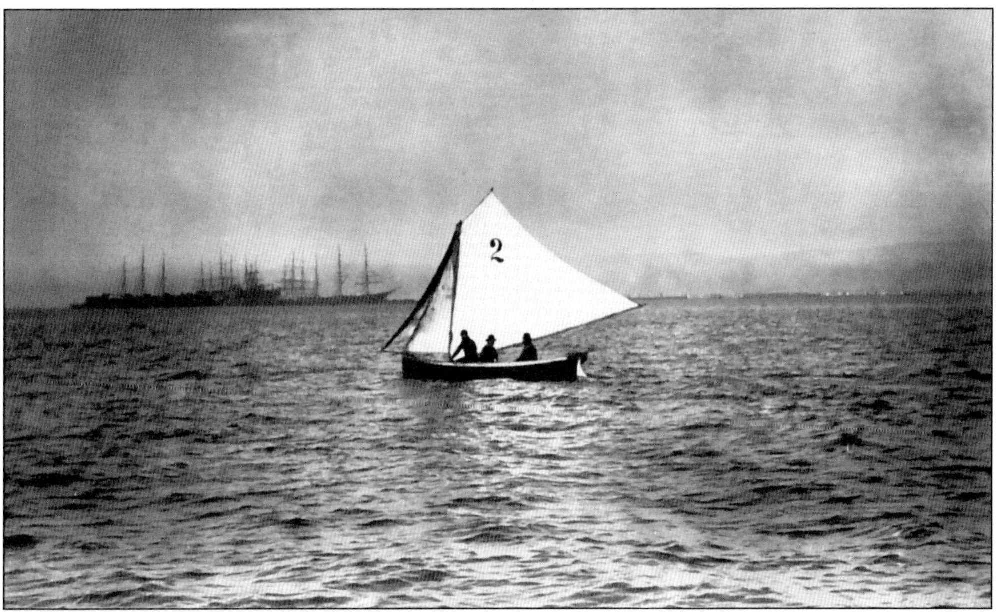

A single Whitehall boat, with its sail up, was photographed during the annual Fourth of July race. The race actually began in 1878, when the city's shanghaiing community established it as a fund-raiser for victims of a yellow fever epidemic in New Orleans. The race's route ran from Union Street Wharf to Fort Point and back again.

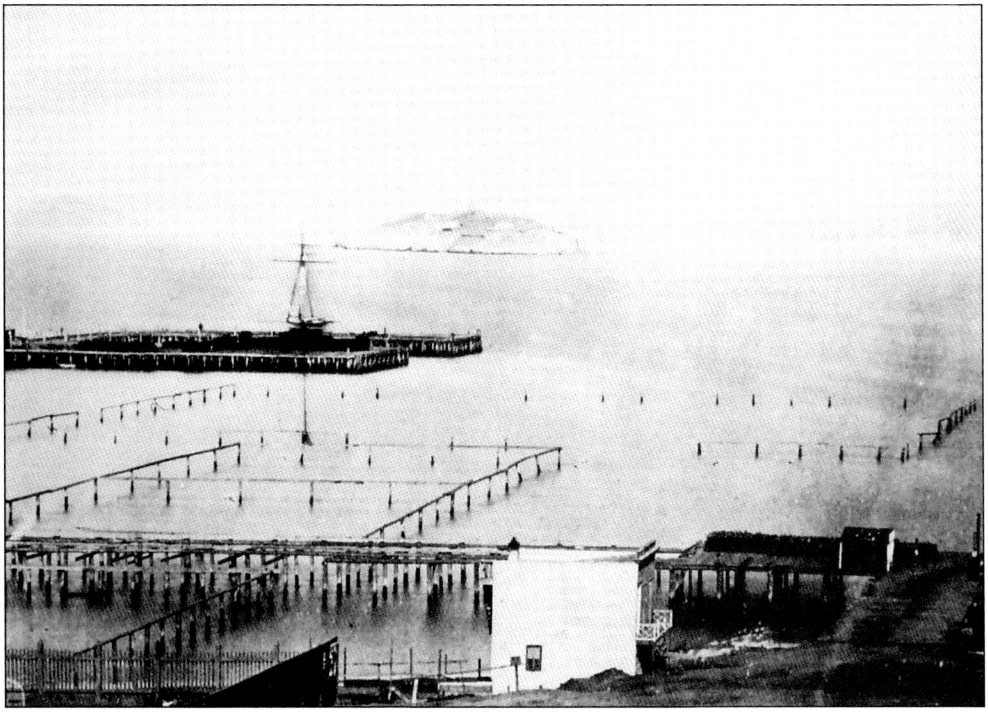

This is a view of Meiggs Wharf water lots.

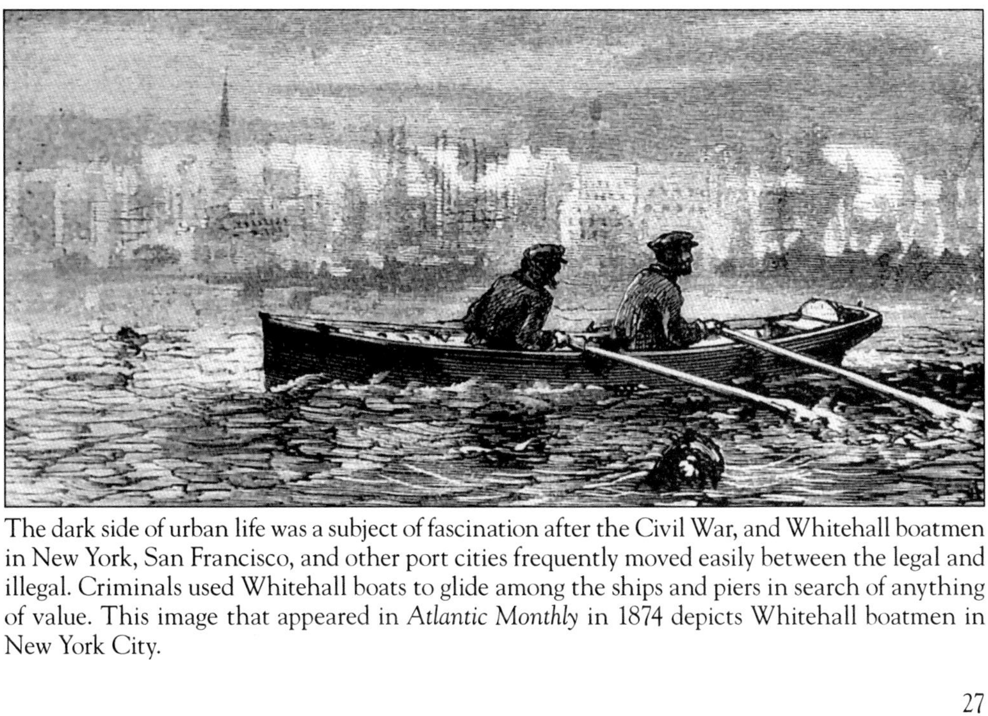

The dark side of urban life was a subject of fascination after the Civil War, and Whitehall boatmen in New York, San Francisco, and other port cities frequently moved easily between the legal and illegal. Criminals used Whitehall boats to glide among the ships and piers in search of anything of value. This image that appeared in *Atlantic Monthly* in 1874 depicts Whitehall boatmen in New York City.

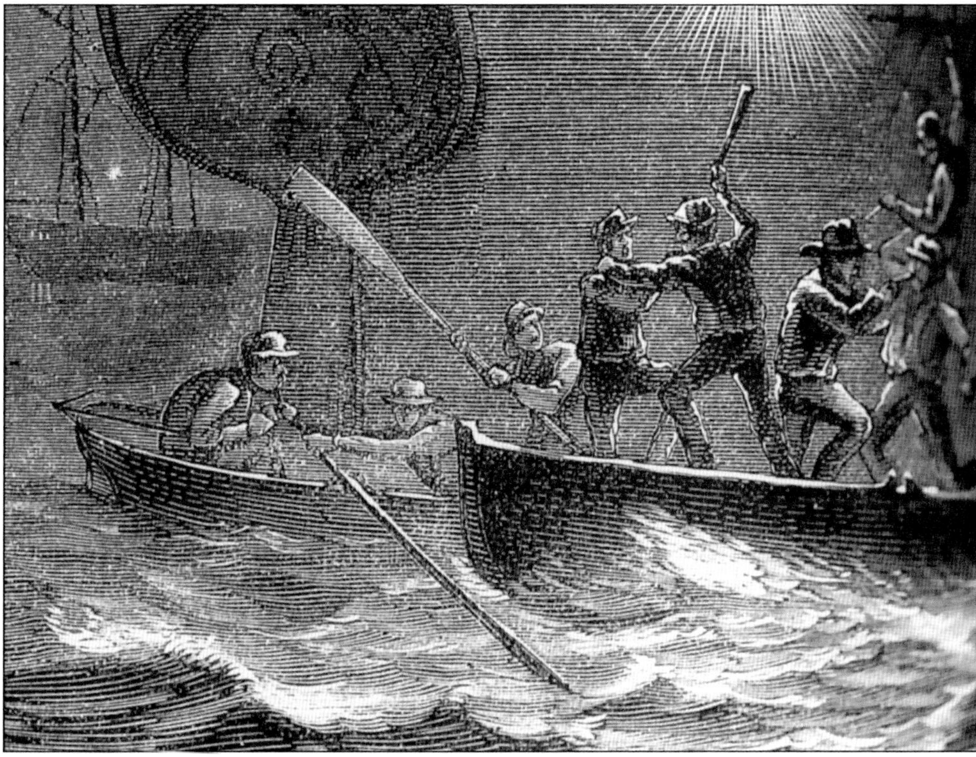

These Whitehall boatmen battle over valuables or turf in what might be a simple gang war.

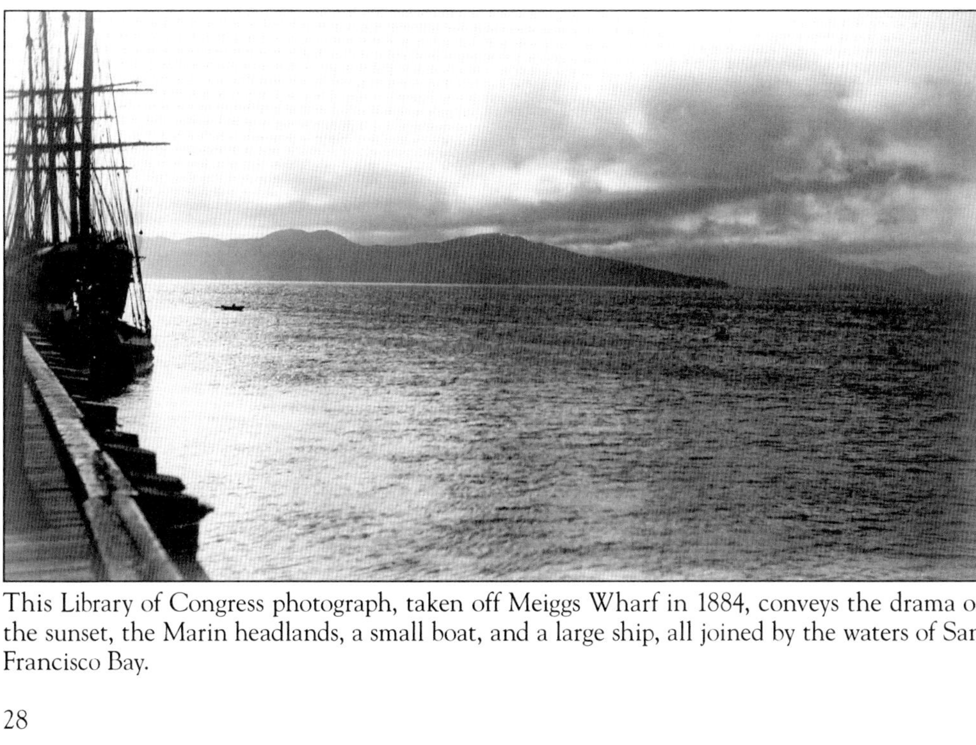

This Library of Congress photograph, taken off Meiggs Wharf in 1884, conveys the drama of the sunset, the Marin headlands, a small boat, and a large ship, all joined by the waters of San Francisco Bay.

Two

A FUTURE PLAYER

An important player in the Aquatic Park story actually spent the first 30 years of its existence at the foot of Third Street. The original South End Rowing Club was founded in 1873 and was located in what would now be the middle of the Third Street Bridge. After its defeat to the Pioneer Rowing Club in a hotly contested race on St. Patrick's Day in 1874, that club went through a series of reorganizations (as the Friendship Club in 1874, then the Neptune Club that same year, and, lastly, as the Golden Gate Rowing Club) until it ceased to exist in 1887. A new South End Rowing Club was started in 1881. A new clubhouse was put up, along with a handball court, only to be sold off in 1903 for its lumber at the behest of the State Board of Harbor Commissioners.

The South End, with its neighbor the Ariel Club, had new boathouses constructed at the foot of Sixteenth Street in Central Basin. Four short years later, the harbor commissioners again drove the clubs from their homes: the South End cooperated, and had its boathouse moved by one of Henry Petersen's barges to Black Point Cove. It rested just west of the Dolphin Club, at the foot of Van Ness Avenue. The Ariels did not cooperate, and their boathouse was demolished on order of the harbor commissioners. Undeterred, the Ariels had another boathouse built just east of the South End.

Daniel Hudson Burnham revived the old Frederick Law Olmsted concept of an Aquatic Park for the people of San Francisco in his 1905 plan drawn up for the city. The 1906 earthquake and fire derailed any action by the City of San Francisco, but the idea of an aquatic park had taken firm hold among members of the clubs as an idea whose time had arrived.

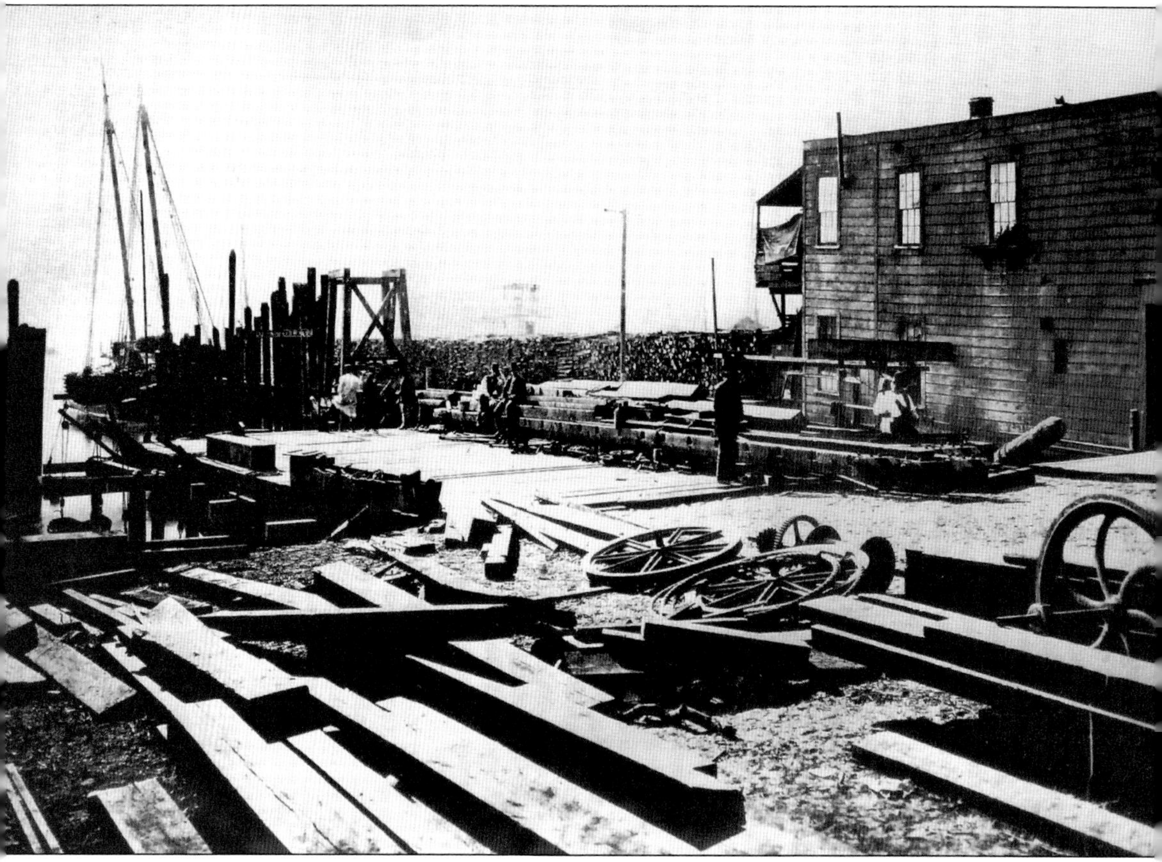

In 1873, the home of the South End Rowing Club was in this building. At the foot of Third and Berry Streets, the club counted boatmen and other working-class citizens as it membership in 1873 and 1874. The competitive fortunes of the club took a dramatic turn upwards when Fred Plaisted, a boatman from Maine, joined the club in fall of 1873. Fred, recently returned from a sojourn of six years in China, rowed under the name Charles Brown. Fred beat the Pacific Coast singles champion in November of that year, and was a critical part of the South End's four-man crew that faced the Pioneers in a grudge match on St. Patrick's Day. Fred collapsed from exhaustion during the race, and his crew lost by a nose. They also lost $550, equal to a man's annual wages in 1874, and the club lost its identity through several reorganizations.

Plaisted moved back East where there were more rowing races and bigger purses. In 1878, he faced off against world champion Ned Hanlon in a widely anticipated race in Toronto. Stephen Roberts, New York City alderman and Whitehall champion in the 1830s and 1840s, served as referee. Hanlon won easily.

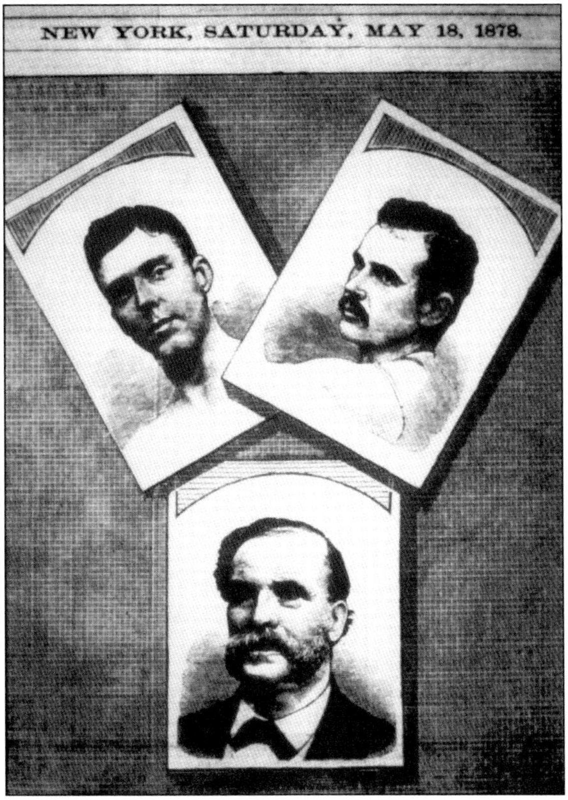

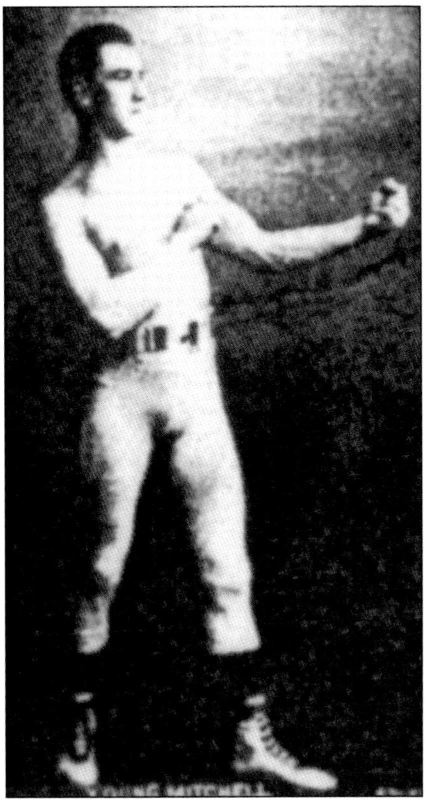

John L. Herget was the son of German immigrants. Born on Telegraph Hill, he took up boxing at an early age, and achieved fame and some fortune. Known as "Young Mitchell," after the English champion Charley Mitchell, Herget picked up the name for the sharp tongue he taunted opponents with, and his utter lack of fear. Once threatened by a butcher knife if he defeated his opponent in the ring, "Young Mitchell" promptly knocked his opponent out.

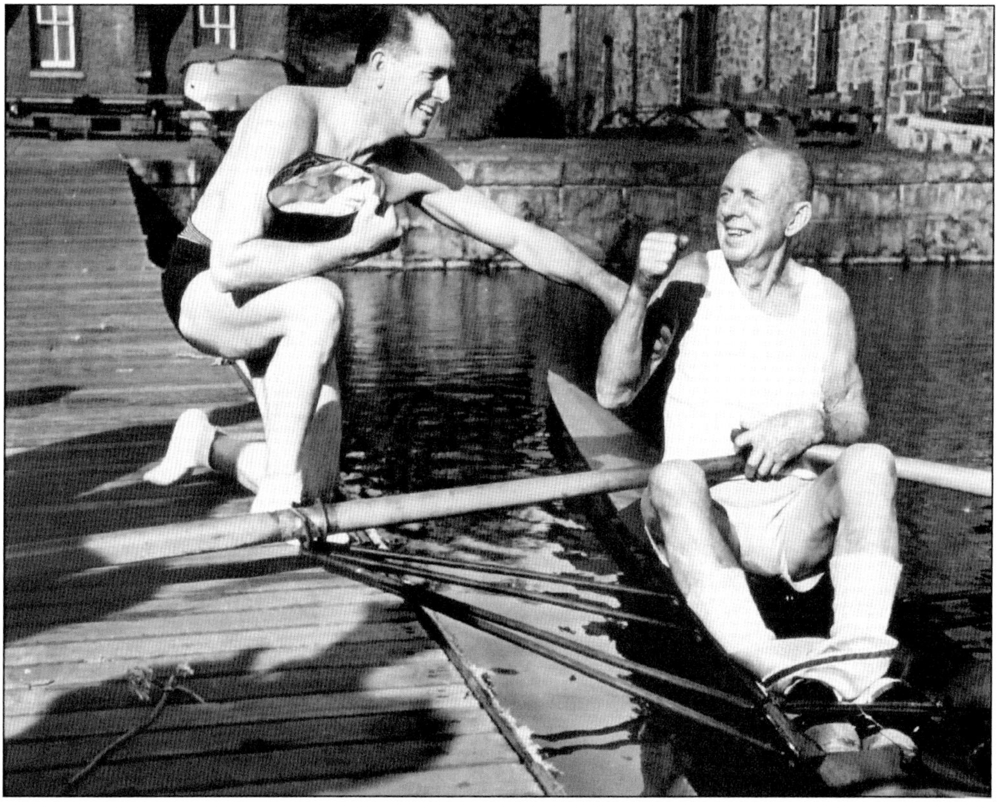

Fred Plaisted, with John Kelly, is on Philadelphia's famed Boathouse Row in the 1930s. Fred had just beaten Kelly, a champion rower and father of Grace Kelly, in a race on the occasion of Fred's 89th birthday. Fred continued rowing until his 96th year, when he passed away. Fred was such an inspiration that a hall was built in his name. The hall is now gone, but rowers on Boathouse Row still vie for the Plaisted Mug, emblematic of rowing superiority.

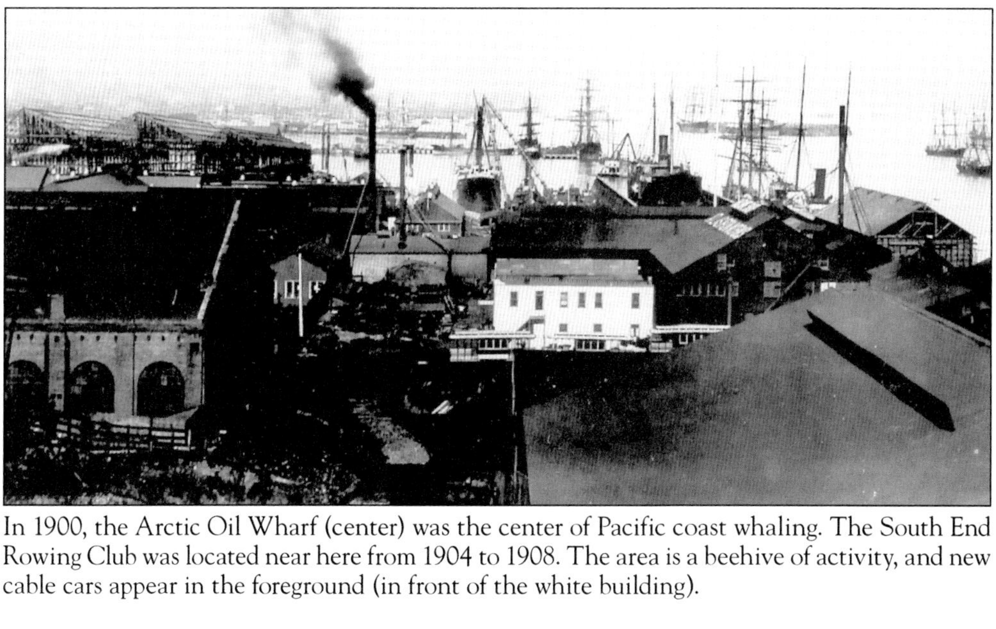

In 1900, the Arctic Oil Wharf (center) was the center of Pacific coast whaling. The South End Rowing Club was located near here from 1904 to 1908. The area is a beehive of activity, and new cable cars appear in the foreground (in front of the white building).

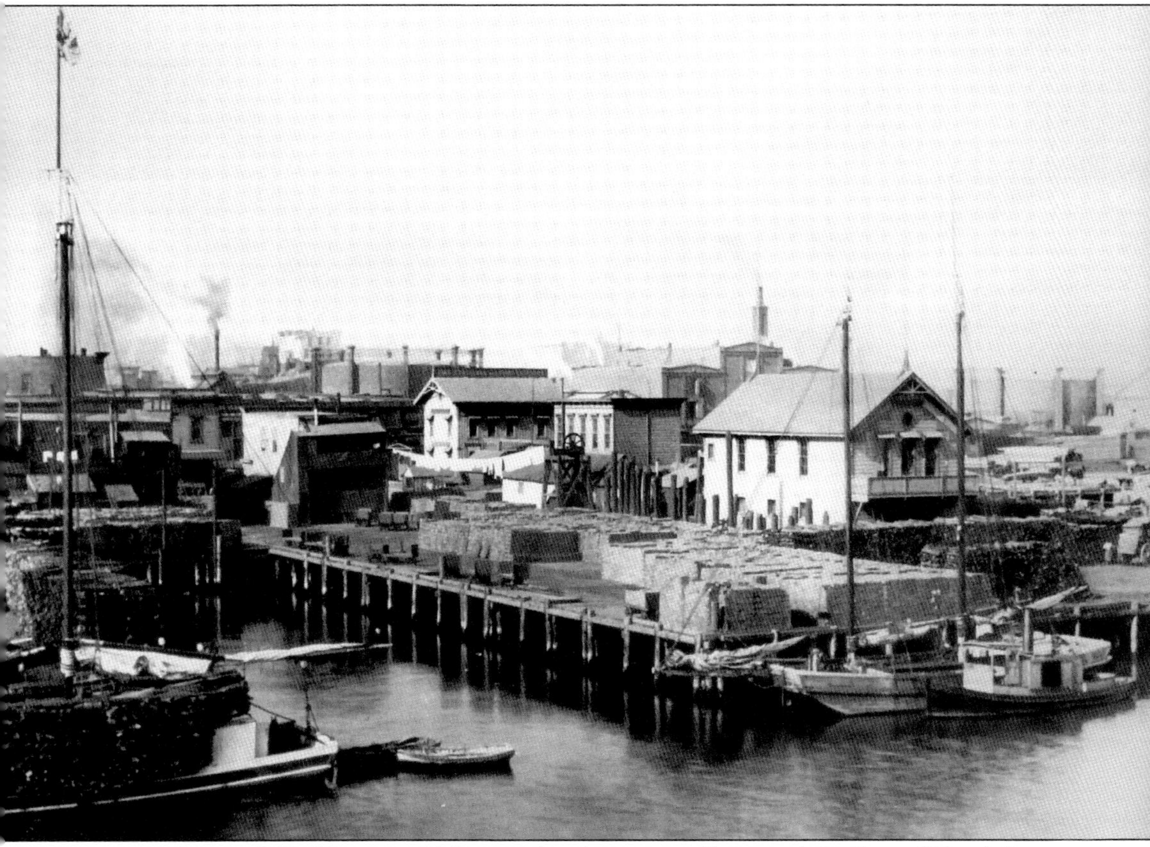

In 1886, the South End Rowing Club's new boathouse proudly graced the foot of Third Street. Right of center, with a balcony, the boathouse shared the wharf with wood, hay, and bricks (note the wagon with wood to the far right). Third Street was the entry point for the city's bulk cargo trade. Dozens of saloons catered to the thirst of men who put in a hard day for their pay. The more fortunate among them parlayed their physical prowess to a career as a boxer or professional rower, or talked their way to a political career in the equally rough and tumble world of San Francisco politics.

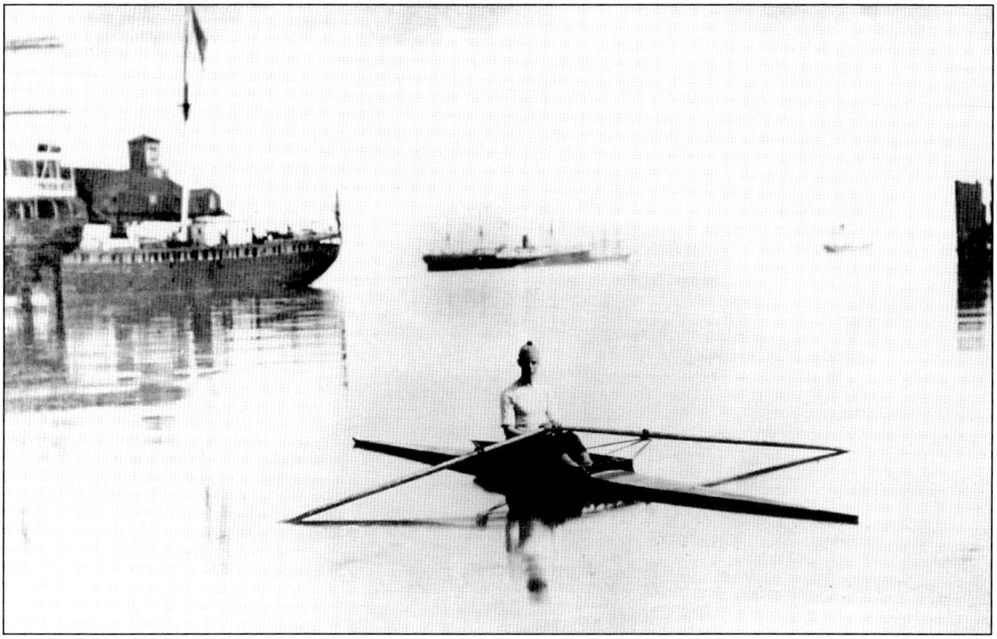

The Nautilus Rowing Club, at the foot of Second Street, was strictly dedicated to amateurism in the sport of rowing. This Nautilus rower poses with his shell about 1881, as a Pacific Mail steamer towers over him in the background.

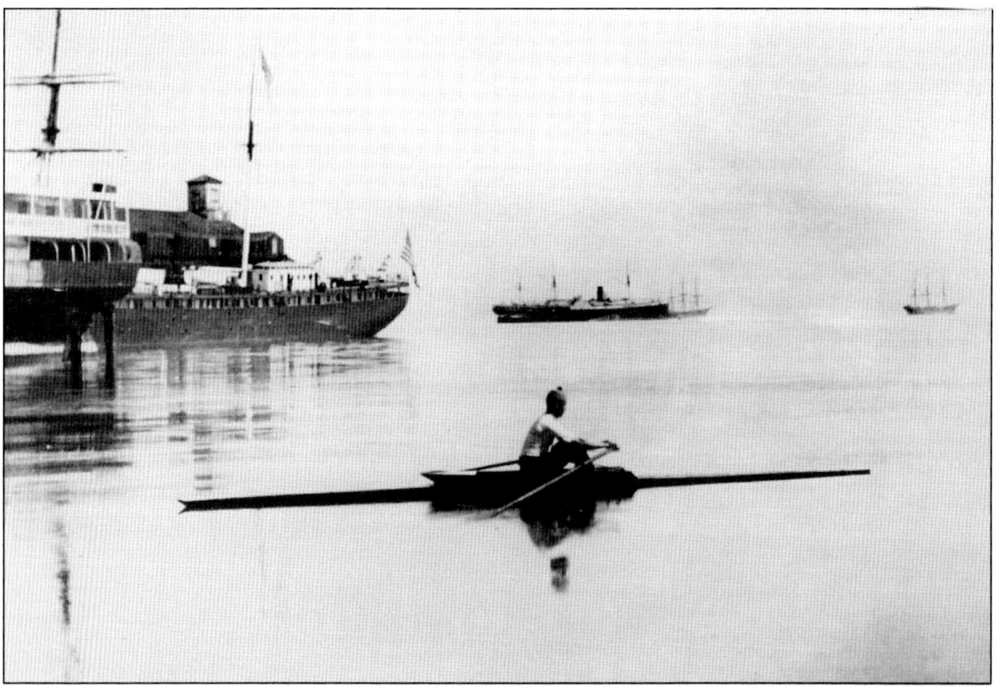

Rowing clubs that decided to follow amateur rowing only soon disappeared from the San Francisco sporting scene. The Nautilus Rowing Club existed for only a few years. The most successful clubs, like the Ariel and South End, combined professional and amateur rowing under one roof.

Henry Peterson graduated from success as a Whitehall boatman to the owner of a fleet of gasoline launches on San Francisco's waterfront. Peterson was bought out by the top businessman to rise from the ranks of Whitehall boatmen—Tom Crowley Sr.

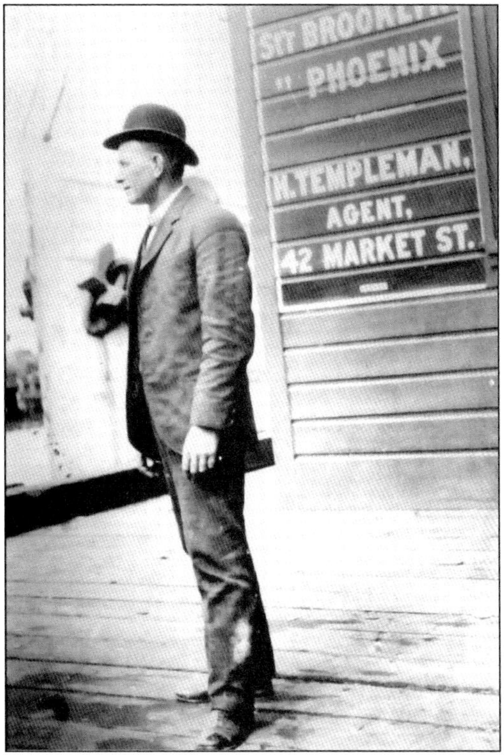

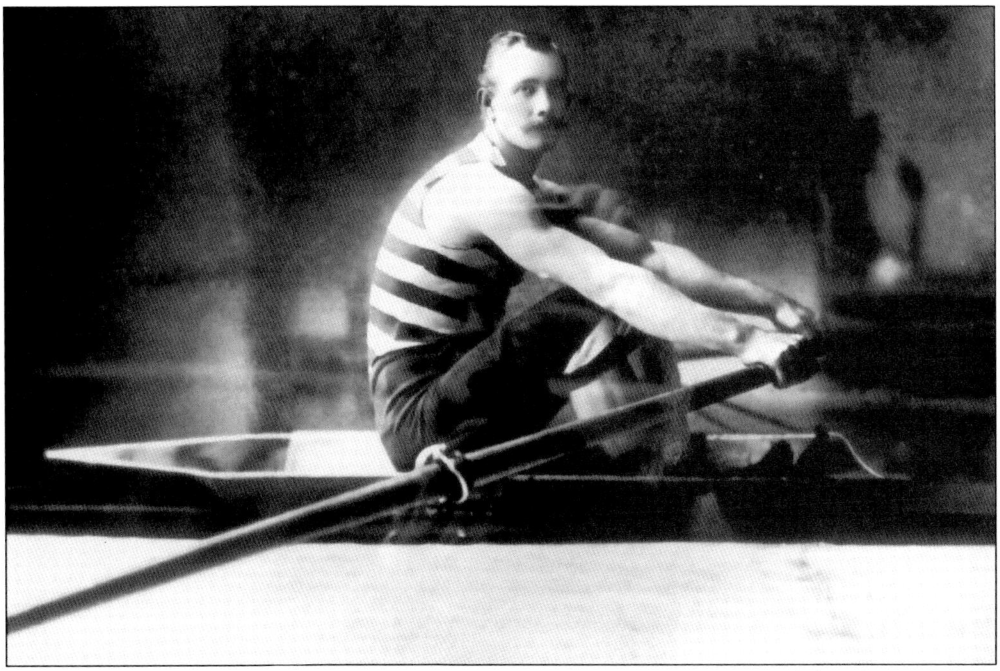

Henry Peterson was the best oarsman native to San Francisco. He presented this photograph to the South End and Dolphin clubs to commemorate his widely publicized race against Canadian William O'Connor in 1888. Peterson's fame as a boatmen stemmed in part from the many people that would have drown had he not rescued them from the frigid waters of San Francisco Bay.

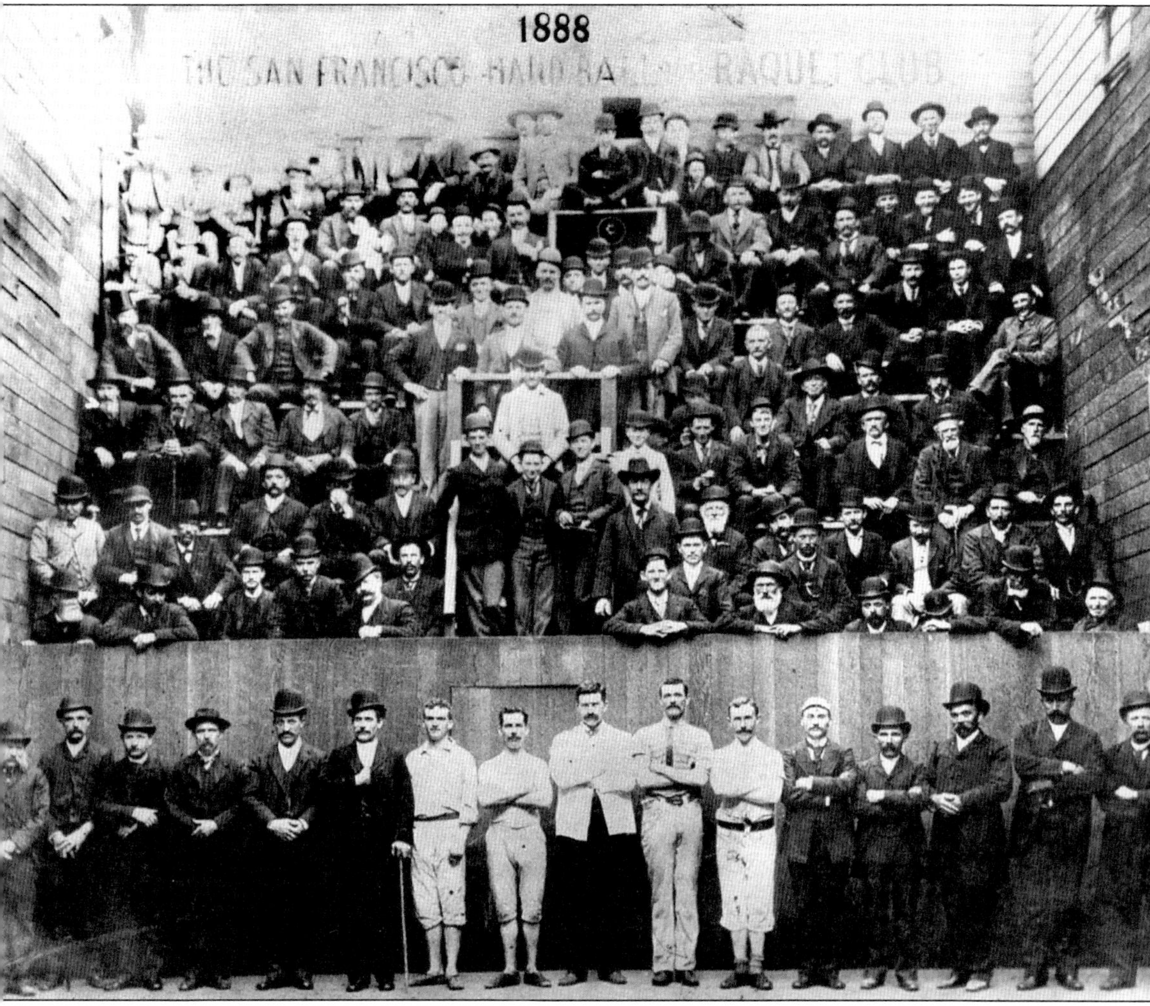

Handball was a very popular working class sport, and courts thrived South of Market. In 1888, the San Francisco Handball and Racquet Club stood on Howard Street. In the 1890s, the South End Rowing Club put up a handball court on their premises. The sport carried the club in the 1950s and 1960s, until swimming supplanted handball in dominance in the 1970s.

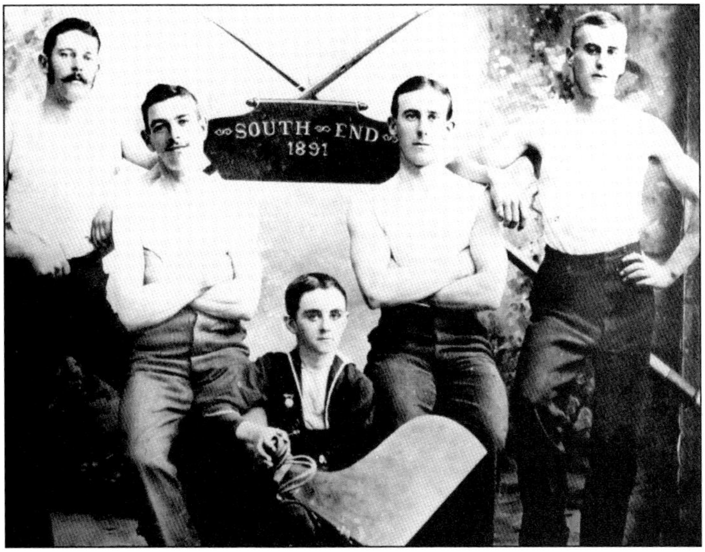

This 1893 South End championship crew, from left to right, includes William La Chappelle, Al Fritz, Henry Bode, Frank Duplissea, and George McGrill, coxswain. The nameplate is from the barge *South End*, built in 1891. Al Fritz was a nephew of saloon keeper and political boss Alfred J. Fritz, who ruled San Francisco during much of the late 1870s (he threatened to turn his Gatling guns on the Workingmen's Party at one point). With the elder Fritz' death under very mysterious circumstances, the way was cleared for "Blind Boss" Buckley to ascend to the top of the political heap. The younger Fritz became a judge, where he served on the bench for over 50 years. Frank Duplissea was a son of the longtime stroke of the South End's extremely successful professional four man crew, George Duplissea. Frank was a great oarsman and became wealthy in later years. George suffered the loss of Frank and another son Walter when they were fairly young.

Fred Plaisted is pictured here in 1922 after his defeat of Jim Riley. Plaisted was 73 at the time, and Riley was 79. The men were two of the last surviving professional rowers in the 1920s.

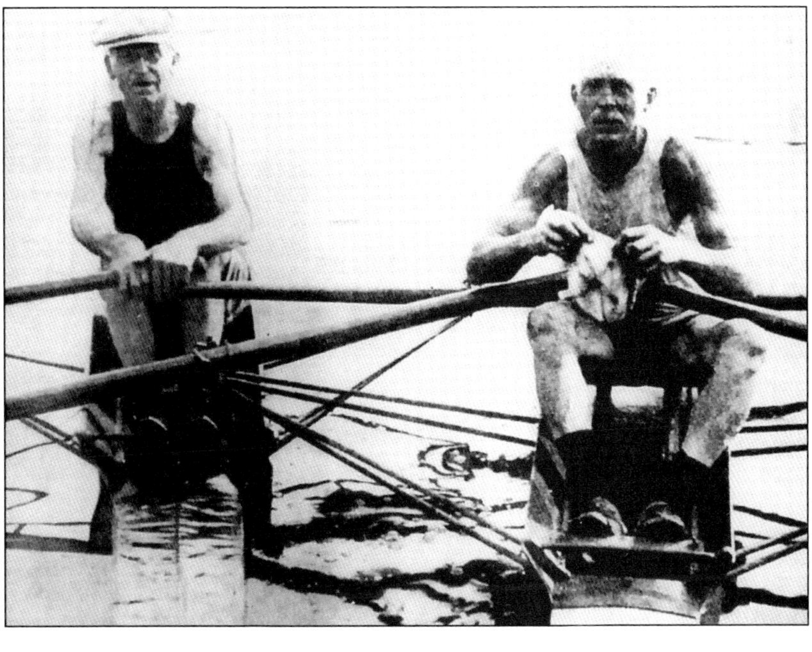

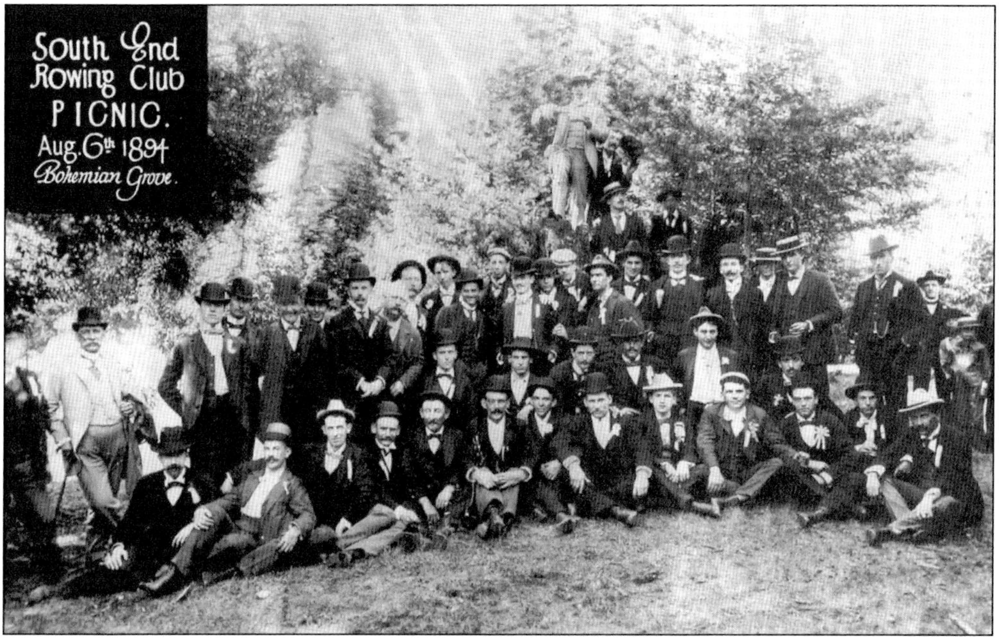

Social occasions were almost as important as sporting competitions for San Francisco's sports clubs. Contacts were made or reinforced, business or politics might rear their head, or dates were allowed, such as on a Ladies' Day where the day could be spent courting.

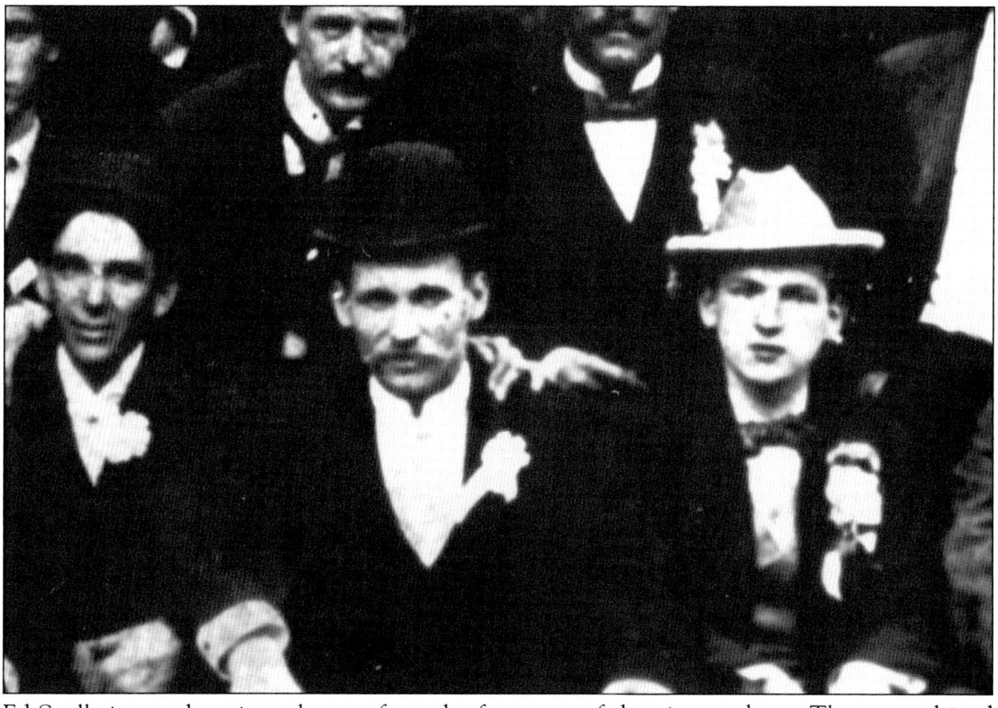

Ed Scully is seen here in a close-up from the front row of the picture above. The mustachioed man in the middle, Scully was first a carpenter, then a general contractor (he built St. Brigid's Church on Van Ness Avenue). Scully led the fight to make Black Point Cove the Aquatic Park, but did not live to see his dream realized.

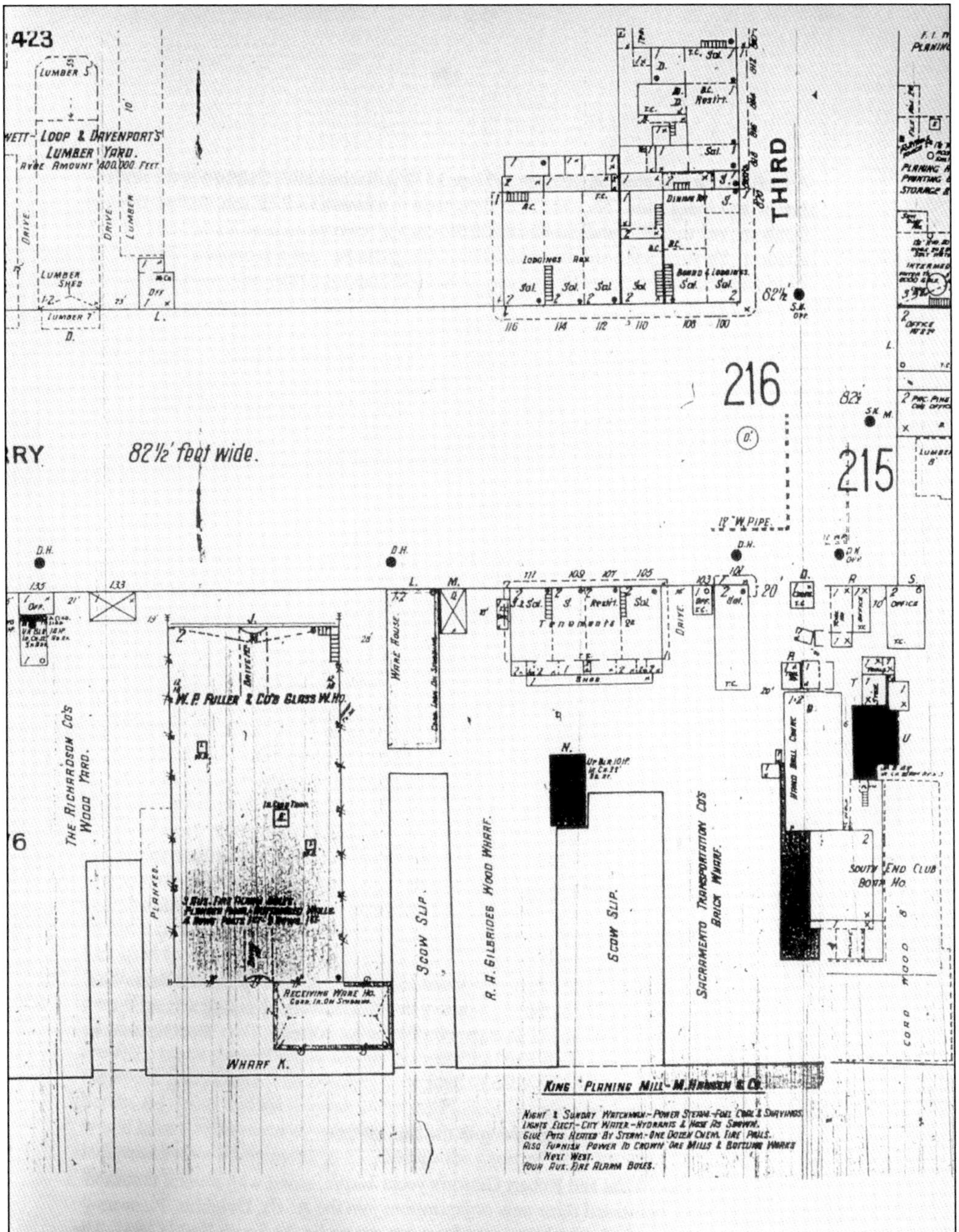

Map C-Sanborn Map of 1899 showing the South End Boathouse (in the bottom right corner) at the foot of Third Street. The handball court begun in 1897 and completed in 1899 is just above and to the side of the boathouse. The 15 "S"s at the northwest and southwest corners of Third and Berry streets denote saloons. (San Francisco History Room, San Francisco Main Library)

The South End Rowing Club appears on an 1899 Sanborn Insurance Map. At the bottom right hand corner, the club's handball court was at the rear of the boathouse. Fifteen saloons waited on thirsty patrons within a block of the boathouse.

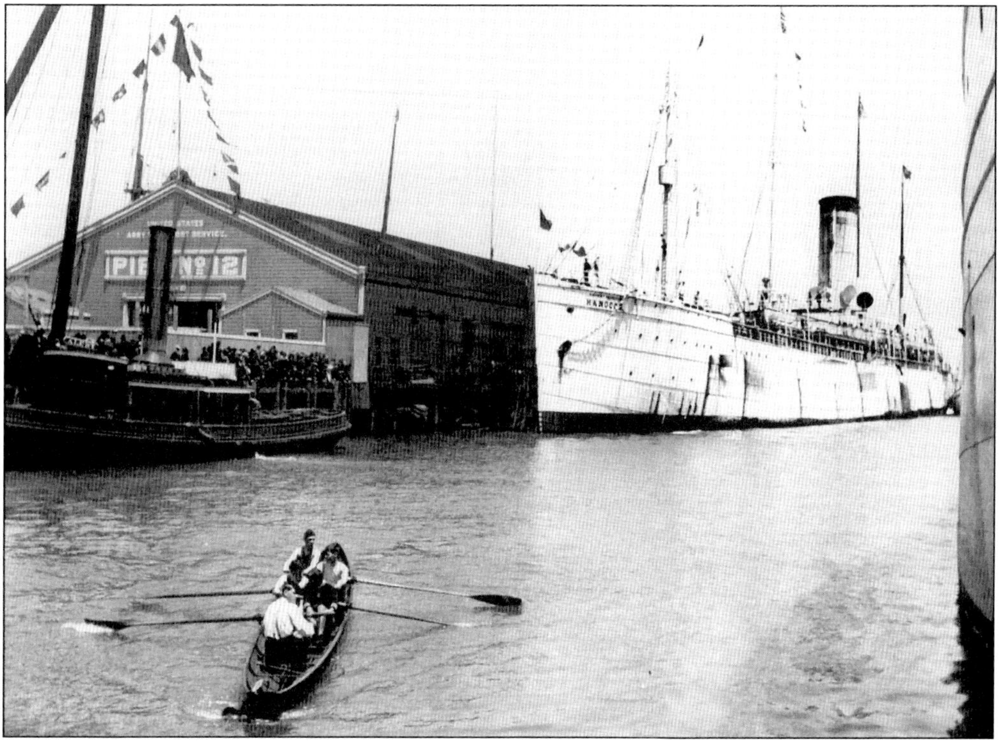

In 1898, a four-man barge with coxswain rows out to see the *Hancock*, back from the Spanish-American War. The South End was near Pier 12, so this could be a South End crew.

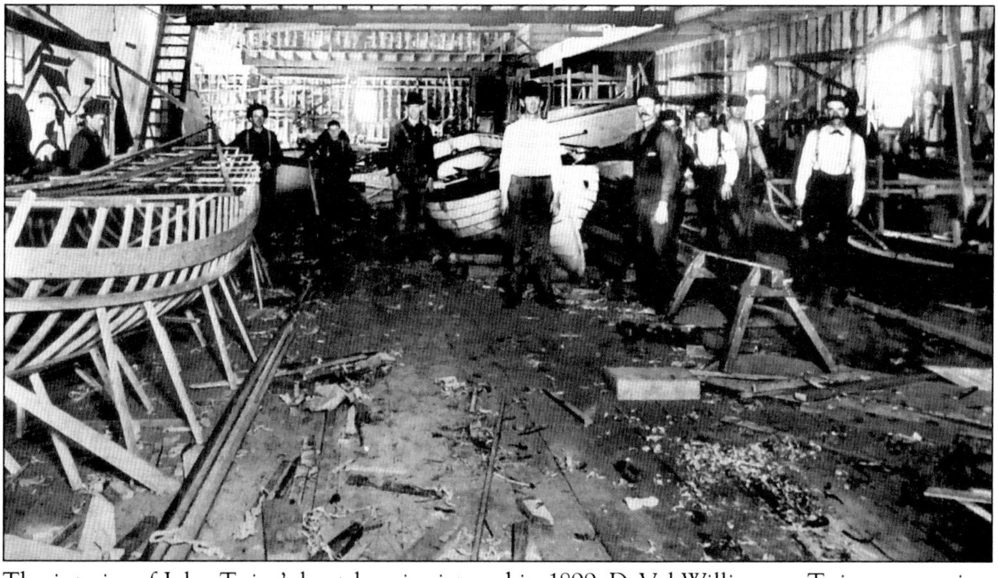

The interior of John Twigg's boatshop is pictured in 1899. DuVal Williams, a Twigg apprentice, gave a long oral history of his life and the Twigg shop 60 years later to San Francisco Maritime Museum volunteer Jack McNairn. John Twigg was a boatbuilder of great respect in San Francisco, but he is best known for making the most dependable gasoline launches in the 1890s, and just after the beginning of the 20th century, launches that propelled Tom Crowley Sr. to fame and fortune.

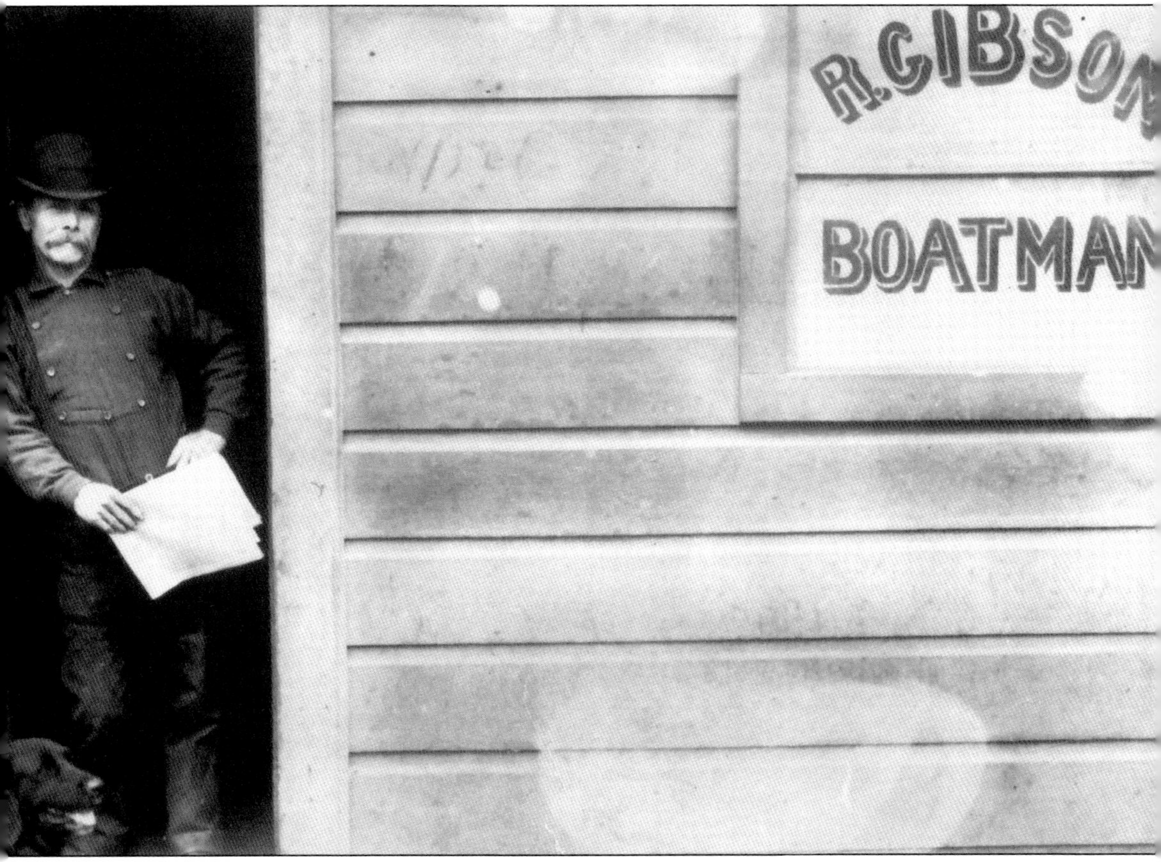

Robert Gibson was a Whitehall boatman at the foot of Third Street for decades. He owned and rented out a sailboat, and also took his friends from the next door South End Rowing Club on hunting trips up the Sacramento River. Gibson developed a small gasoline launch presence, but he was a bit too old and not as aggressive as Crowley. He is seen here with a good friend at his boathouse.

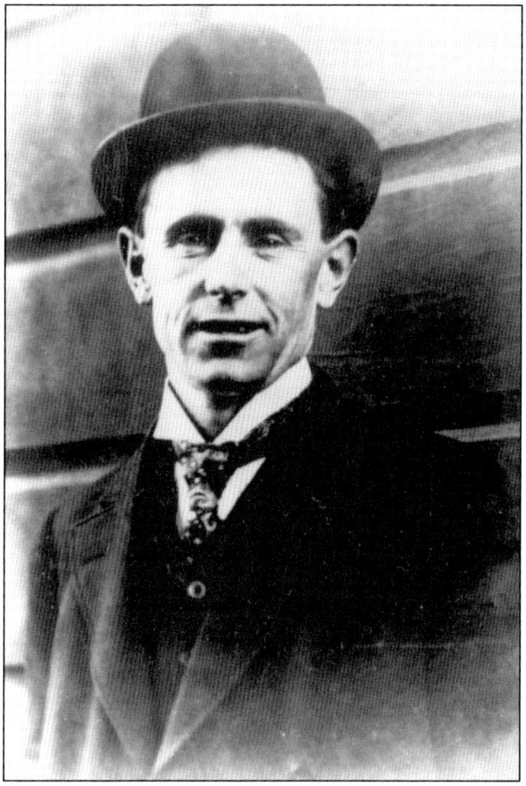

Tom Crowley Sr. was a feisty Whitehall boatman who had the vision to turn to the new technology of gasoline launches in the mid-1890s. By World War I, Crowley was a millionaire. He became an Olympic Club member to learn the subtle points of boxing, a skill he sometimes put to good use on the wild waterfront.

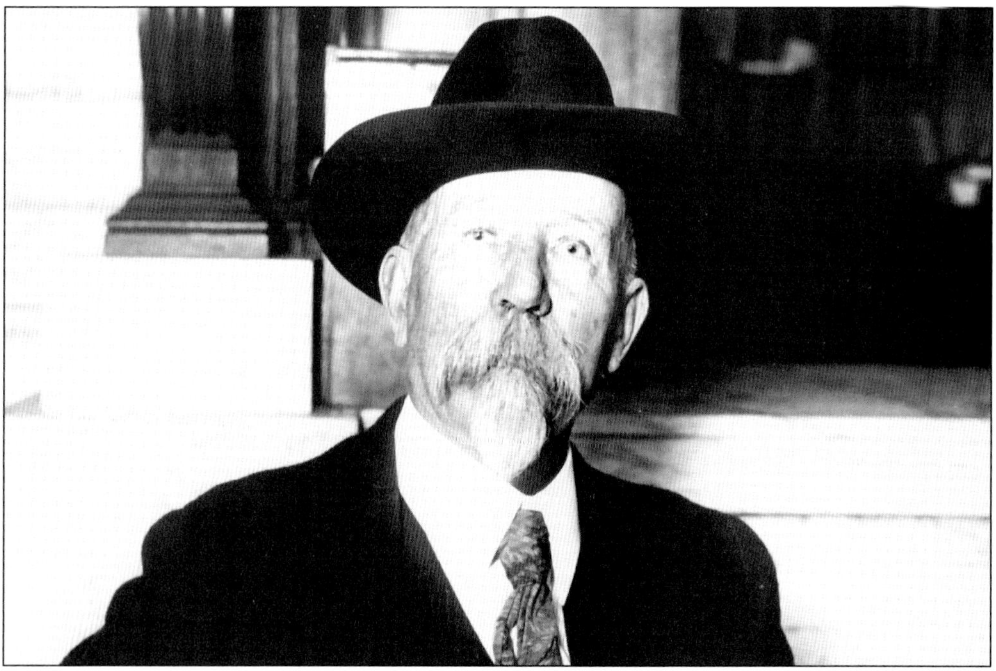

A Pioneer Club rower in the 1870s, William Alexander (W. A.) Coulter suffered a severe injury to an ankle. He turned his eye to painting and sketches for the *San Francisco Call* and created an important record of Bay Area waterfront life in the late 1800s.

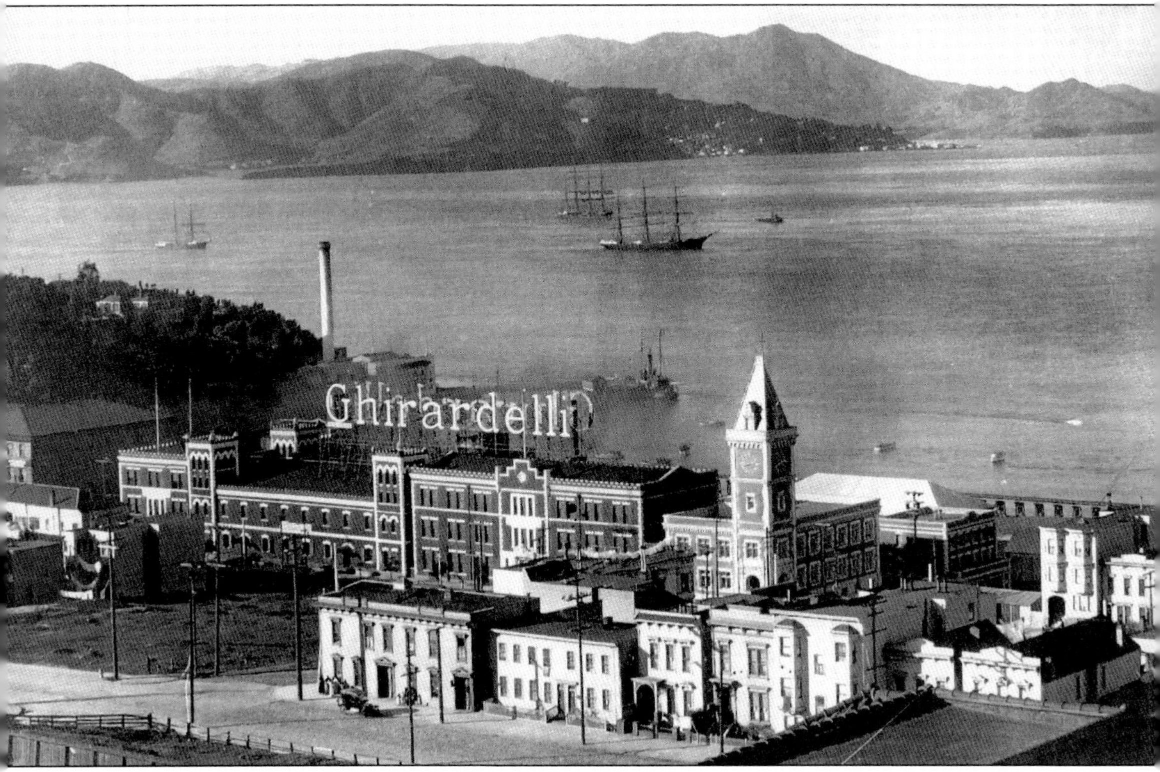

After the 1906 earthquake, the Ghirardelli Chocolate Company was a bustling chocolate manufacturer off Black Point Cove. At the government dock, a boat filled with water and provisions is about to set off for the prison at Alcatraz, while three-masted vessels have furled their sails as they head in to port.

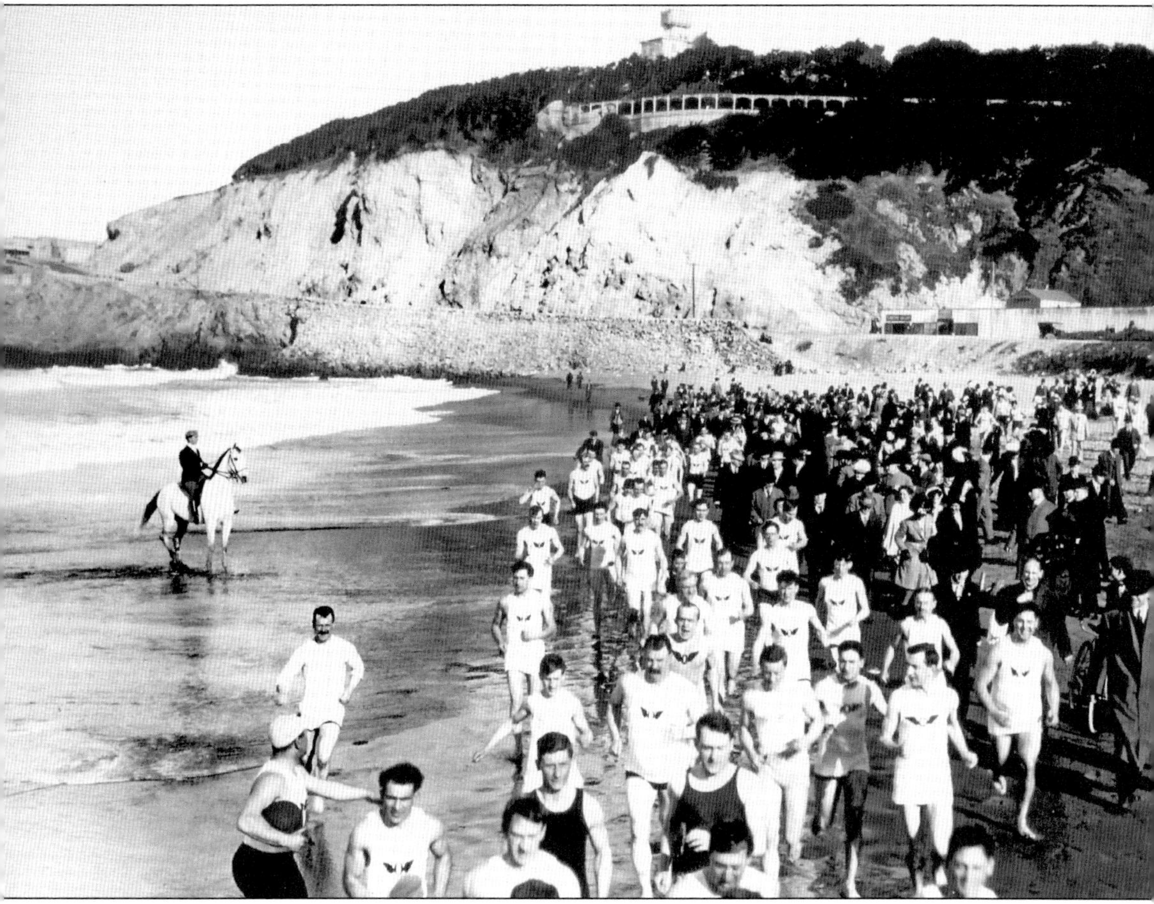

The Olympic Club held an annual run that may be the "forerunner" to the Bay to Breakers run. This 1905 photograph shows club members as they head down Ocean Beach, south of the Cliff House.

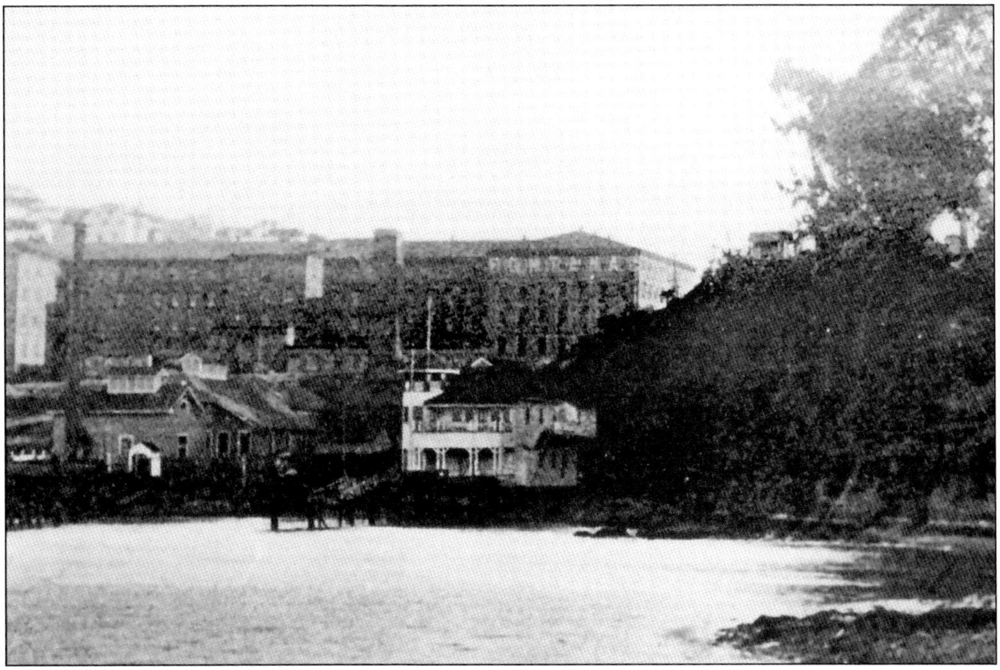

In 1904, the Dolphin Club sits almost alone at the foot of Van Ness Avenue. The Fontana Warehouse looms in the background.

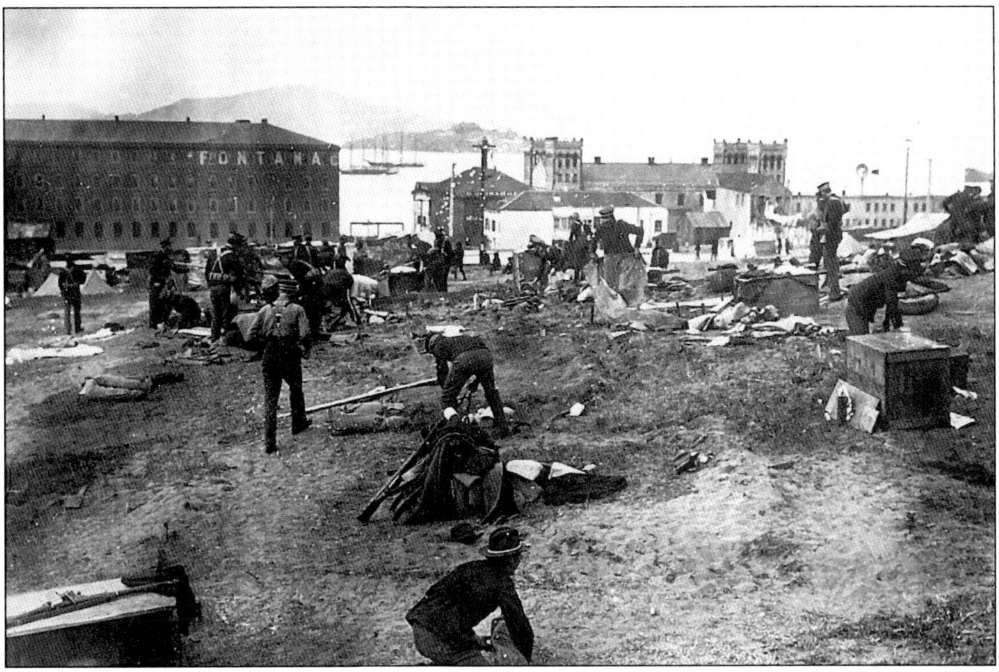

National Guard troops set up camp south of Black Point Cove as flame destroys much of San Francisco after the 1906 earthquake. The troops were brought in to maintain public safety and order after much of the city was destroyed. Camps for the newly homeless were located at Fort Mason, Golden Gate Park, and many other sites around the city.

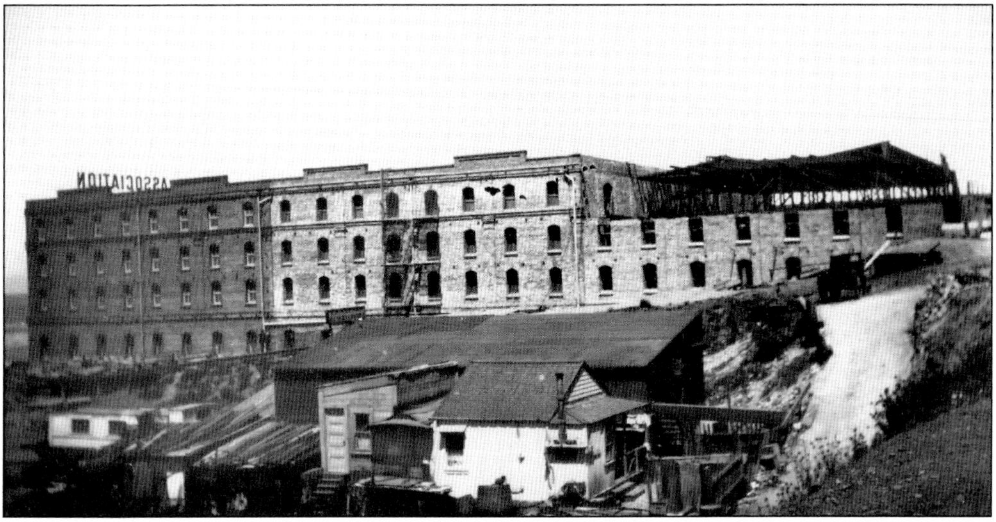

In 1907, after the Selby Smelter came down, the Haslett Warehouse was built. The warehouse was part of the California Fruit Canners Association complex at the west end of Black Point Cove, and fit well with the commercial and industrial character of the environs. When the Golden Gate National Recreation Area (GGNRA) was created by the federal government in the 1970s, the Haslett Warehouse became part of the GGNRA. The structure suffered a disastrous fire before it rose from the flames as the Argonaut Hotel.

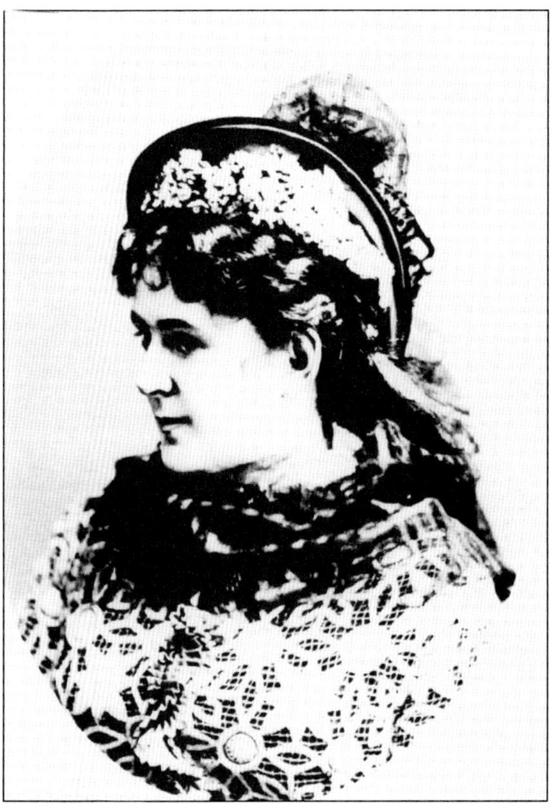

Around 1874, actress May Howard was a member of the California Theatre Boat Club, one of the most colorful rowing clubs in the city. They did not win many races, but the group's social events were sure to see plenty of champagne toasts and chowder. May Howard even had a barge named in her honor.

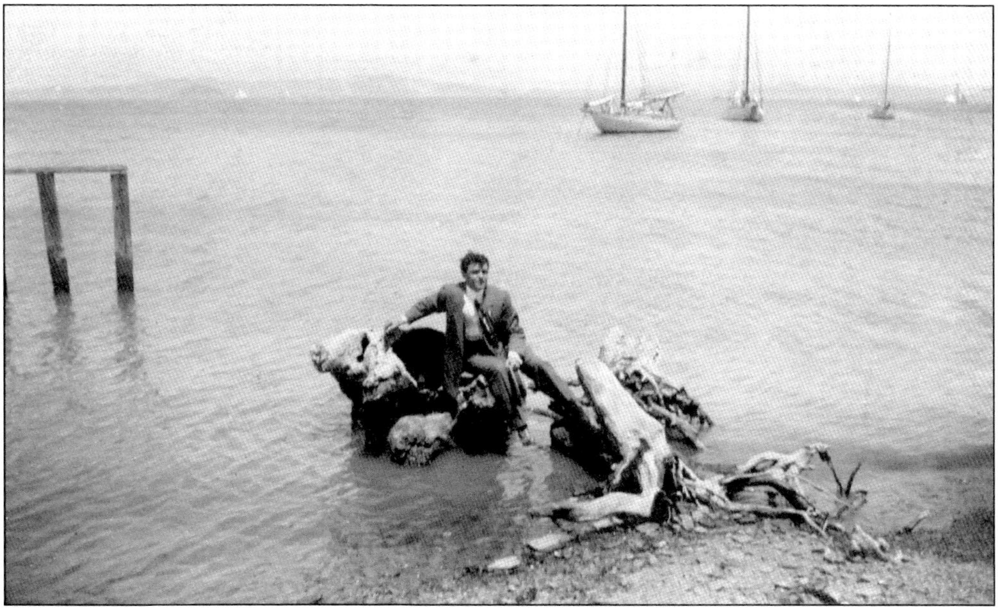

In 1907, a Dolphin Club member relaxes on gnarled tree stumps next to the club.

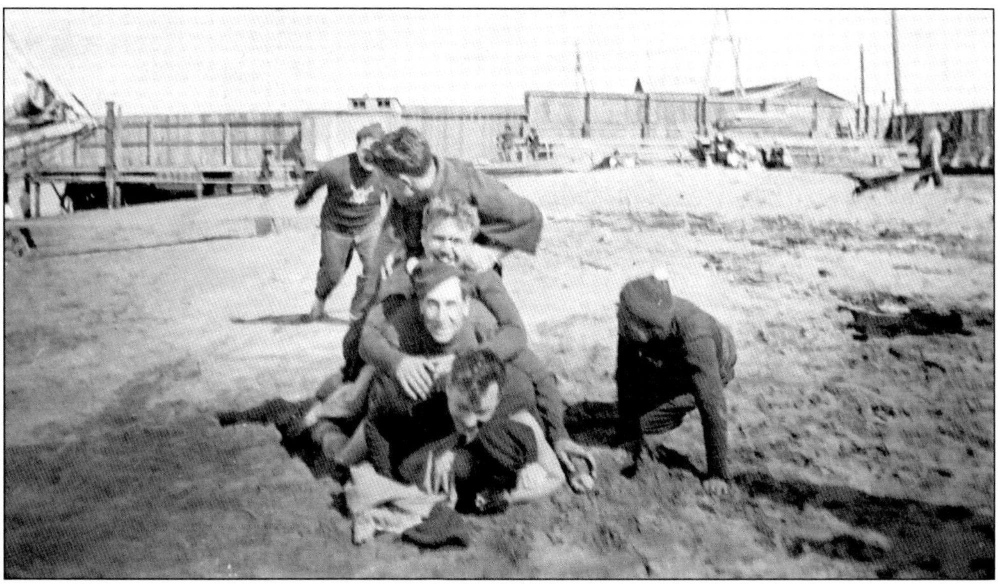

Dolphin Club member Guido Ghiselli poses with friends east of the club. Ghiselli was part of the Wharf Rats, a waterfront gang of sorts, who gravitated to the Dolphin Club. His mother must have steered them in the right direction, even though she was involved in shanghaiing from her sailors' clothing store on Jackson Street. Shanghaiing had pretty well died out by 1907, and the Dolphin Club provided the social structure that opened some doors toward upward mobility.

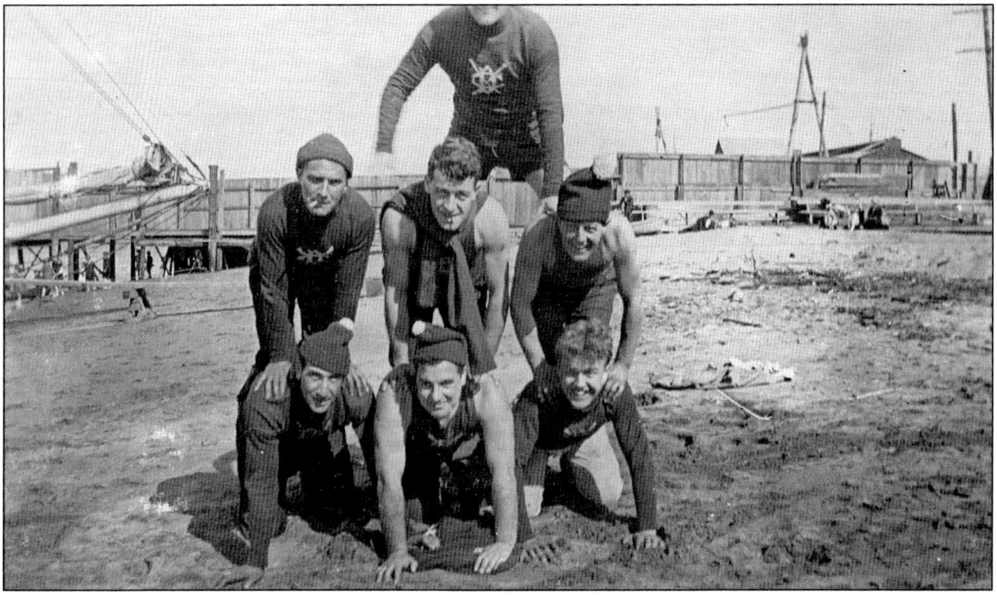

The Ghiselli gang made a great pyramid, but the photographer could not quite keep all the heads in the picture. A good pyramid was no reason to put out a better smoke, as attested by the man on the left in the second row.

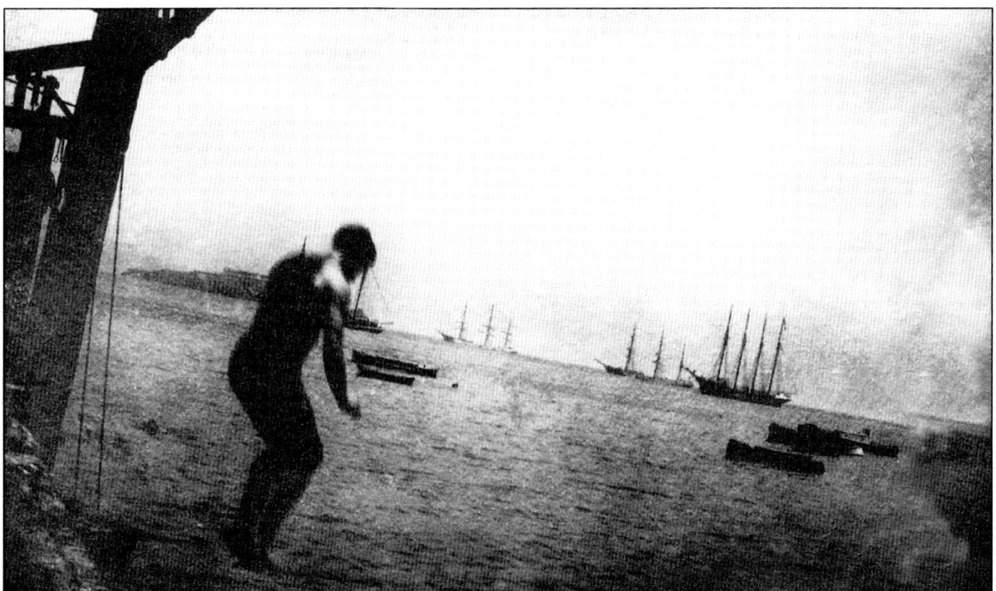

One of the Wharf Rats jumps from the dock of the Dolphin Club, with Alcatraz looming in the background.

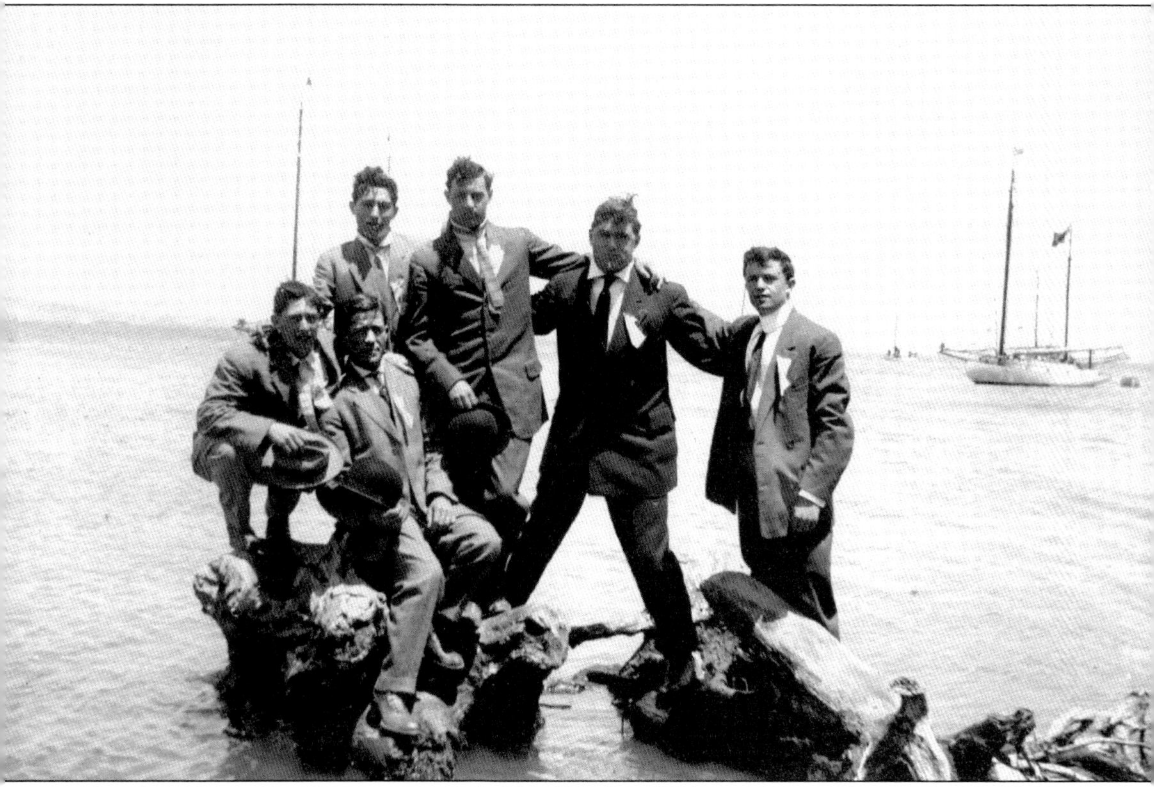

Ghiselli and partners share stumps in their high-collared shirts. Dress was much more formal in those days and a suit and tie were very common, even among the working class.

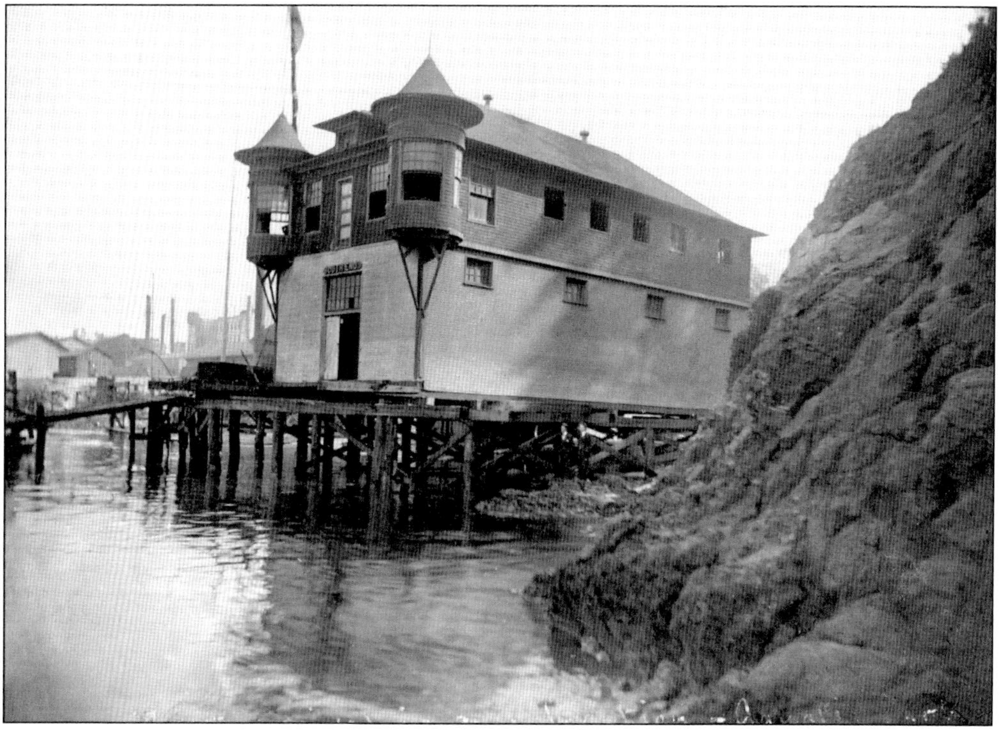

With arrival of the South End boathouse in Black Point Cove in 1908, a new era began. Ed Scully at the South End, Charles Farrell at the Dolphin Club, and others envisioned an aquatic park and set out to see their vision become reality. The South End boathouse was designed by Frank Van Trees, who had also designed numerous landmarks around town. The dual towers were a South End landmark until a fire in 1964 destroyed the left one. It was unfortunately never rebuilt.

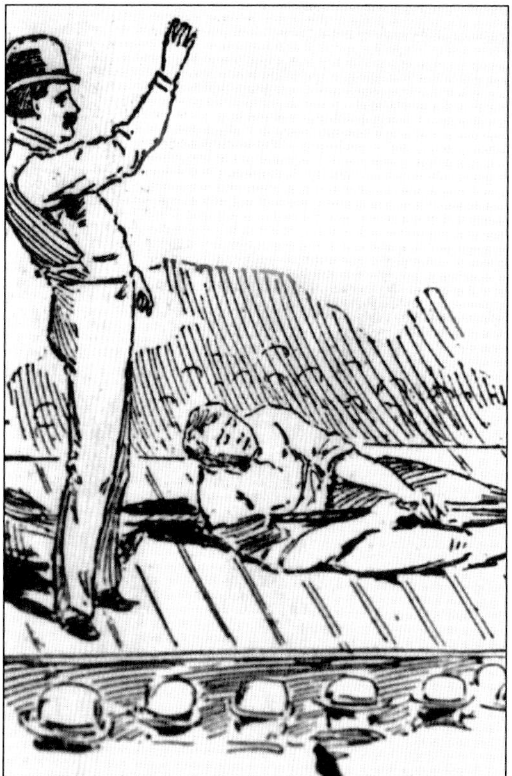

The Canadian Captain signals for victory.

In this etching of a tug-of-war match, the man standing is the captain, while the man on the ground in front of him anchors the team. International tug-of-war enjoyed a fervent, if brief, craze in the mid-1890s, with men of various nationalities uniting to win bragging rights for their country. South Ender George Duplissea captained the Canadian team.

Three

The Aquatic Park Idea Takes Root

The idea of an aquatic park for the people of San Francisco gained a huge boost when the three rowing clubs formed the Aquatic Improvement Association in 1909. Aquatic Park Days, sponsored by the clubs, with regattas, swimming exhibitions, and high diving, were open to the public. The press and local politicians supported the concept.

Developmental interests stepped up their efforts to deny use of the cove for recreational use as first the Belt Line Railroad trestle was built through the cove. The Southern Pacific Railroad applied to fill in the cove to have piers built for their trans-Pacific steamers. The State Board of Harbor Commissioners applied to the board of supervisors to fill in the three blocks of the cove, which would have forever ruined the possibility of an aquatic park. Supervisor McLaren, however, proposed the preservation of Black Point Cove as the site of the future aquatic park. The Harbor Commissioners application was denied, but a great deal of work lay ahead. Title to land had to be acquired, and financing found to actually build an aquatic park.

On the recreational front, the South End supported the first woman to accomplish a swim of the Golden Gate, Hazel Lagenour. Other women's swims followed. In February 1915, the recreational barge *South End* was launched. It still exists today.

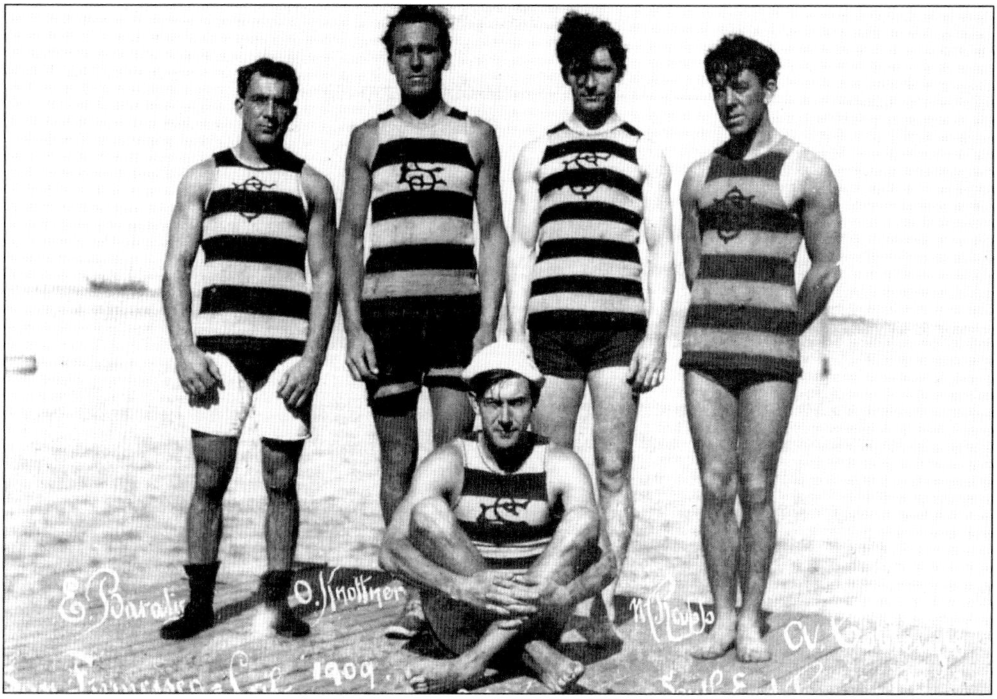

This is a South End crew from 1909.

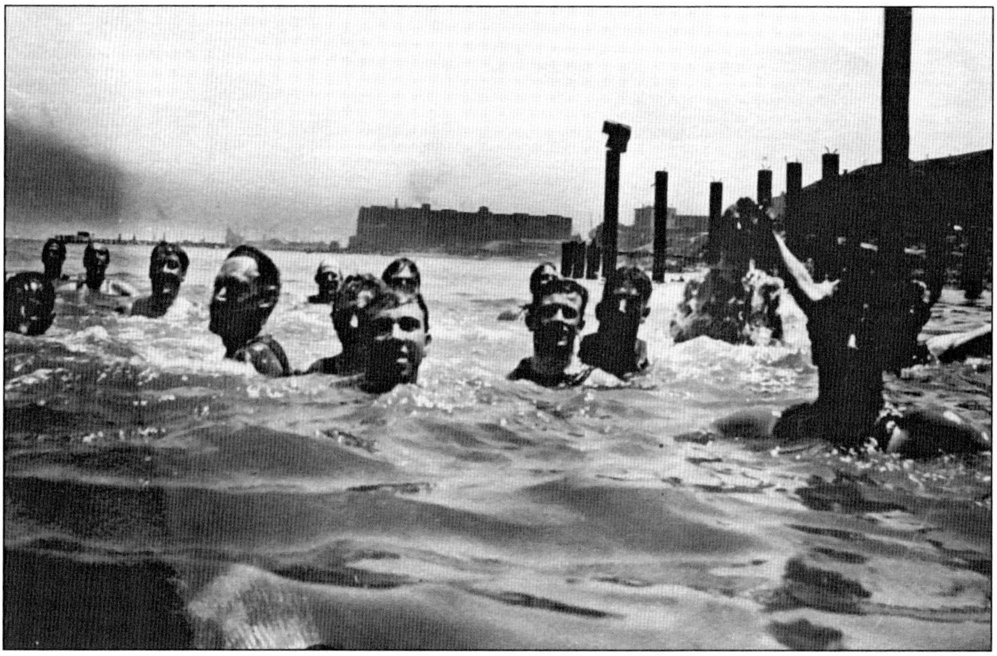
The Ghiselli Dolphin Club gang reach to us from a century ago as they enjoy the invigorating thrill of the chilly San Francisco Bay water. The Haslett Warehouse in the background and lack of an Ariel boathouse date this photograph to 1907.

John L. Herget, formerly known as "Young Mitchell," used his seat on the board of supervisors to help gain political backing for the aquatic park idea. He also sponsored, for many years, the Herget Cup for the best South End rower.

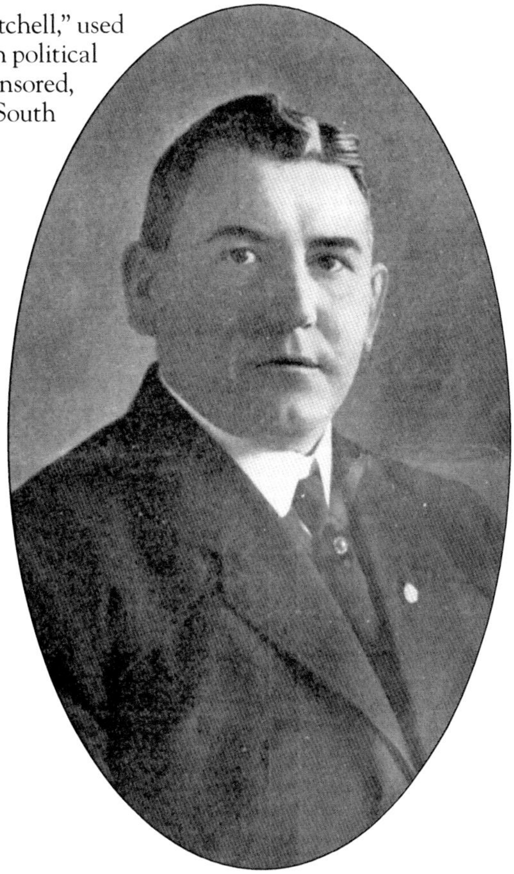

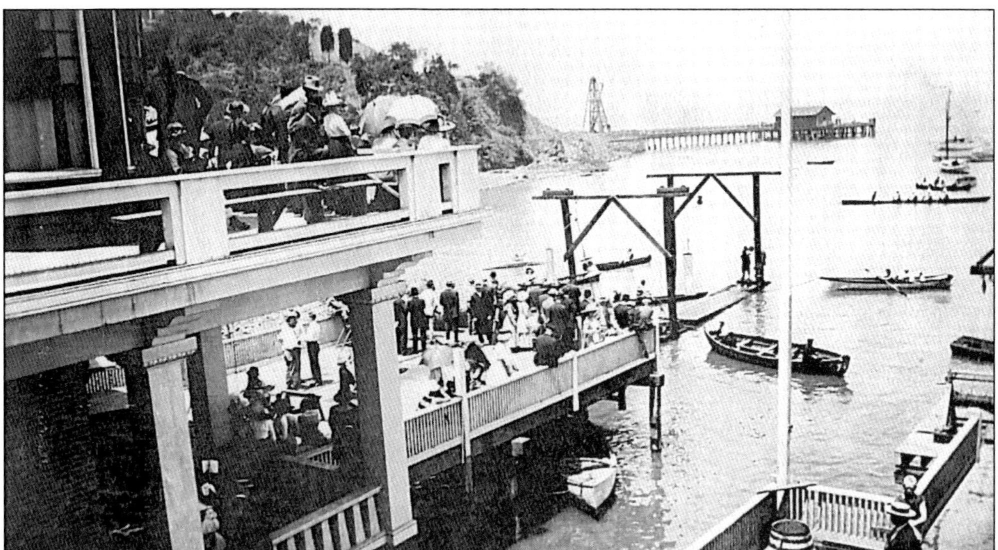

Crowds begin to arrive for the 1909 Aquatic Park Day. Ladies with umbrellas gaze out from choice seats on the second balcony of the South End as derricks are brought into place for the high-diving exhibition.

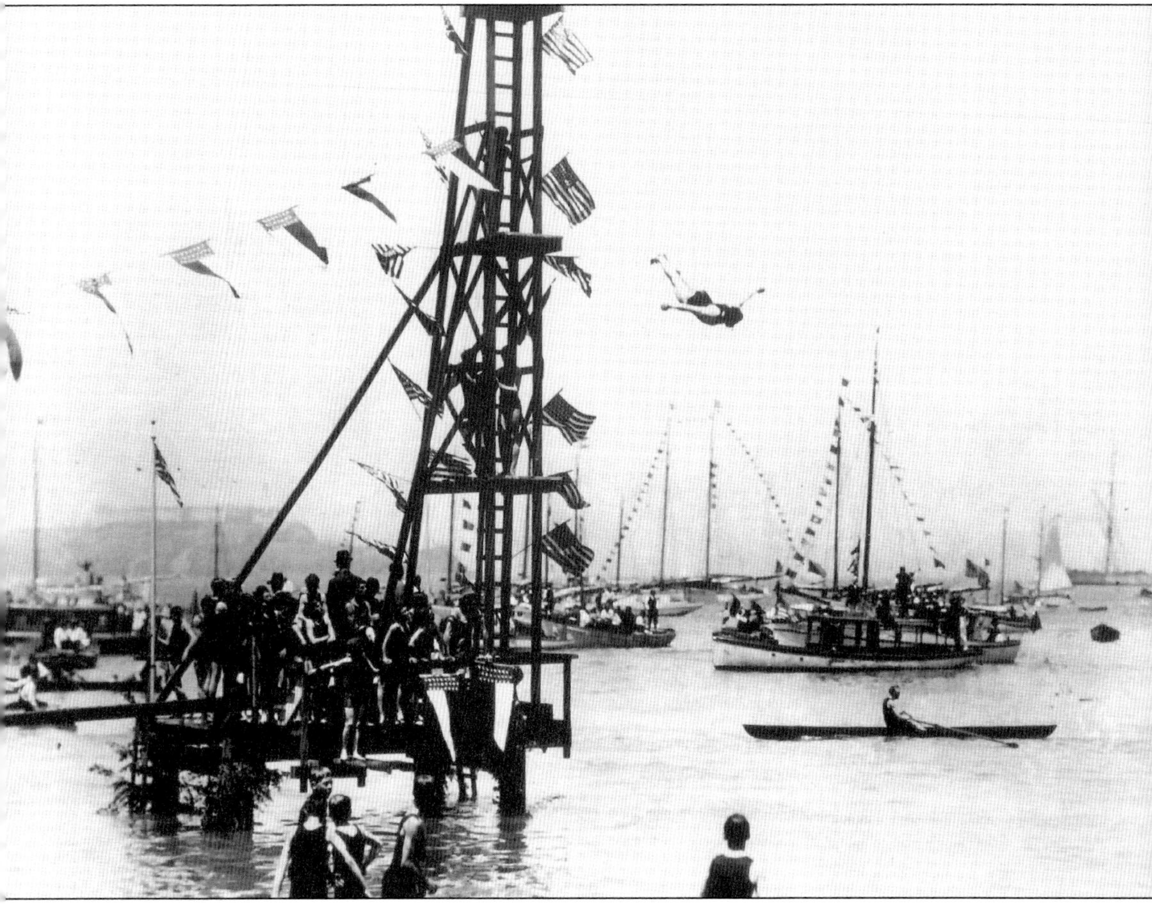

In an amazing scene from Aquatic Park Day, a high diver is photographed in mid-dive. Lookers-on from the beach, the derrick, at the clubs, on rowboats, launches, and sailboats take in the excitement as the diver plunges toward the water. Entertainment like this created a swell of public support for Aquatic Park.

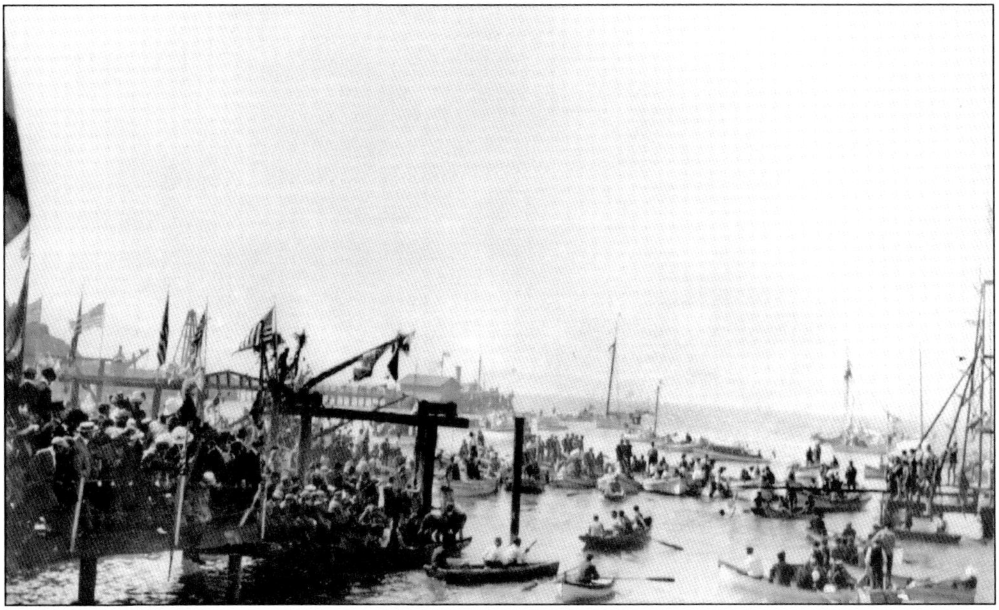

Club docks are filled to capacity and rowboats jockey for position as another Aquatic Park Day event is about to begin.

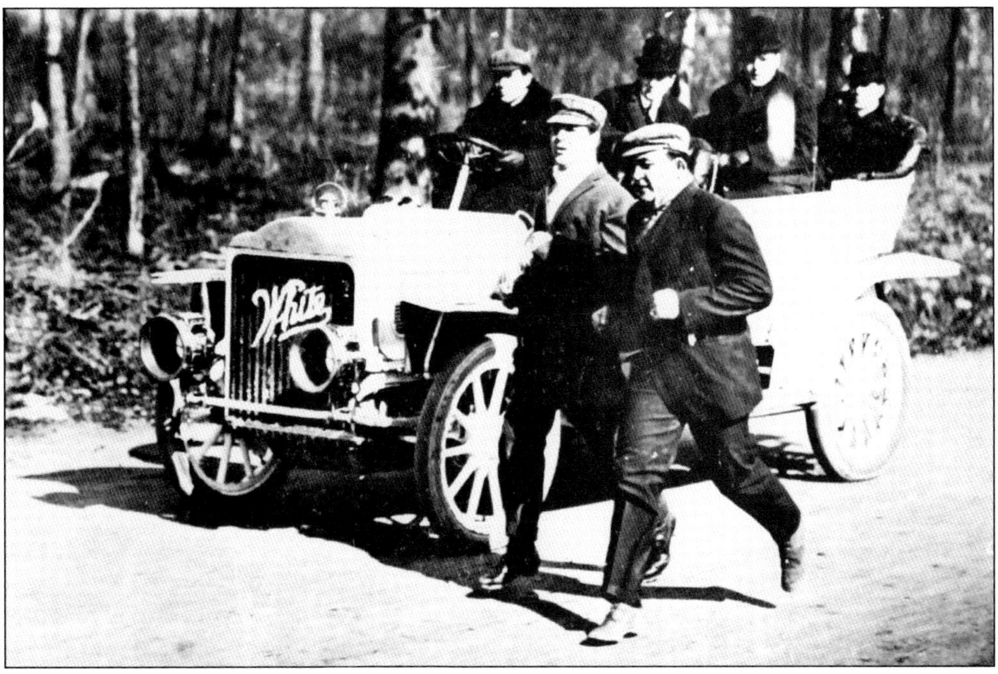

South Ender Sam Berger, left, jogs next to Jim Jefferies as Jefferies trains for the Great White Hope fight against Jack Johnson in 1910 in Reno. Ironically, the vehicle trailing is a White motor car. Berger, an accomplished boxer at the Olympic Club, trained Jefferies against Johnson. Johnson was too much for the aged former champion and won easily.

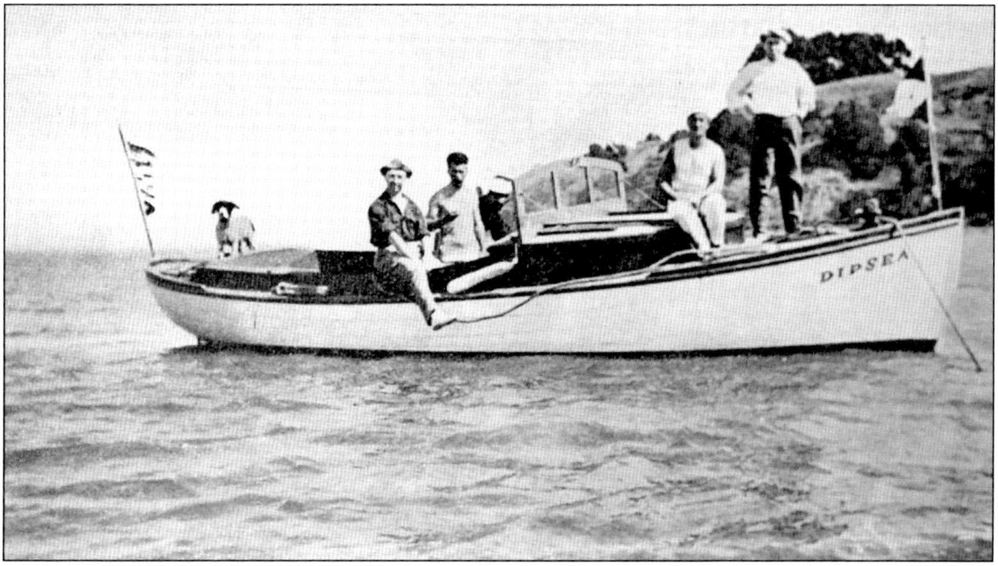

South Ender Timothy Ignatius Fitzpatrick is at the controls of the powerboat *Dipsea*. Fitzpatrick joined the South End around 1893 and was a founder of the Dipsea run. He sat on the bench in San Francisco for over 60 years.

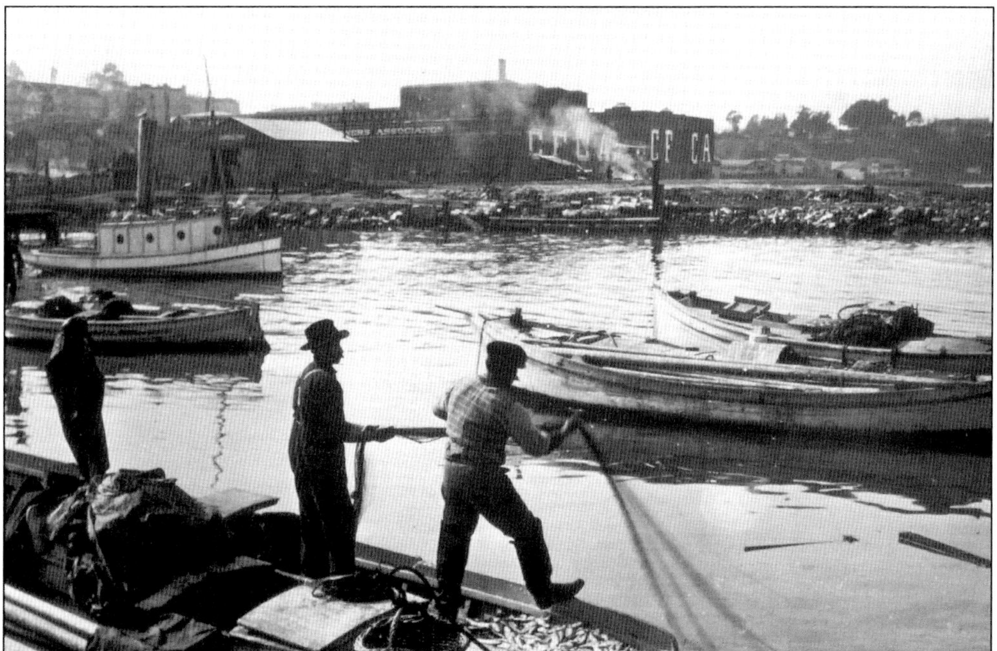

Around 1910, this is Fishermen's Wharf just east of Leavenworth Street. The rowing clubs are in the distance to the right.

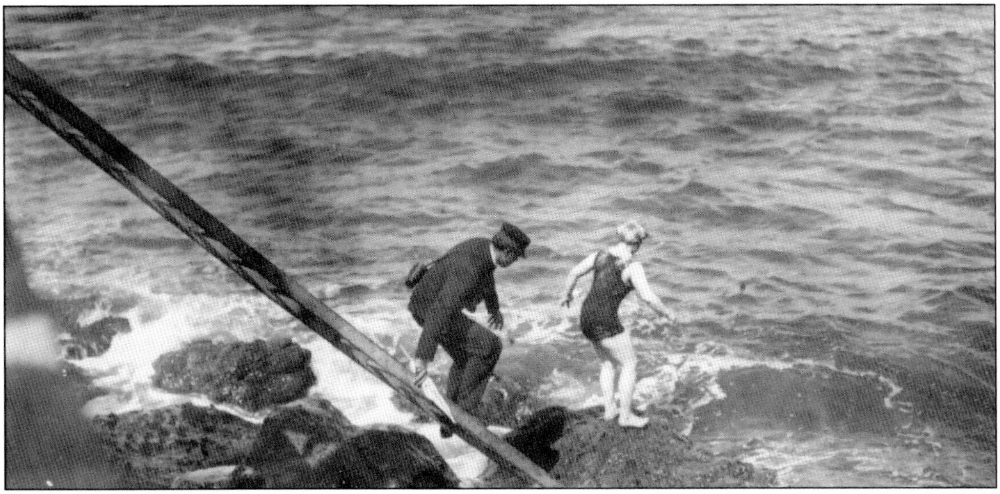

Hazel Lagenour appears about ready to begin her attempt to swim the Golden Gate. She had agreed to meet three other women to make the try on a Sunday in August 1911, but actually made her swim on Saturday—even if she was not the fastest, she would always be the first. She was successful, and her father, a state senator who also owned a film studio, recorded the swim for posterity in a 1911 reenactment.

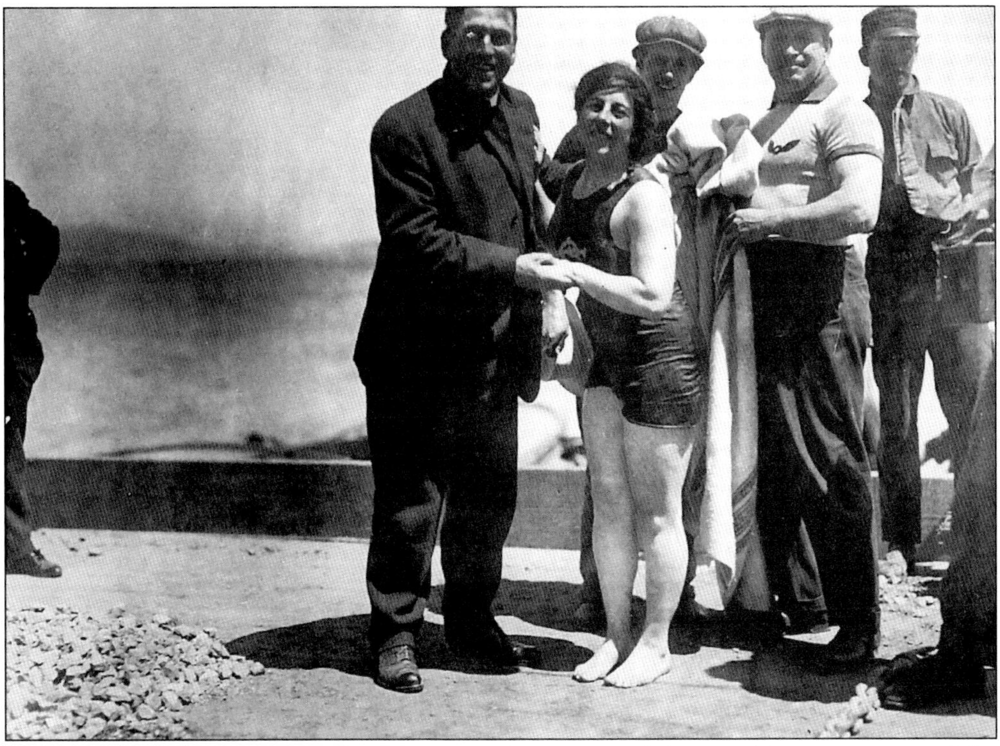

Hazel and her father pose atop Fort Point after she conquered the gate. Newspapers around the country and in London, England, and Sydney, Australia, proclaimed her feat. Hazel parlayed that triumph to a vaudeville career, where she swam in a huge tank and did various acrobatics before the crowd. Her act was banned in Boston, where Hazel was accused by shocked city fathers of doing the tango underwater.

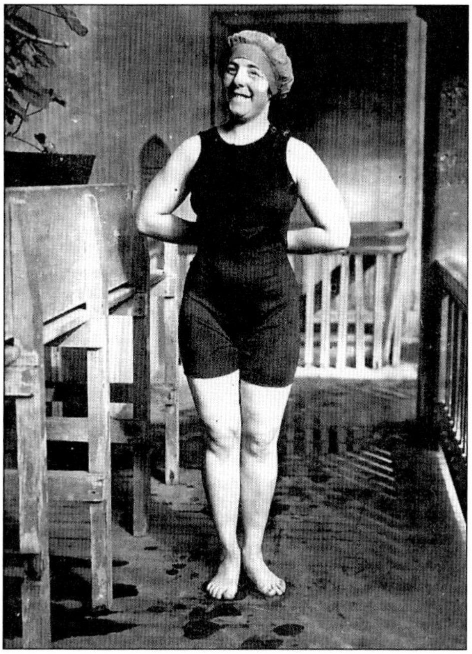

Hazel poses for the cameras at the South End boathouse. The South End provided boats and pilots to ensure her safety during the swim; the Dolphin Club would have nothing to do with it. Hazel was said to have the perfect body for a woman of 1911. The film of her Golden Gate swim opens with several minutes of the young Lagenour flexing her calf muscles and biceps for the film.

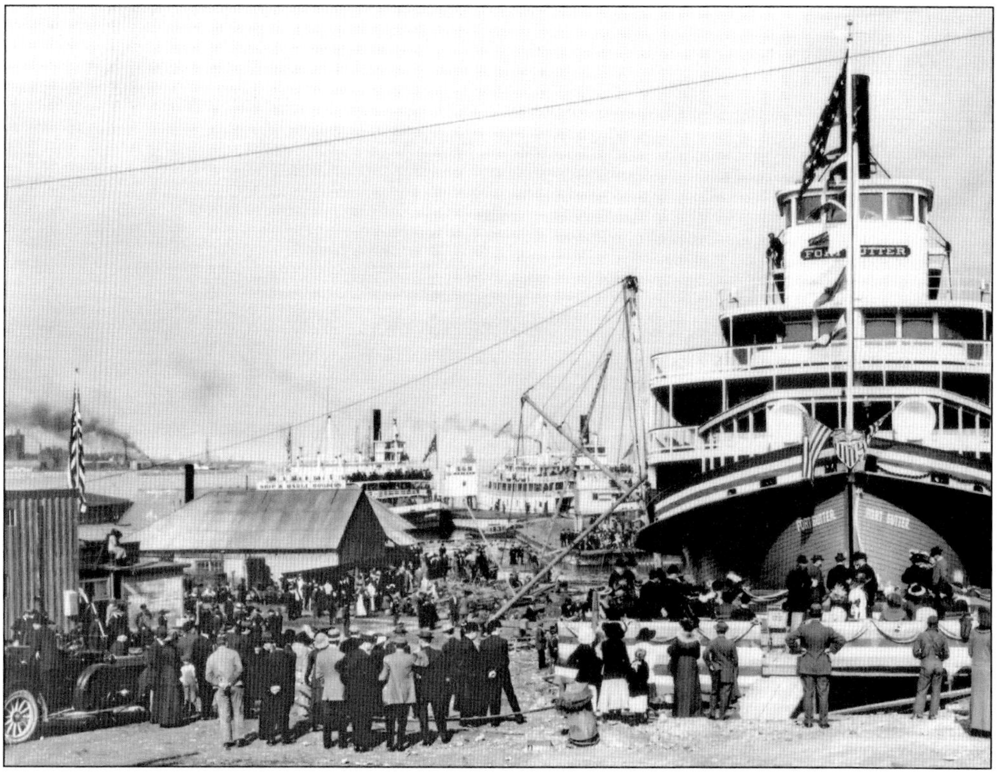

In 1911, the launch of the *Fort Sutter* was a grand occasion. The boat did the run from Sacramento to San Francisco for several years, and played a major role in the conflict in the cove decades later. A young lady won a prize for her essay on how the *Fort Sutter* was a step forward in western civilization.

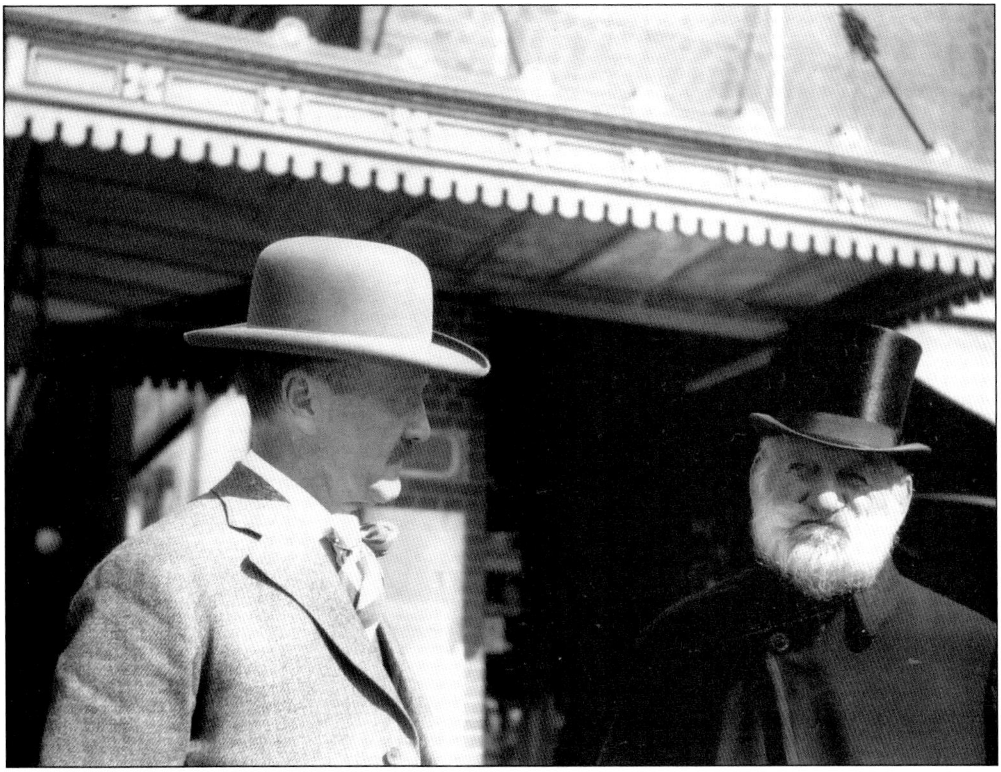

The second president of the South End, Alex M. Robertson (left) stands in front of his Union Square bookstore in 1915 with pioneer Theodore Hittell. Hittell was the author of *Gentle Ben.* Robertson left San Francisco for adventure in Tombstone, Arizona Territory, and Grants County, New Mexico Territory. He was in Tombstone at the time of the OK Corral shootout.

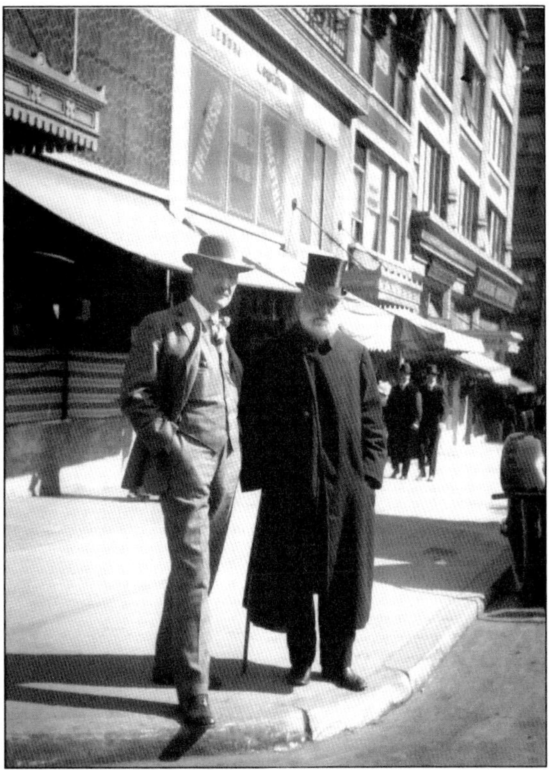

Hittell in his top hat and greatcoat add a touch of antiquity to this photograph. After his time in the territories of the Southwest, Robertson returned to San Francisco, where he started a fine book publishing company. He published George Sterling, Ina Coolbrith, and was the first to publish *Man With a Hoe*. Ironically the author of *In the Footprints of the Padres* recounts his adventure as a boy walking the old redwood flume on Black Point.

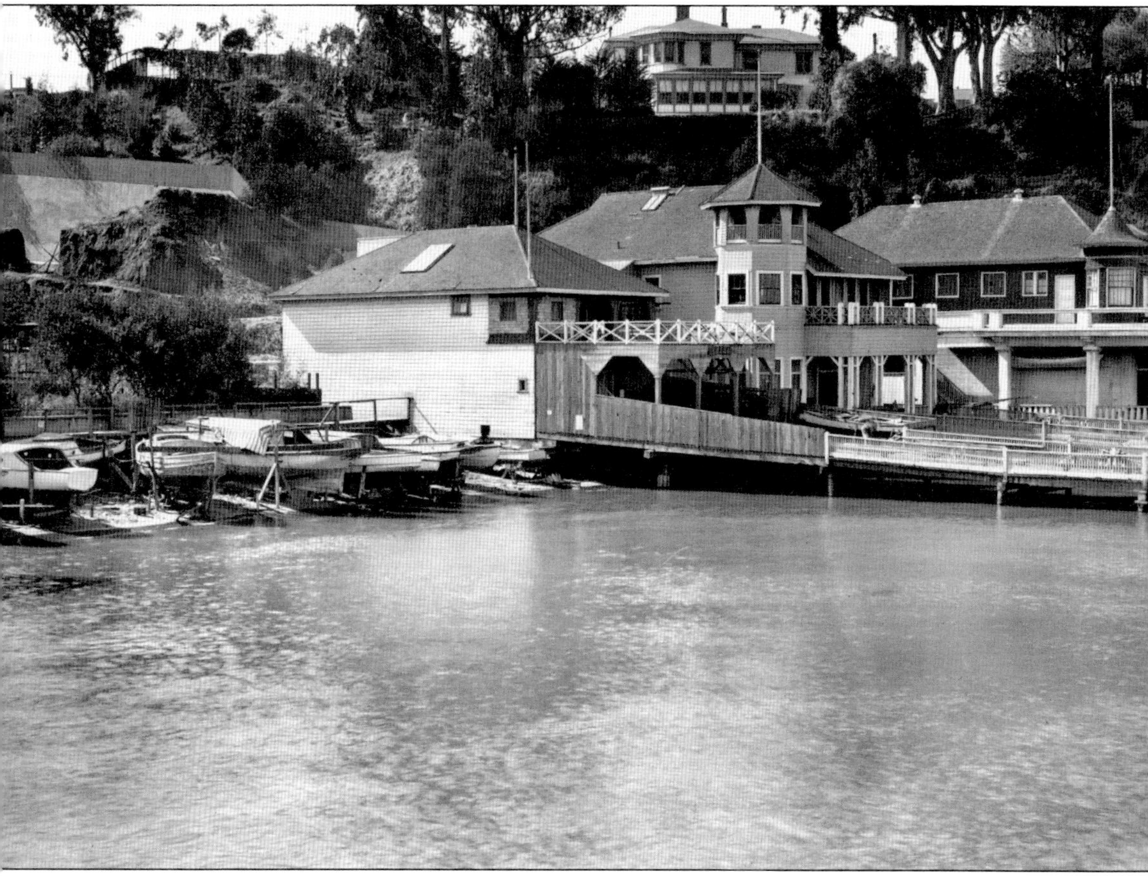

This amazing dual print captures the full sweep of the western side of Black Point Cove in 1918. The Belt Line Railroad trestle runs just above the docks of the clubs—a derailment would have ended the clubs. Borings from the Fort Mason Tunnel, which allowed the Belt Line to continue on to the Marina District are to the rear of the clubs. Pictured, from left to right, are the Ariel,

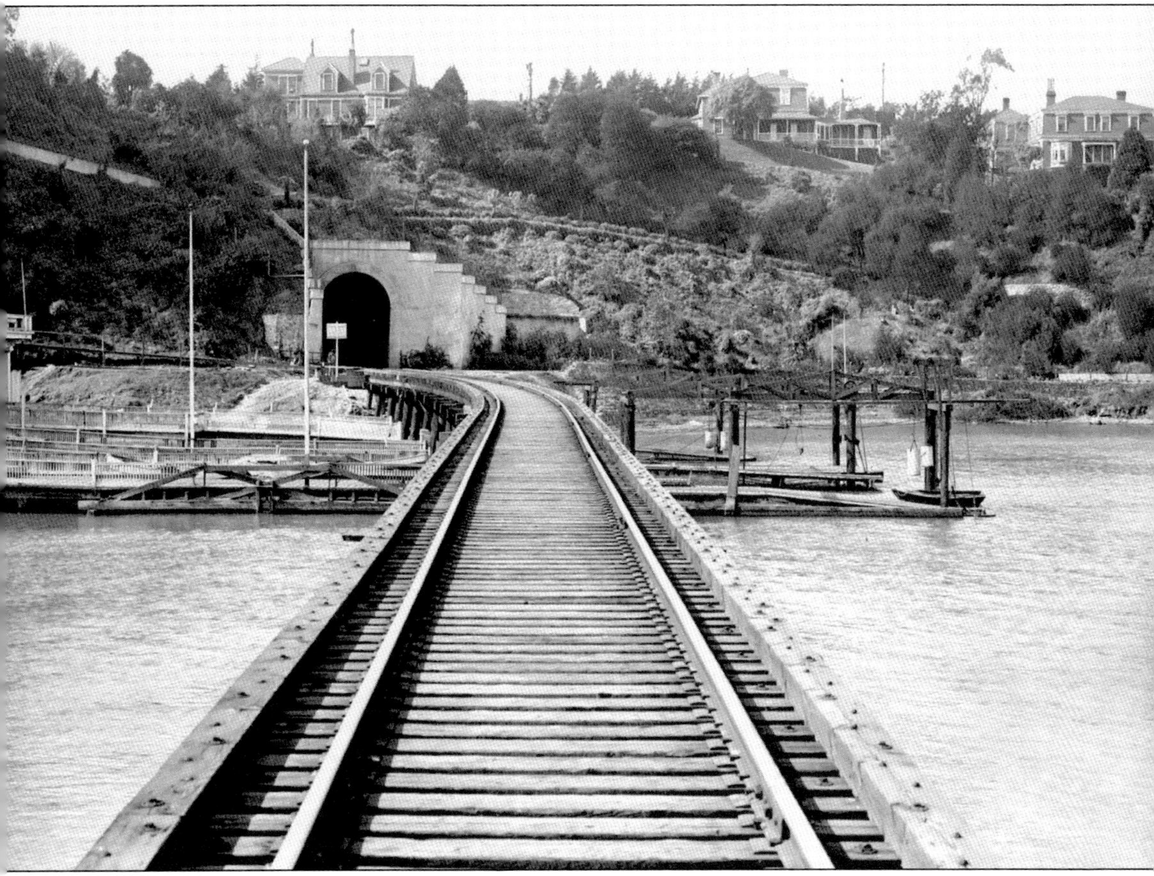

Dolphin, and South End clubs, while various homes and halls in Fort Mason overlook the cove. Van Ness Avenue still did not extend down from North Point, which made deliveries to the government wharf expensive; due to the fact that wagons had to go to the far side of Fort Mason and down the steep road to the wharf far below.

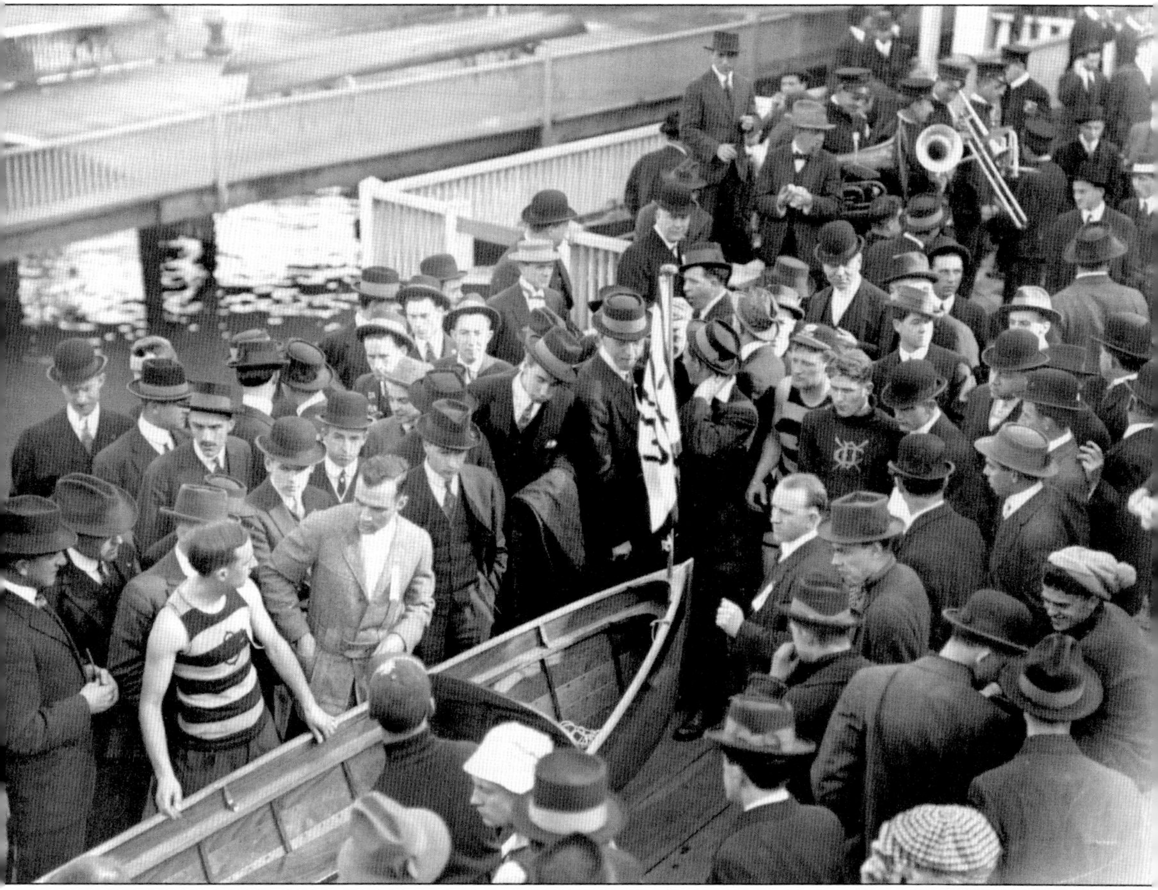

The launch of the barge *South End* in February 1915 called for a brass band and big celebration. It was a product of the boatshop of Al Rogers of Oakland. Rogers had fabricated boats on San Francisco Bay since the 1880s, including some race boats for the South End, and one of his skiffs can still be seen at Lake Tahoe. Still in use, even though the boat is important only because of its age, it does have its supporters.

In May 1917, Haslett Warehouse came just to the edge of the bay. It was not until the boat clubs were moved from the west to the east side of the cove and Aquatic Park completed that Jefferson Avenue was extended west to Larkin Street.

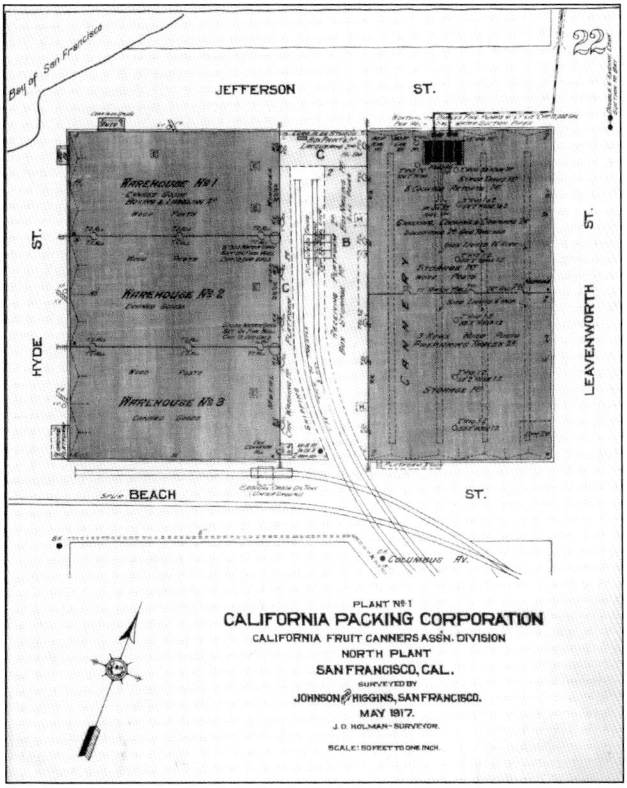

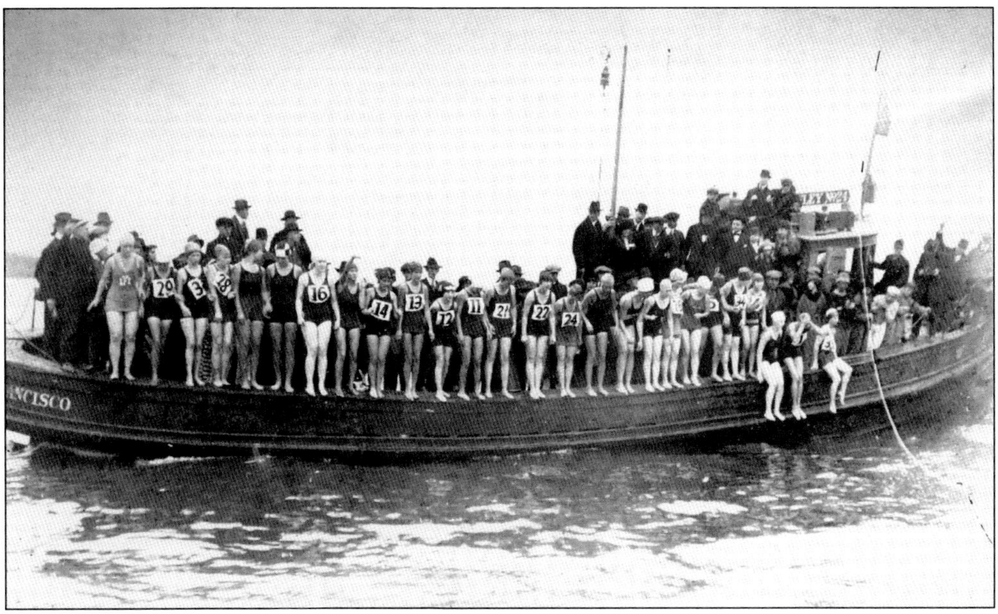

In a moment of quiet, anxious anticipation, over two dozen women wait to jump in the waters of the Golden Gate. Their launch was the *Crowley No. 24*. From the first Golden Gate swim in 1911, with three participants, the swim had grown to 26 women at the time of this photograph in 1920.

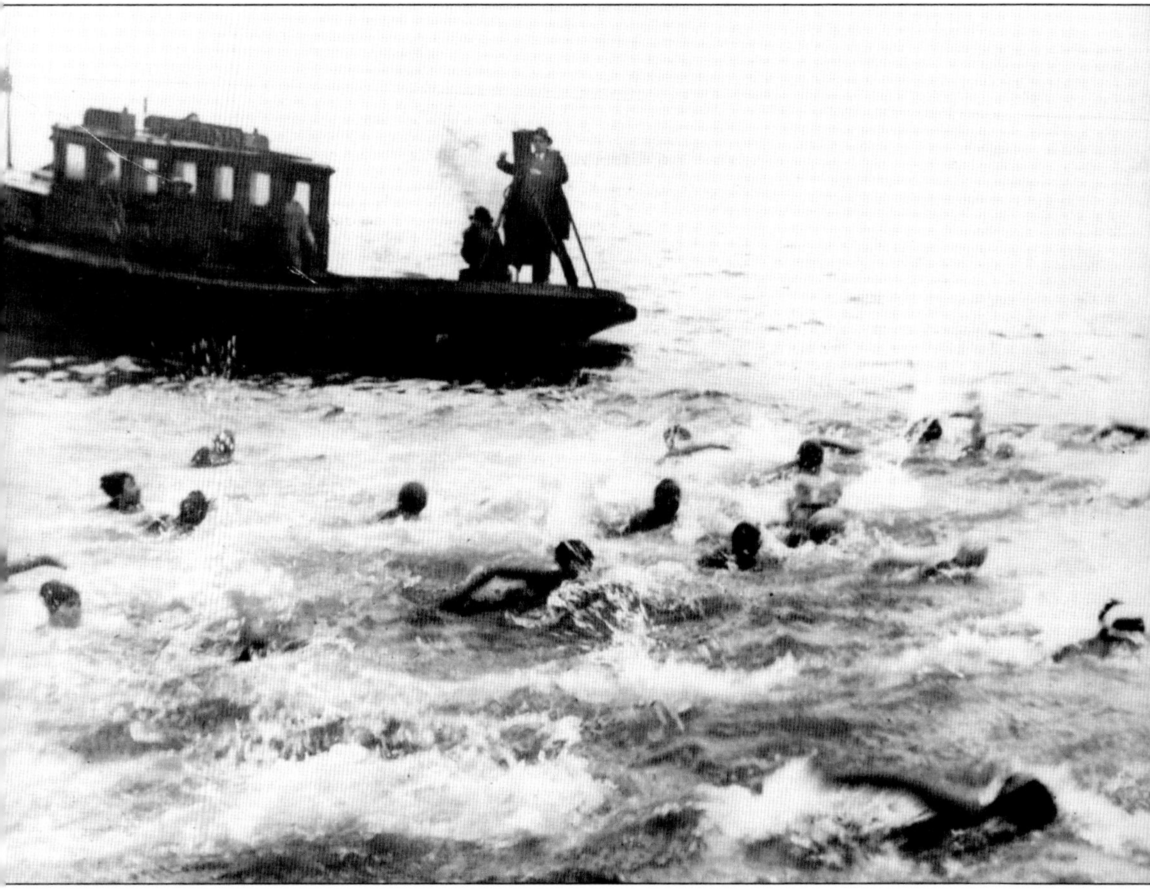

As the women head to the Marin shore, a motion picture camera records the swim.

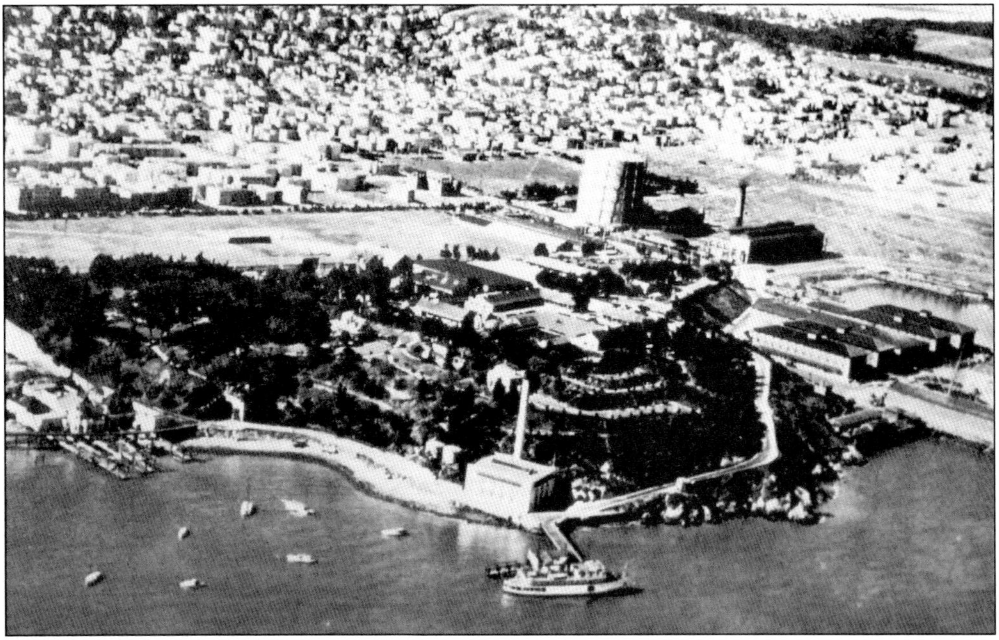

The clubs are to the left as the Alcatraz supply ship ties up at the government wharf in this aerial photograph taken on April 11, 1925. The long road around Fort Mason can be seen to the lower right, and Van Ness Avenue remains to be lengthened. In two years, the clubs would be moved for that extension, to the foot of Larkin Avenue.

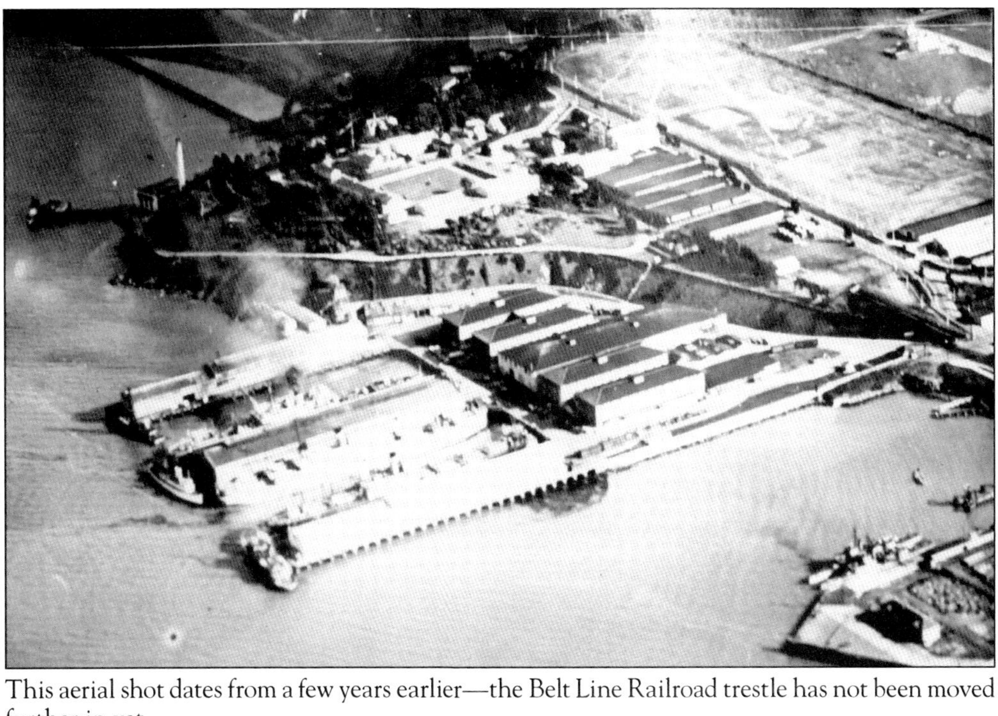

This aerial shot dates from a few years earlier—the Belt Line Railroad trestle has not been moved further in yet.

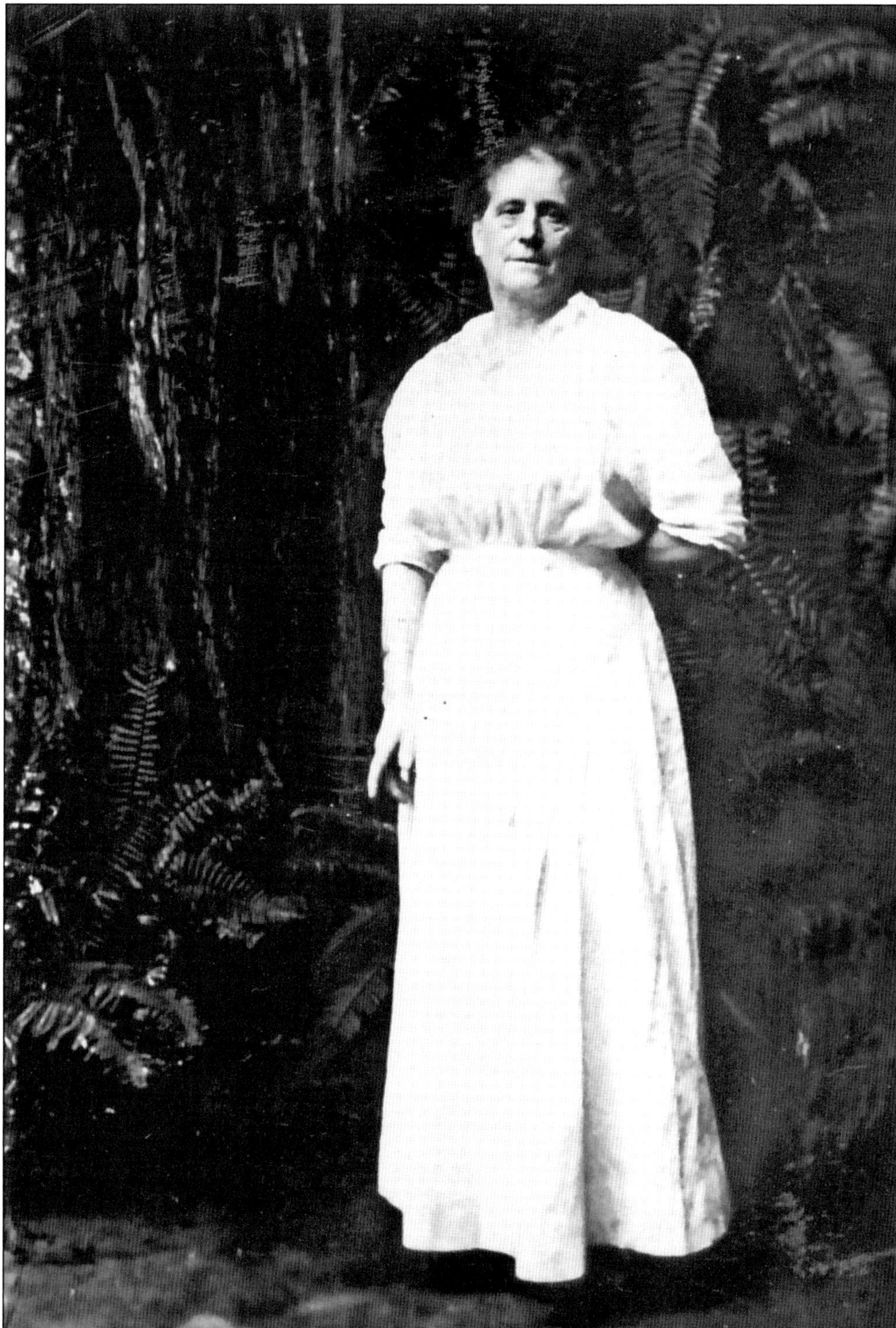

Shanghaier Enrichetta Ghiselli was widowed in the early 1890s and inherited her husband's sailor's clothing store. In 1907, her sons Guido and Anacleto joined the Dolphin Club.

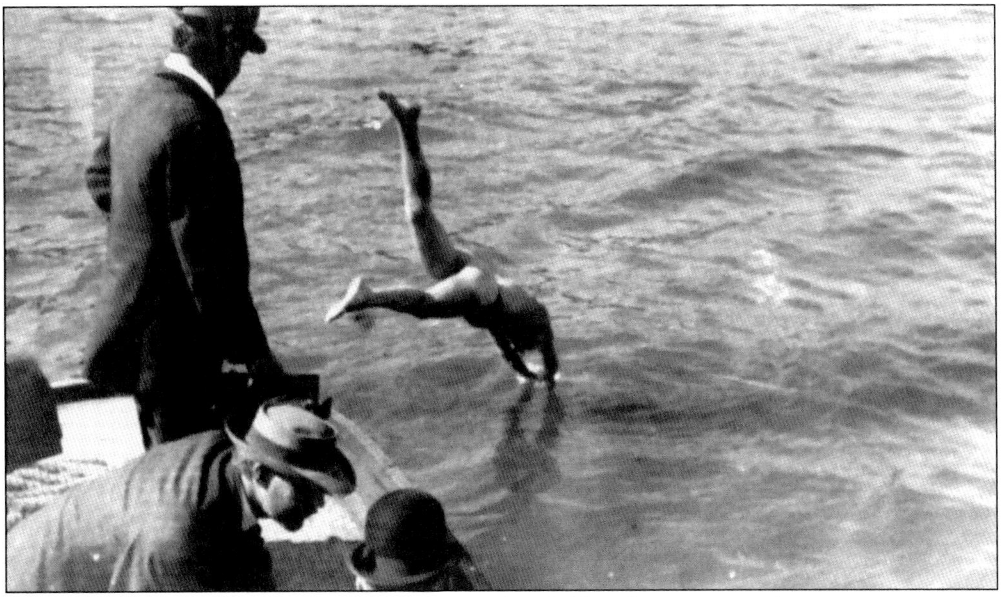

A nude Arthur Cavill jumps into the water at the Golden Gate in an early attempt to conquer the waters. His attempt in 1907 was successful, but it must have been very cold.

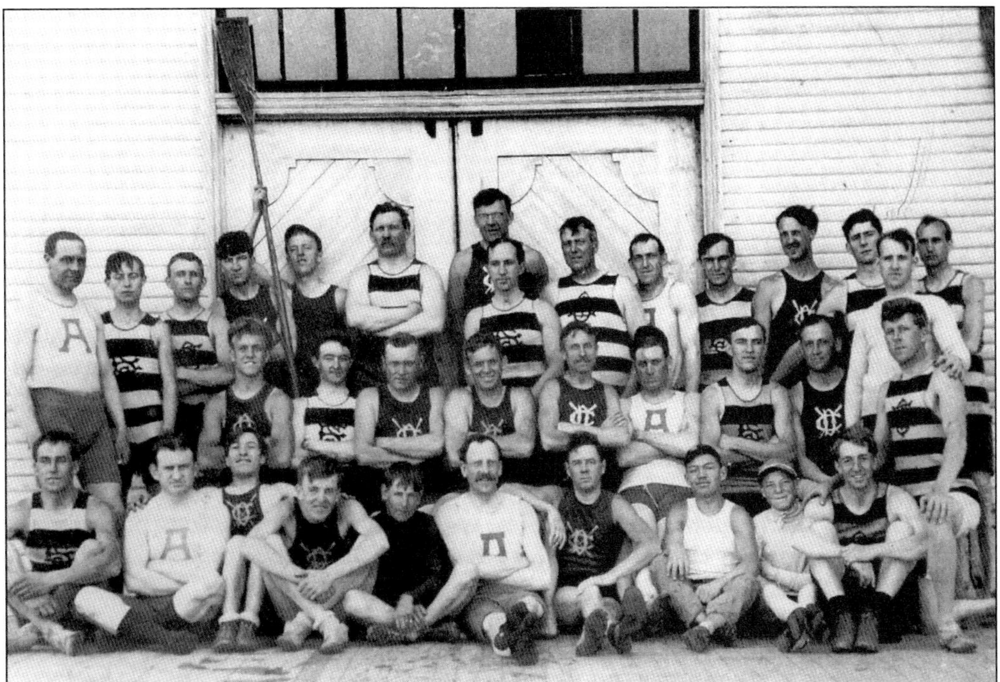

Ariel, South End, and Dolphin Club members pose together in 1920 outside of the South End Rowing Club doors.

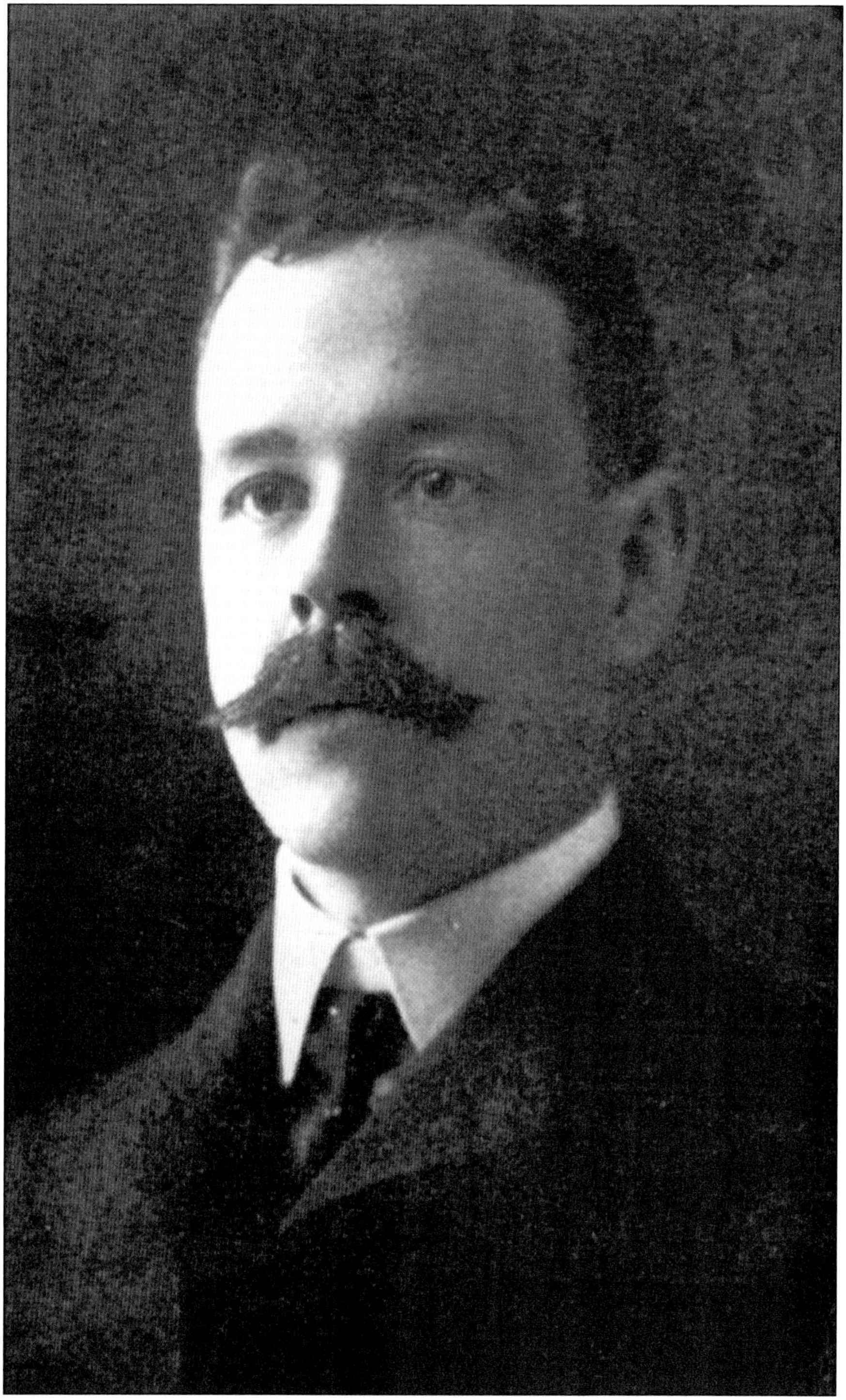

Pictured *c.* 1917, Charles Farrell was an early supporter of Aquatic Park. He was the most prominent Dolphin Club member in the fight to gain an aquatic park at Black Point Cove. Farrell joined with Ed Scully from the South End to achieve this victory.

Four

The Project Slowly Moves Ahead

The years from 1918 to 1935 were years of halting progress for the dream of Aquatic Park. The City of San Francisco had committed itself to the project, but bond issues in 1928 and 1932 were defeated by the city's electorate. The city slowly acquired the land needed, the rowing clubs were moved, Van Ness Avenue extended, and a new government wharf built in 1928 at city expense.

The 1920s saw competing bids for a park design. In 1931, work was started on Muni Pier. The City of San Francisco was able to complete that project, but the Depression meant a long delay for the park. Deeper pockets were needed.

On the east side of the cove, Hyde Street Pier became the embarkation and de-embarkation point for ferryboats that ran to and from Sausalito and Berkeley. The Golden Gate and Bay Bridges had not been finished by the mid-1930s.

Handball, swimming, and rowing flourished. The South End developed its relationship with UC Berkeley and several Olympic gold medal winners pulled an oar for the South End after their college days were over. In 1933, the South End four-man crew won the national championship in Chicago. They were described as having rowed "as if pursued by pirates."

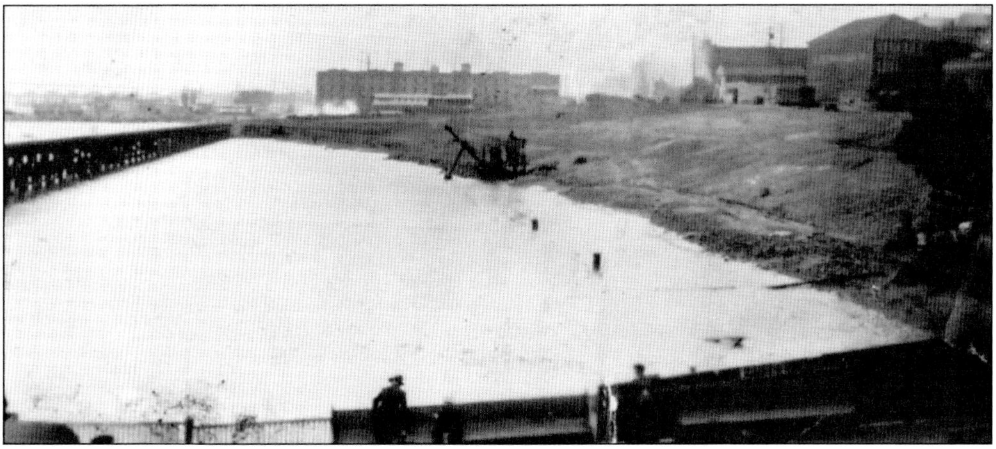

This 1920 view from the Ariel Club shows the first steam shovel in Aquatic Park.

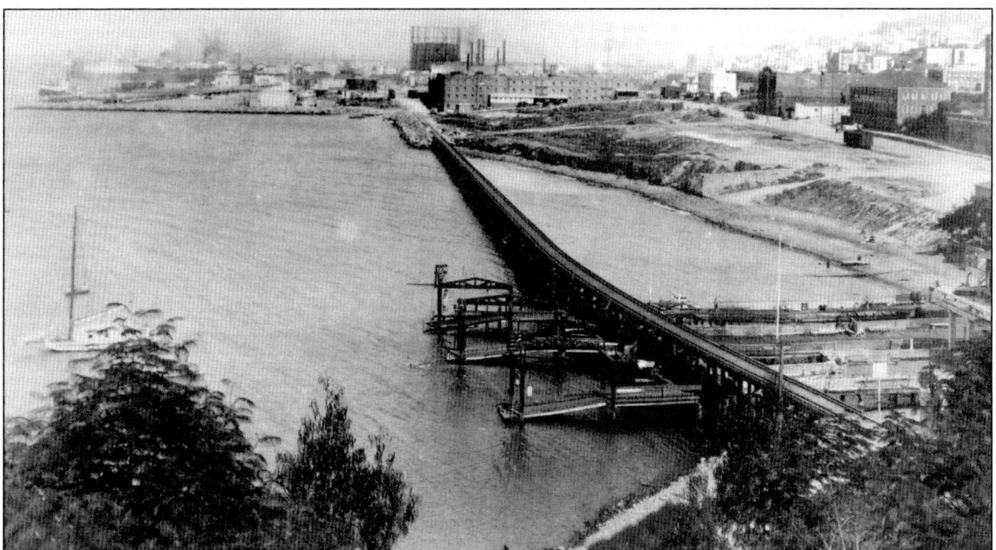

Work had not begun yet to move the Belt Line Railroad tracks behind the rowing clubs, a step essential to the safety of the clubs.

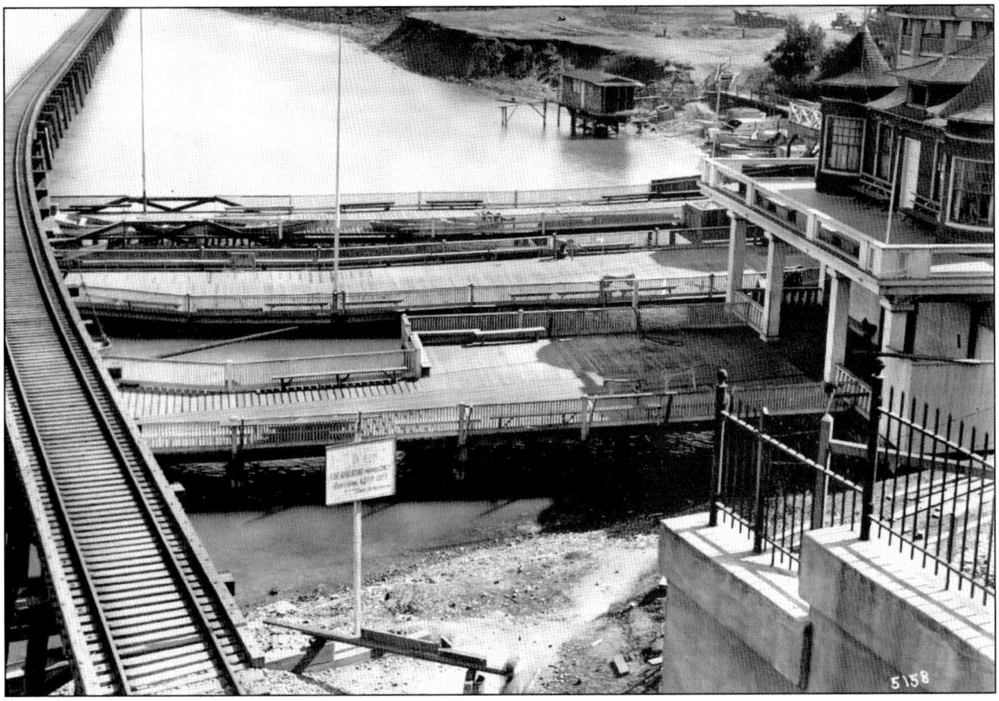

After the destruction of 1906, hundreds of truckloads of debris were dumped in Black Point Cove, and the shore moved out from North Point and Beach Streets nearly to what is now Jefferson. The 20-foot cliff in the background of the photograph attests to the depth of that dumping.

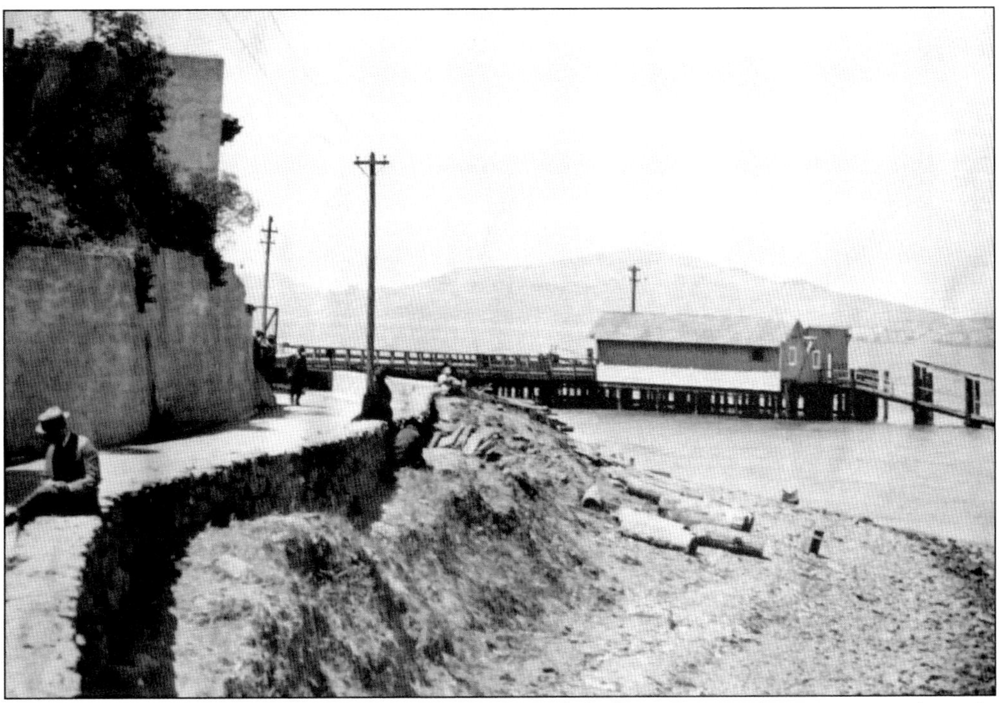

The walkway to the government wharf was a bucolic path before Van Ness Avenue was put through.

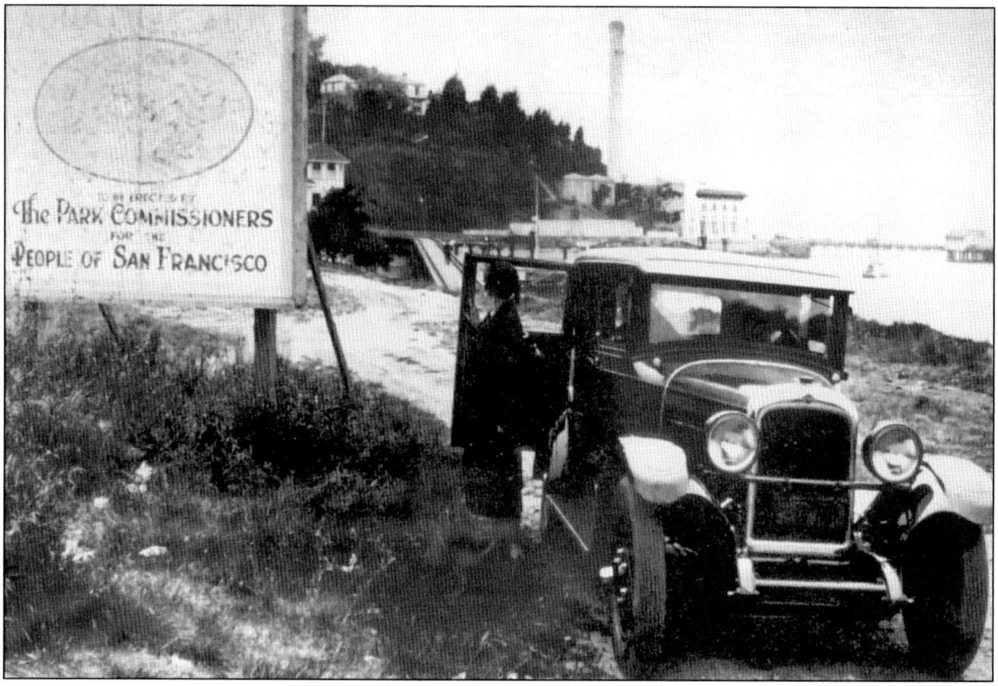

A curiosity seeker in 1925 reads a notice that Aquatic Park will be erected on this site. At this point, a second track for the Belt Line Railroad has been put up further inland.

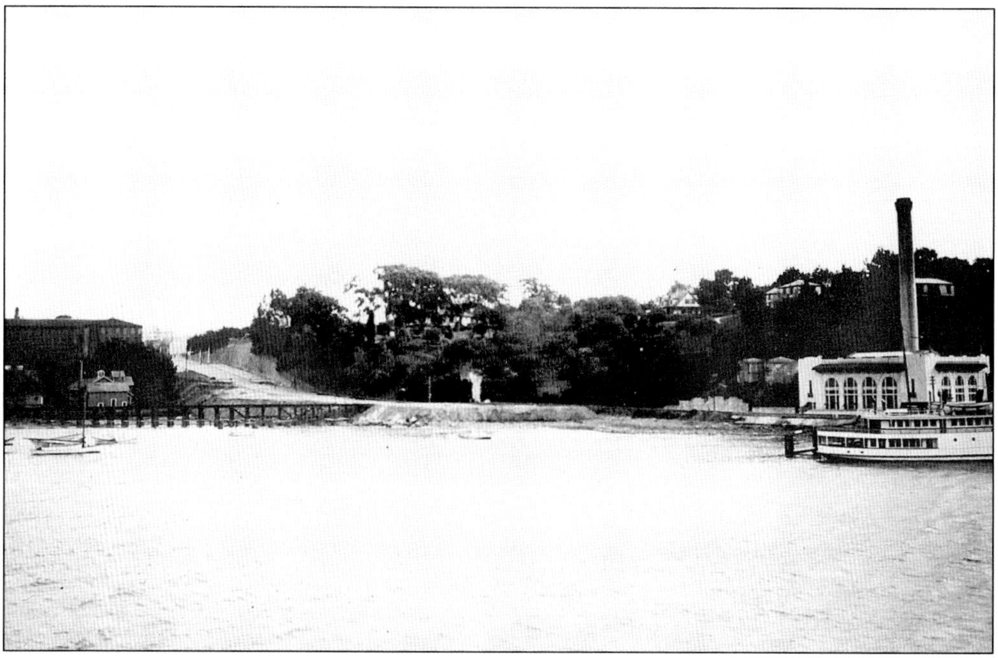

In this post-1927 photograph, the rowing clubs have been moved and Van Ness Avenue extended.

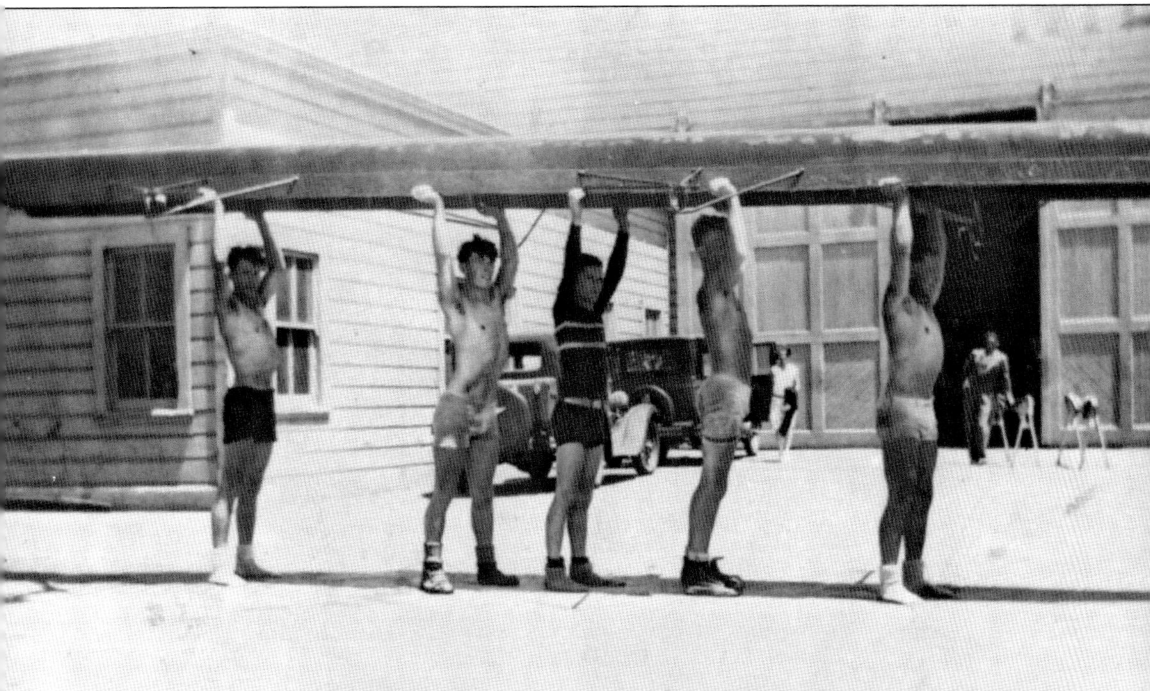

Al Bates, second from left, was a member of the South End crew that beat Olympic champions UC Berkeley in the four-man crew race on July 4, 1928. Al said, "It was the proudest day of my life." Al had joined the South End in 1926 and used to sail with old Judge Fritz. "The judge knew the tides and we would get over to Sausalito in no time under sail."

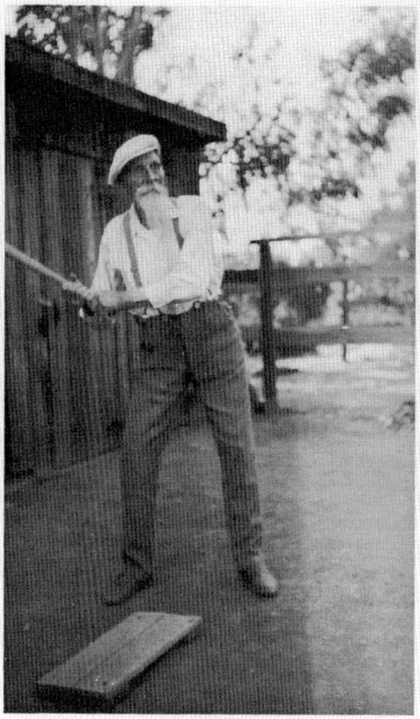

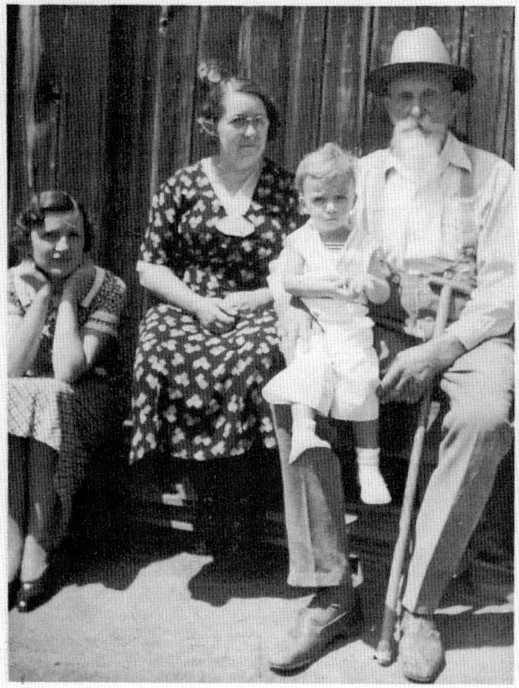

George Duplissea celebrating his 90th birthday on his apricot farm in Los Altos, California, 1934.

Top right ~ four generations of Duplissea's: (from left) Edith ~ granddaughter May ~ daughter Lee ~ great grandson

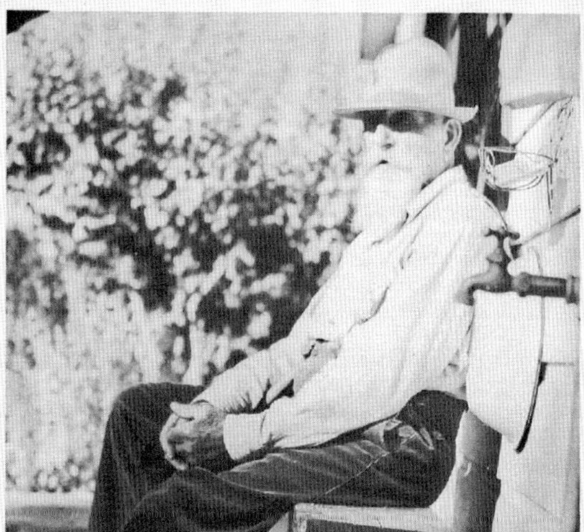

In 1934, "Big George" Duplissea celebrated his 90th birthday with family in Los Altos. As stroke of the South End professional four-man crew, George was a force to reckon with in his mid-1940s. During the 1880s, the South End team swept away all competition. After his active rowing days ended, George formed a Canadian tug-of-war team that had good success during the international tug-of-war craze that engulfed San Francisco in 1894.

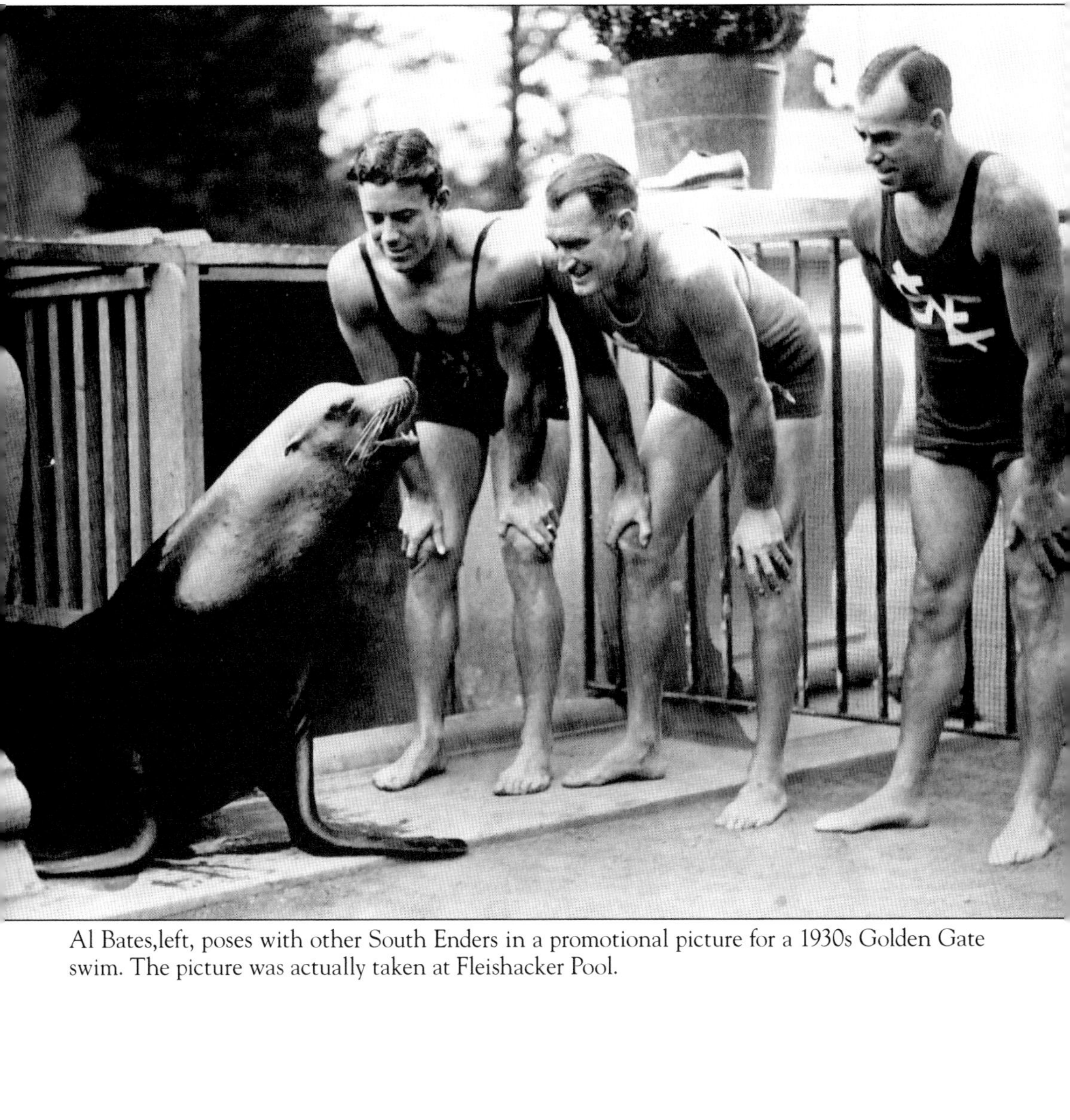

Al Bates,left, poses with other South Enders in a promotional picture for a 1930s Golden Gate swim. The picture was actually taken at Fleishacker Pool.

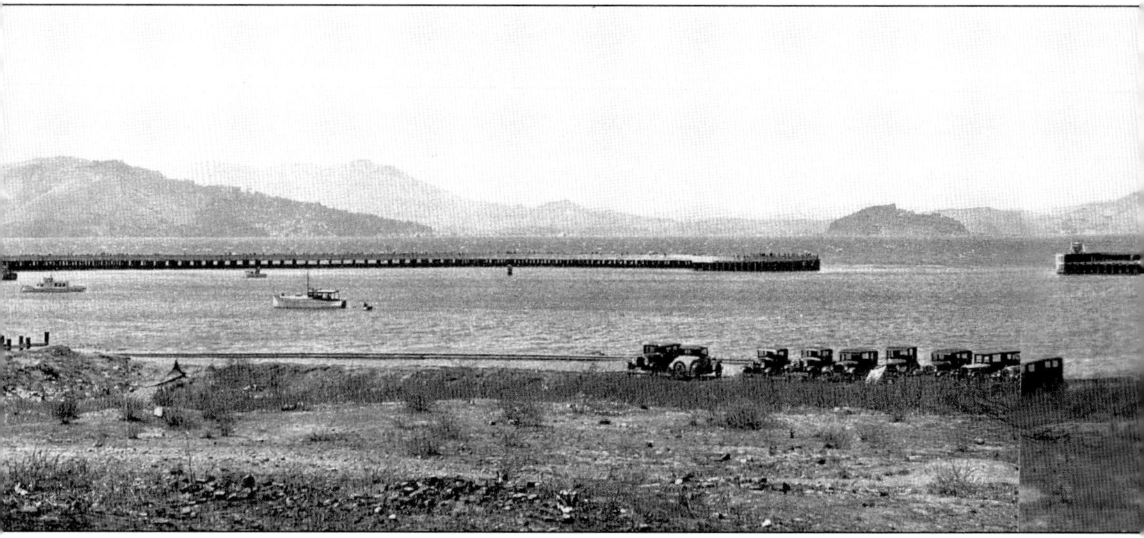

This is a panoramic view of Black Point Cove in 1933. The beach is a convenient parking lot for rowing club members, Hyde Street Pier patrons, and workers at the Haslett Warehouse. The newly

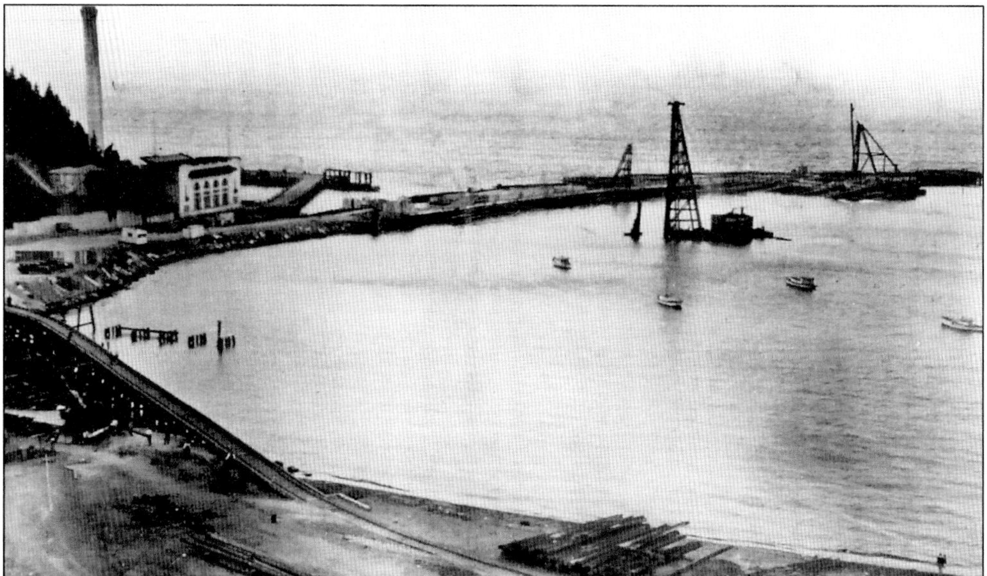

In this November 1932 photograph, Muni Pier appears under construction. The new government wharf, upper left, was built by the city in 1928 in anticipation of Muni Pier and planned Aquatic Park construction.

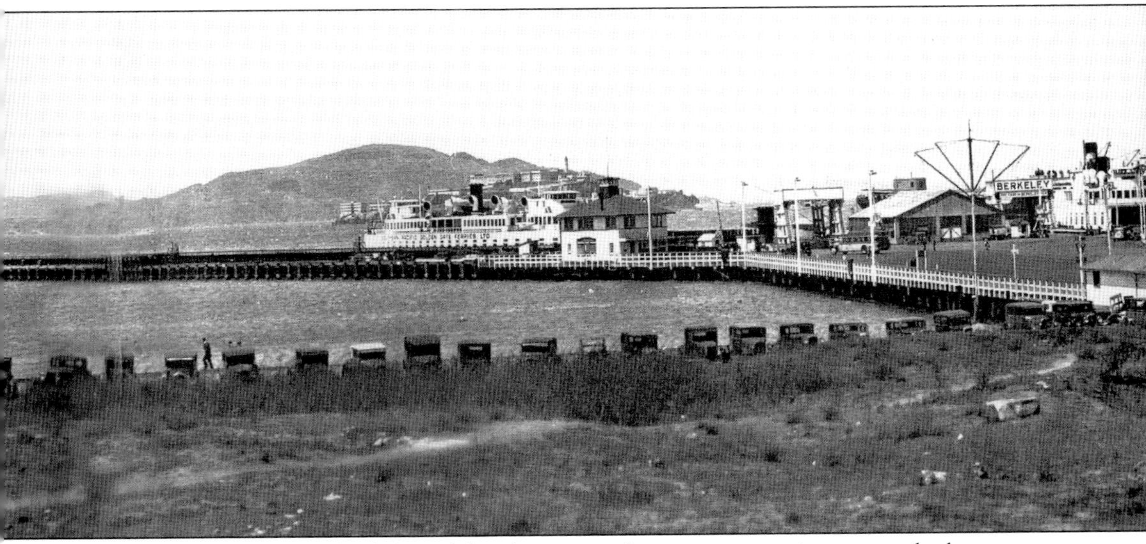

finished Muni Pier is on the left, and ferryboats wait for passengers going across the bay.

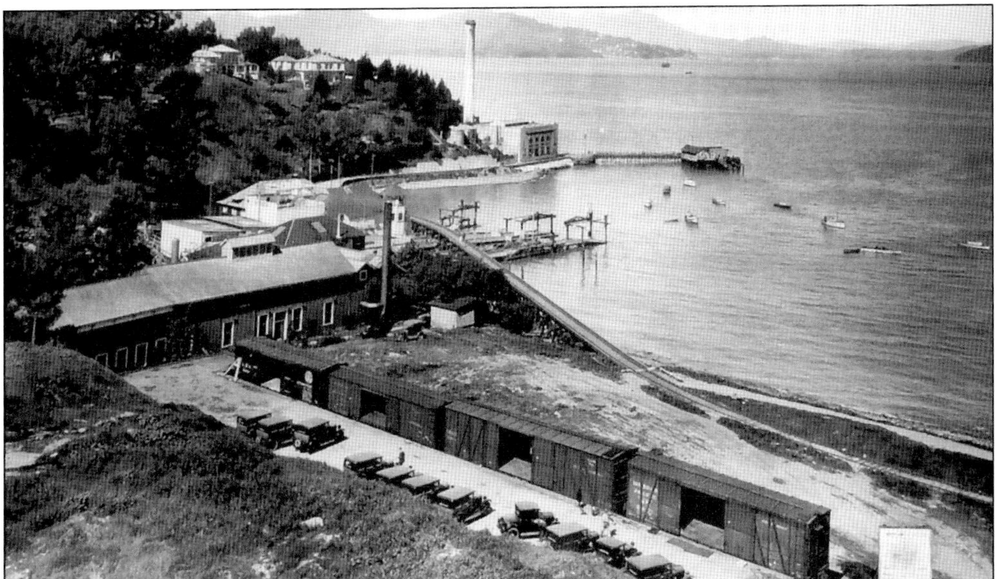

Railcars appear in the foreground of this 1925 view of Black Point Cove. This very detailed photograph gives one an idea of how industrial Black Point Cove still was even several years after San Francisco's board of supervisors had committed to create "a park for the people."

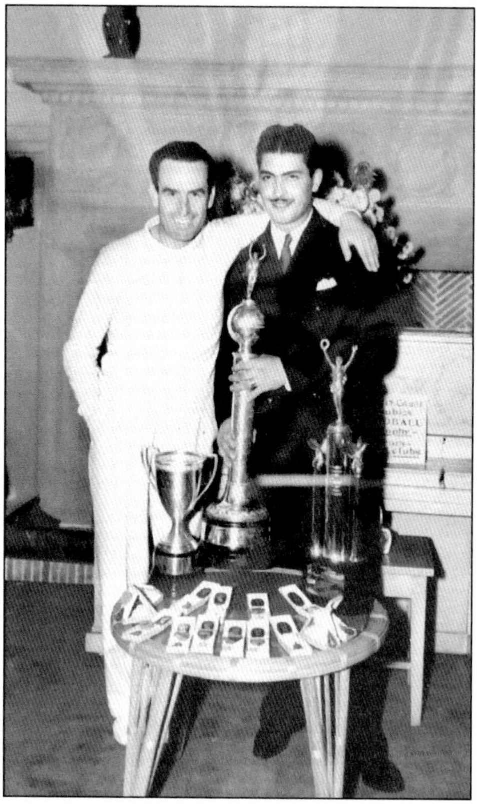

Harold Lloyd, the famed silent film comedian, was an avid handball player. He frequently invited some of the South End's better handball players to play matches at the handball court on his Southern California estate. Trophies were part of the fun.

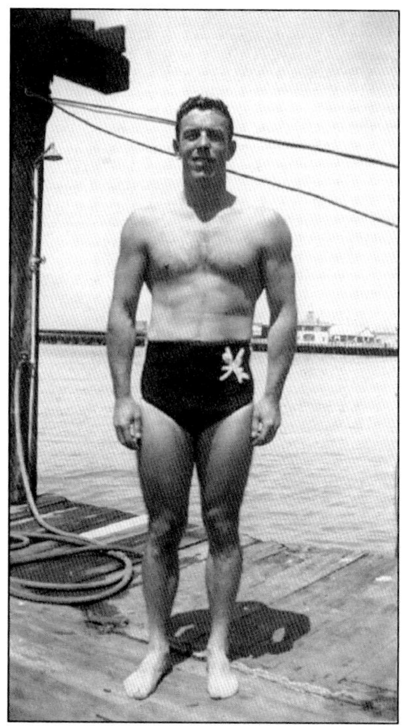

Al Bates, pictured on the South End dock, was nicknamed "Shoulders."

This is Bakewell, Brown, and Bauer's plan for Aquatic Park.

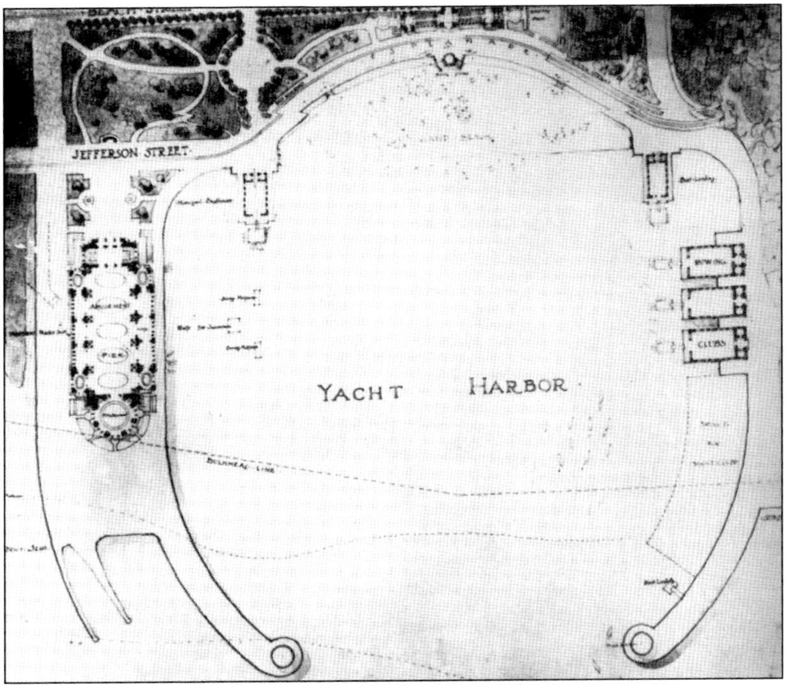

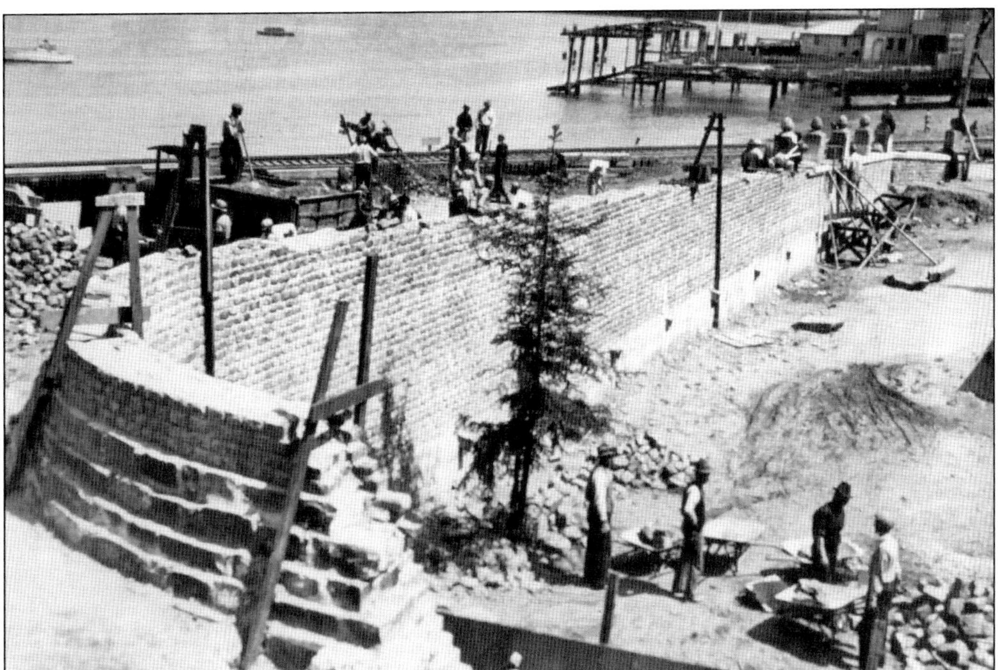

In 1933, looking east from Van Ness Avenue, a State Emergency Recovery Act crew constructs a wall for Aquatic Park. State money, however, dried up after this.

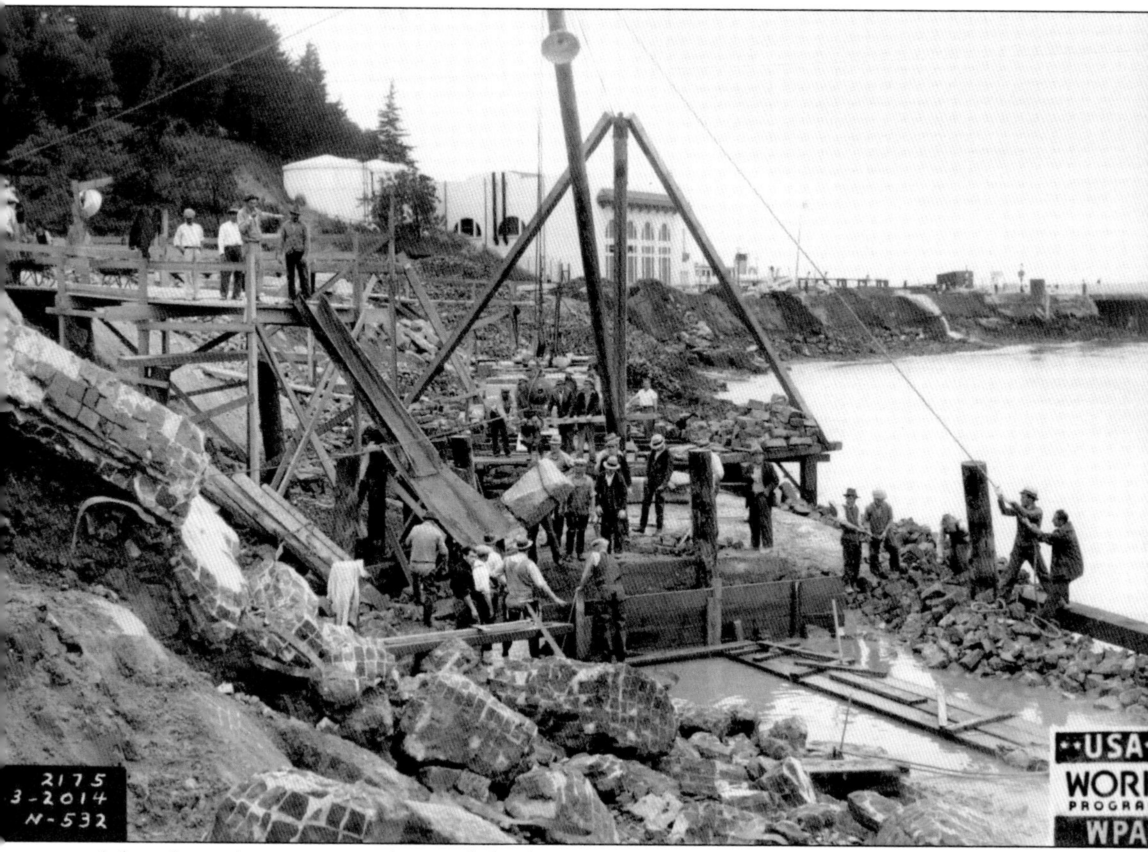

A lot of muscle power is evident as federal WPA money funded the Aquatic Park project from late 1935 until the park's dedication in 1939. A huge block is winched into place as part of the foundation for the seawall. The seawall established the basic configuration of the park.

Five

Building Aquatic Park

With the commitment of the WPA to the Aquatic Park project, the halted work now took off. The seawall was completed and the bathhouse begun. The bathhouse was supposed to be a boathouse, but the rowing clubs declined an invitation to occupy the new building, choosing their old wooden structures. In late 1937, the clubs were moved to their current position on rollers. Some of these rollers still form the foundation of the South End Rowing Club.

Benny Bufano and other artists decorated the interior of the building with murals, and the entire municipal bathhouse had a streamlined Moderne design. William A. Mooser III was the architect on the bathhouse. His father had designed the Haslett Warehouse and Ghirardelli Square, while his grandfather had put his impression on Pioneer Woolen Mills buildings in 1863.

Aquatic Park was dedicated in January 1939 before throngs of enthusiastic San Franciscans. The lease on the municipal bathhouse, for the city, was a nightmare though. The brothers who the city contracted with were terrible tenants, and the city booted them out just as the United States entered World War II.

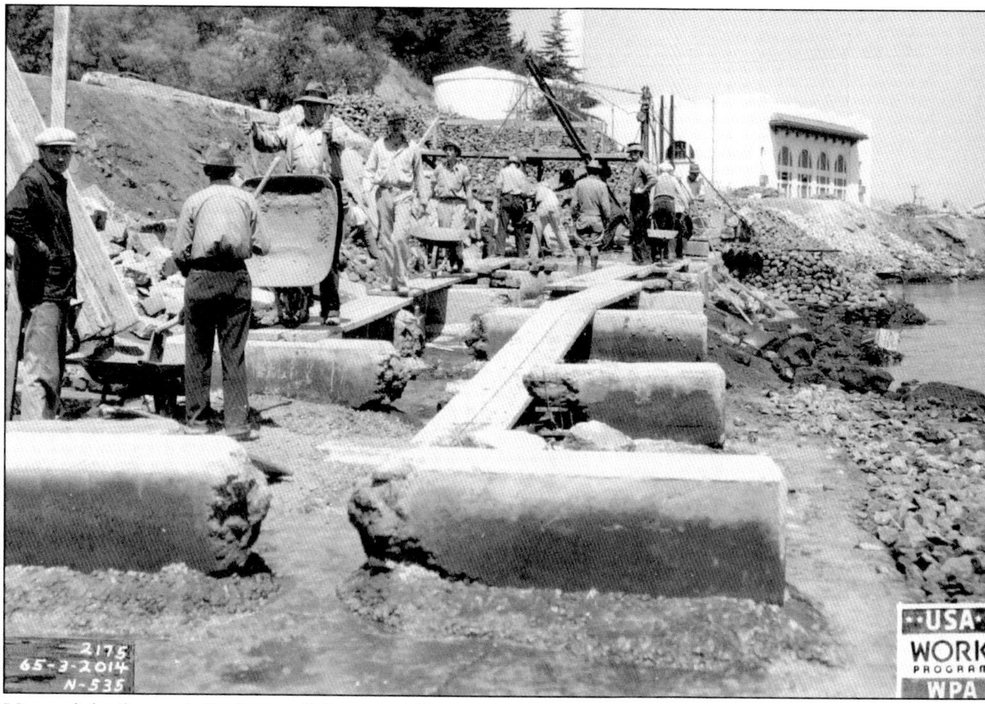

Huge slabs formed the base of the seawall.

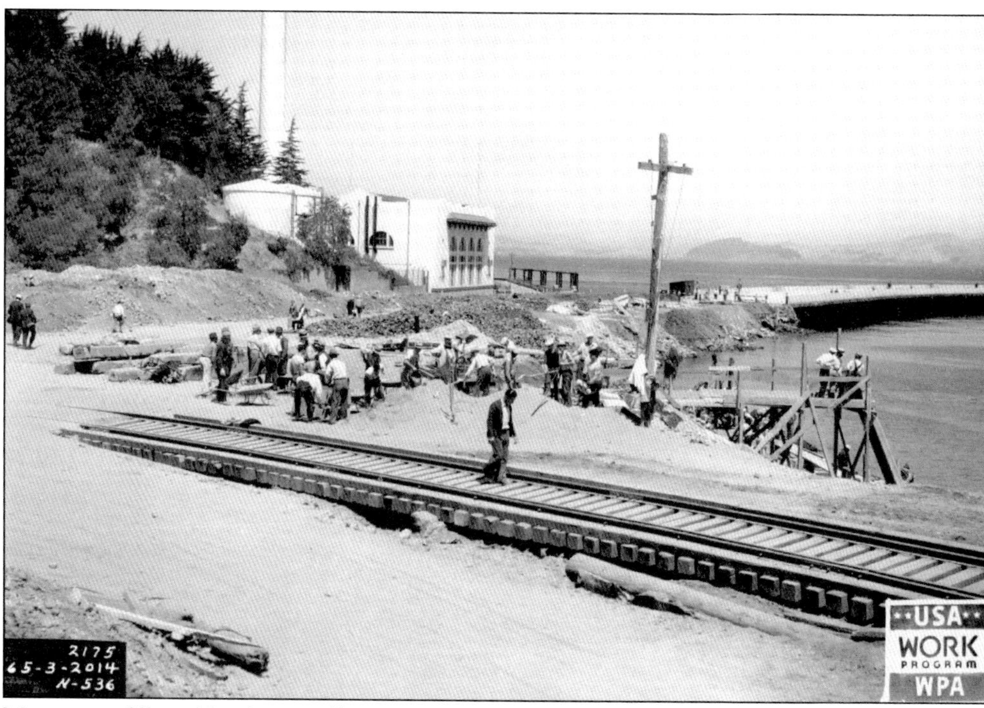

Manpower, fill, and big beams all went into the early construction of Aquatic Park in 1936.

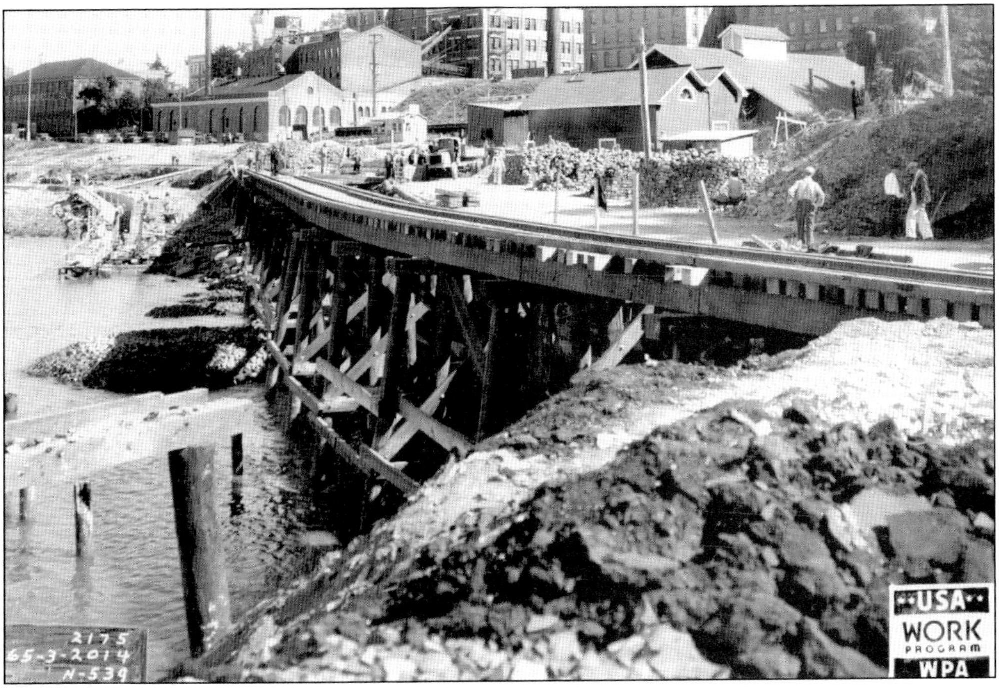

The Belt Line Railroad would soon be enclosed by the seawall.

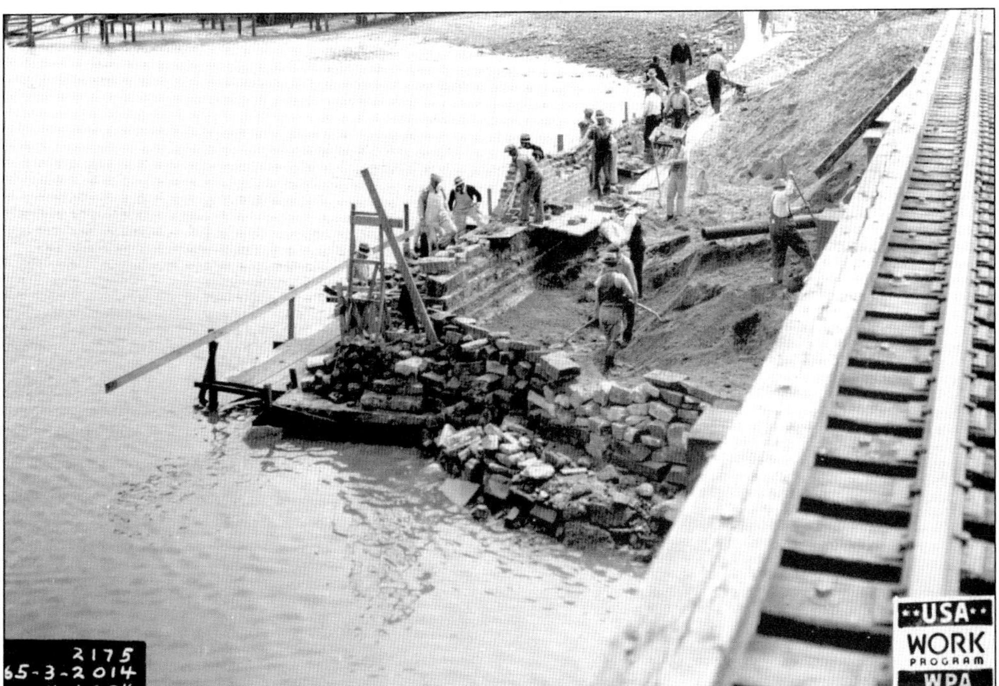

The seawall begins to take shape.

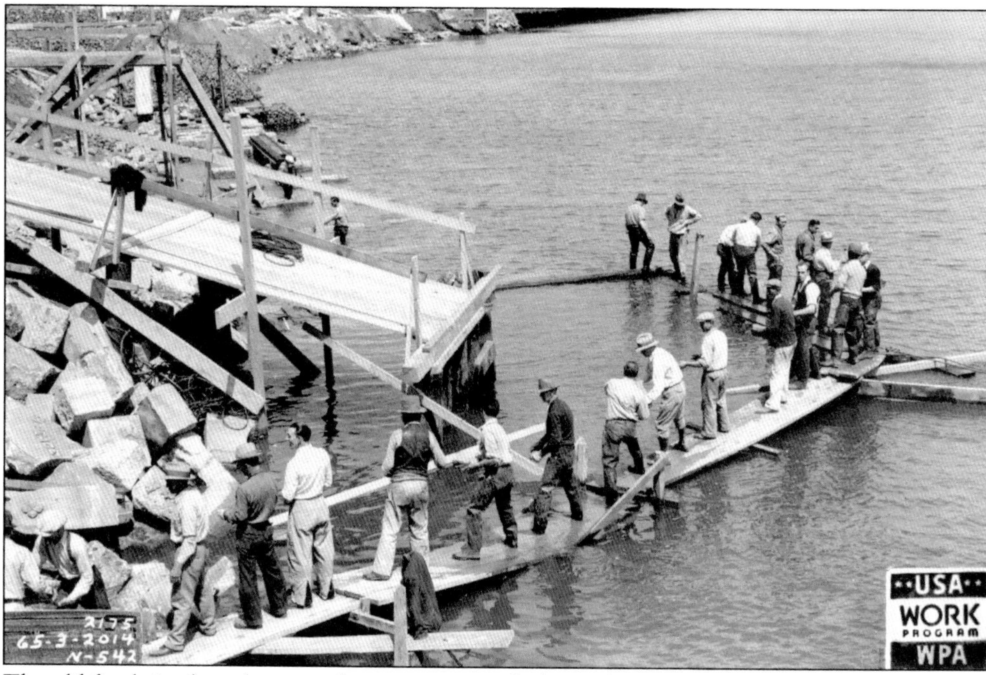

The old fire brigade technique of passing materials down the line was the order of this day.

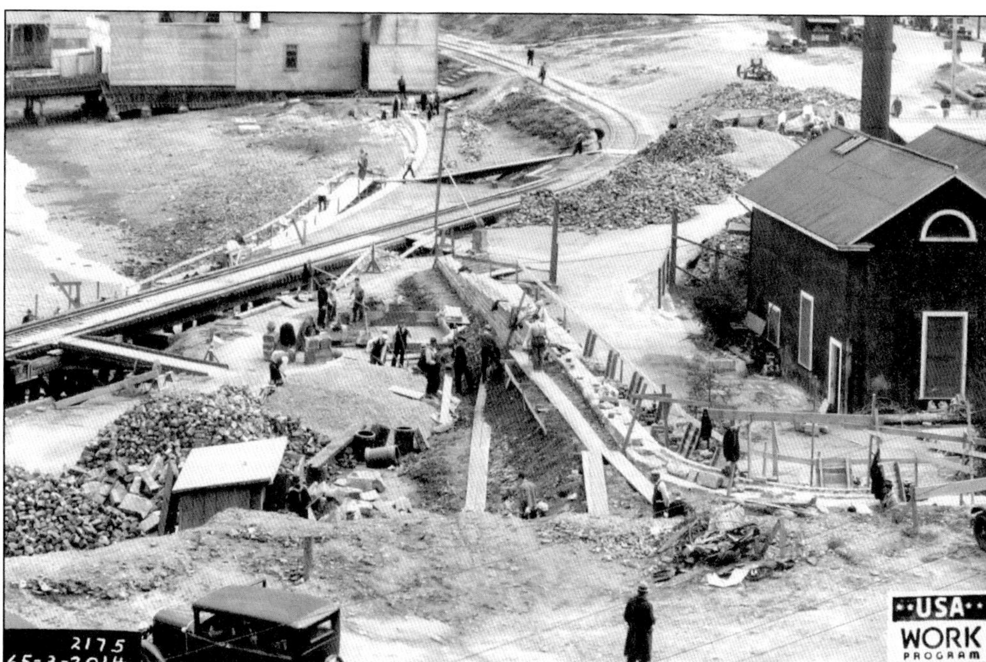

Construction materials are everywhere in this 1936 photograph.

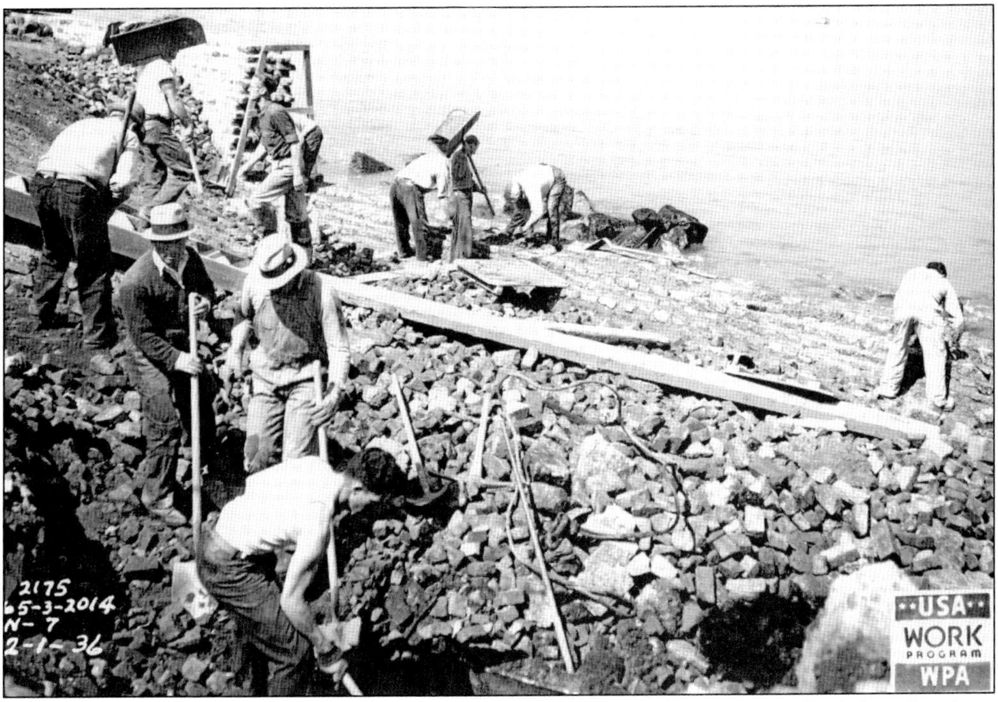

Tons of brick were put into place by men grateful for the work and ability to feed their families.

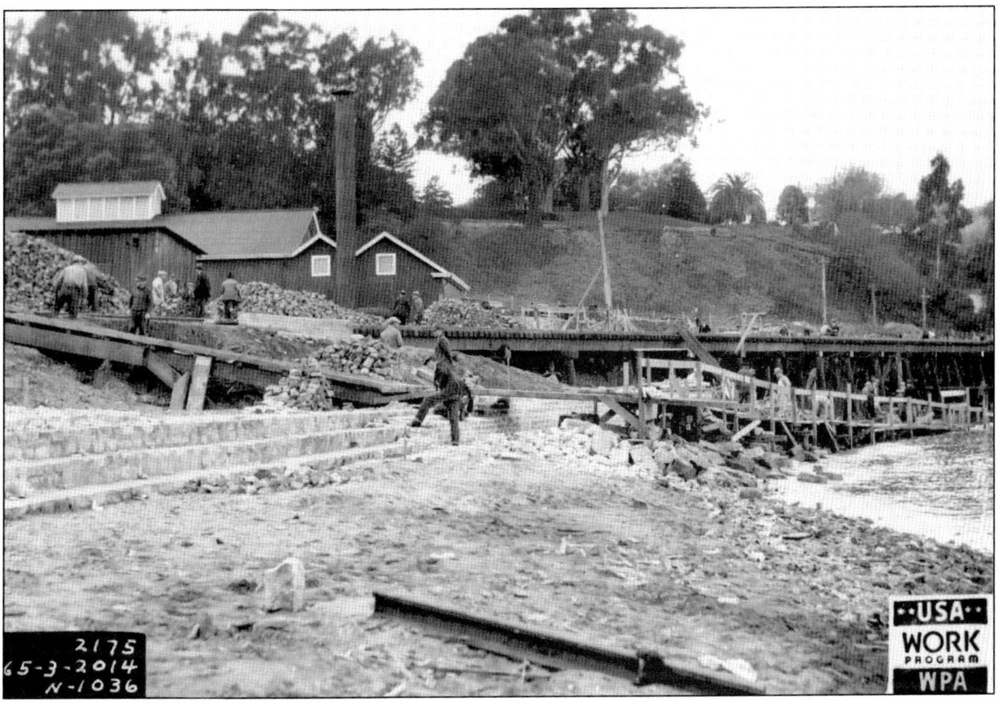

A temporary wooden scaffold served as a platform to build up the seawall.

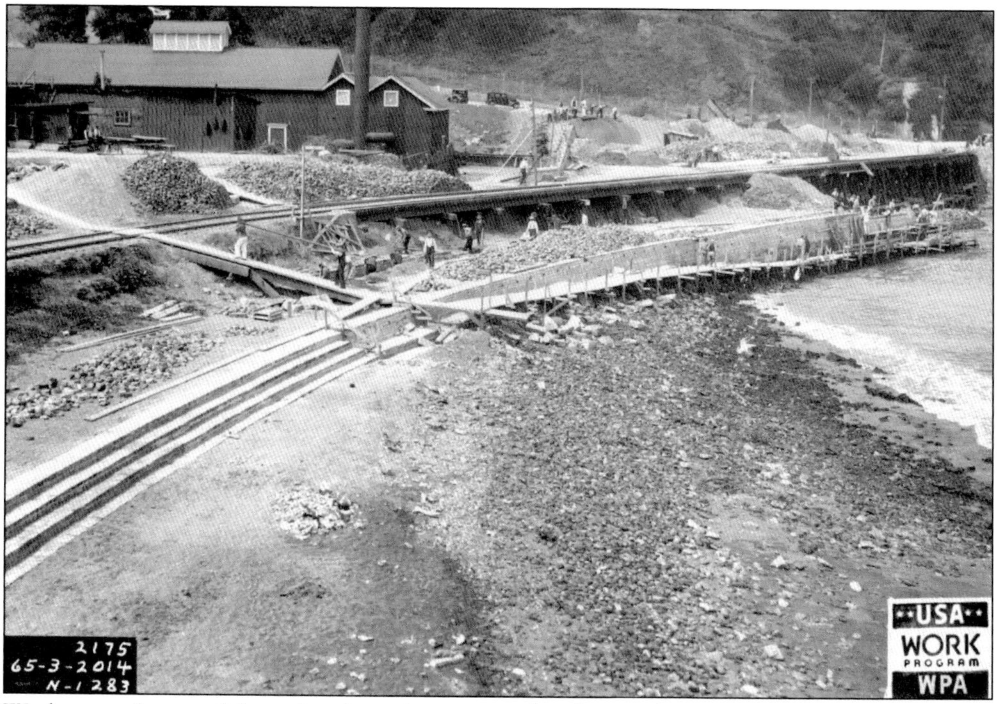

Work on enclosure of the railroad trestle progressed well in early 1936.

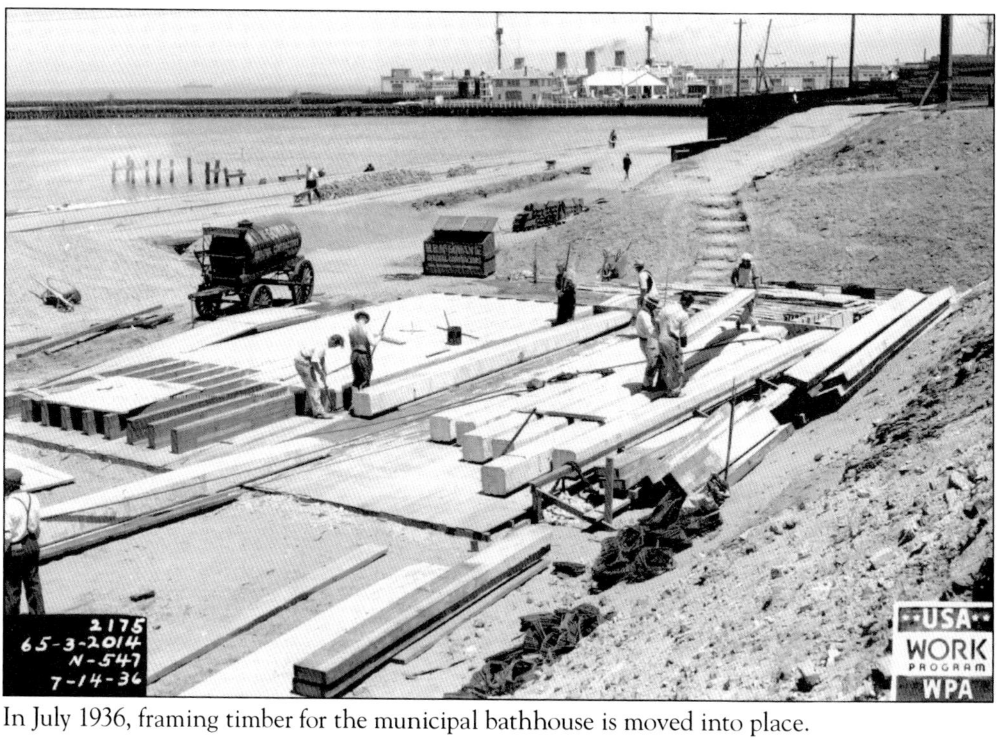

In July 1936, framing timber for the municipal bathhouse is moved into place.

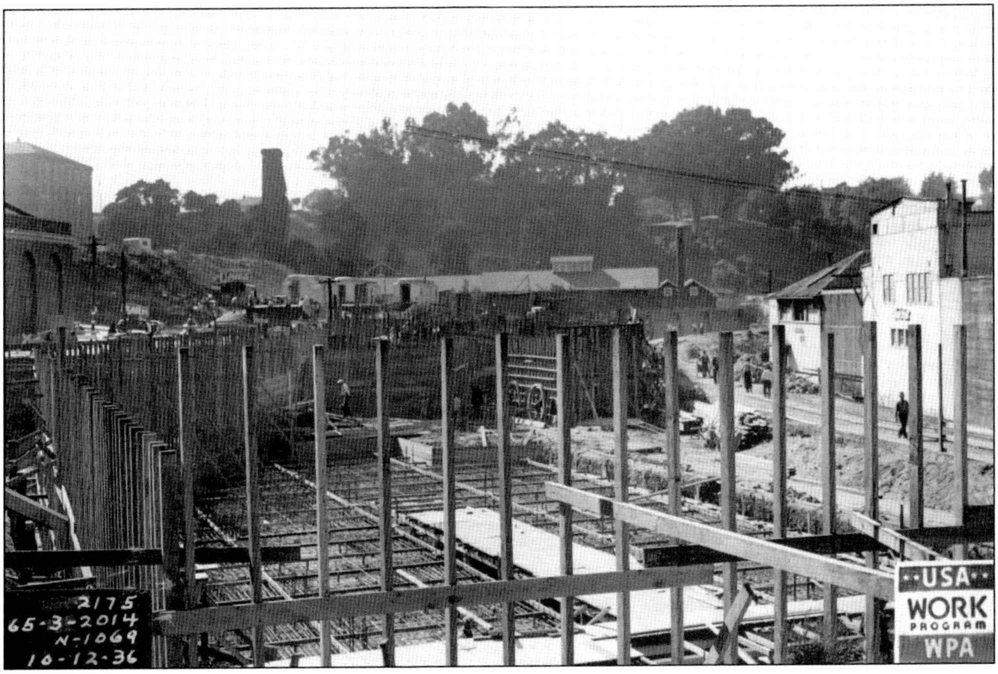

As the rowing clubs look on, framing continues in late 1936.

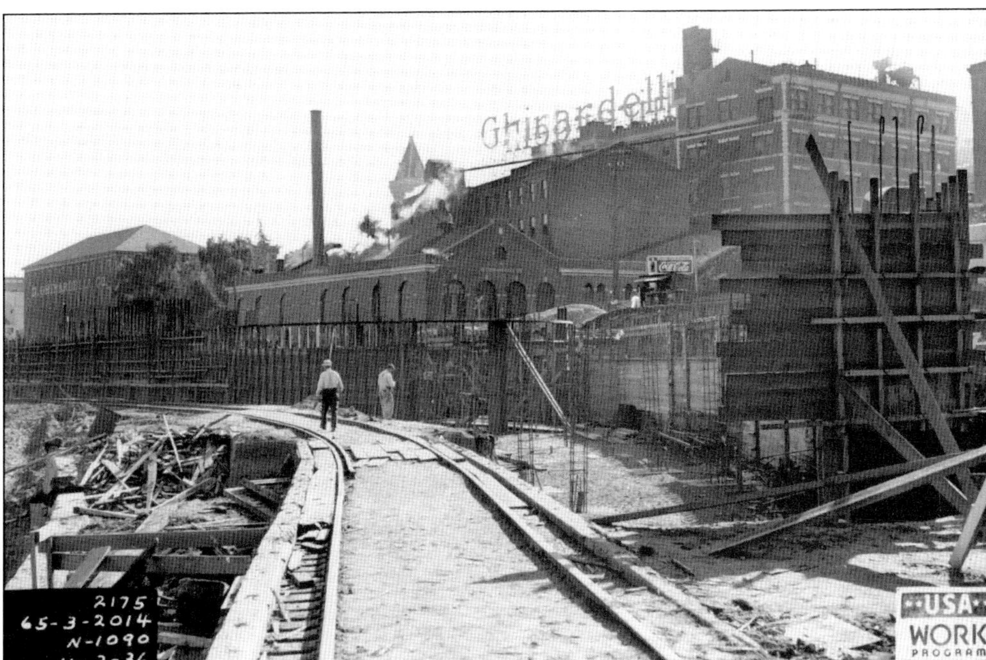

Steel reinforcement rods are now in position.

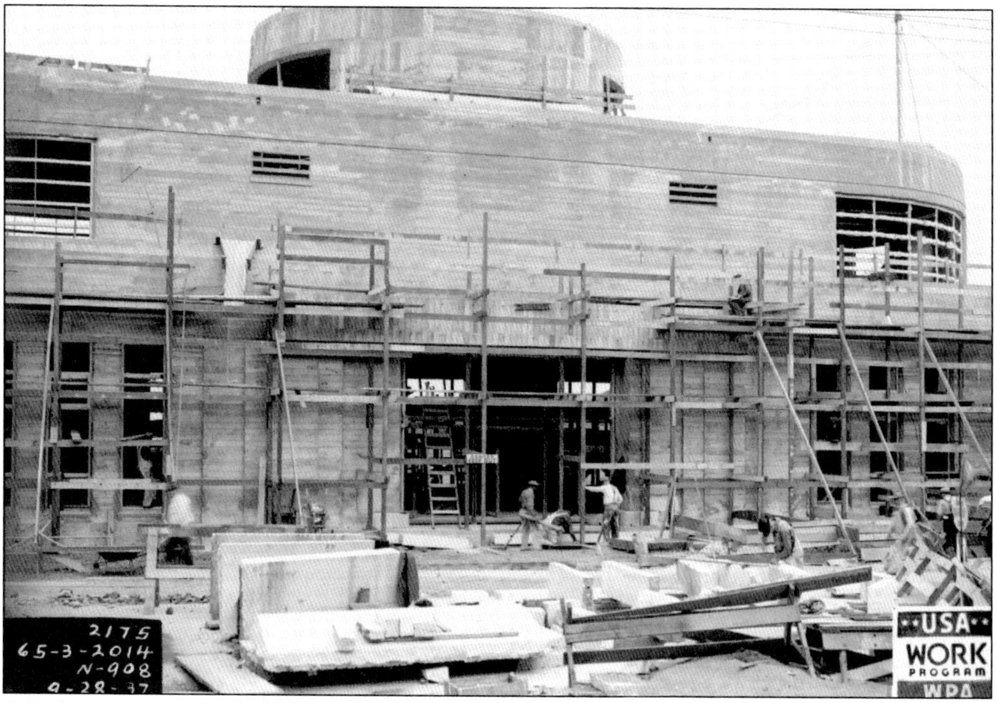

A little over a year and a half into the project, the municipal bathhouse had taken form.

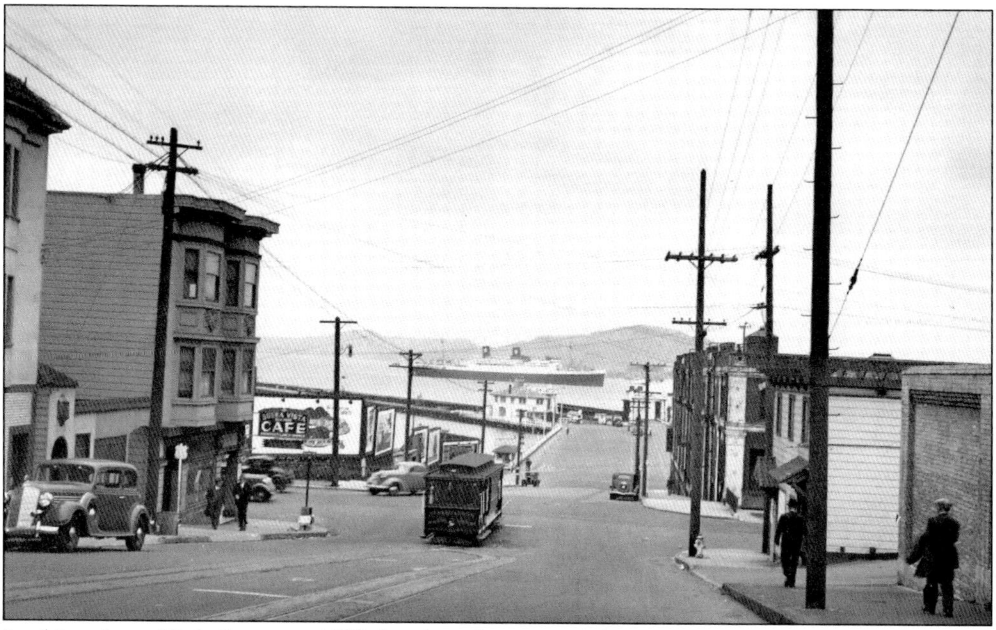

Looking down Hyde Street in 1935, familiar elements of the Buena Vista and cable car are still part of the Hyde Street scene.

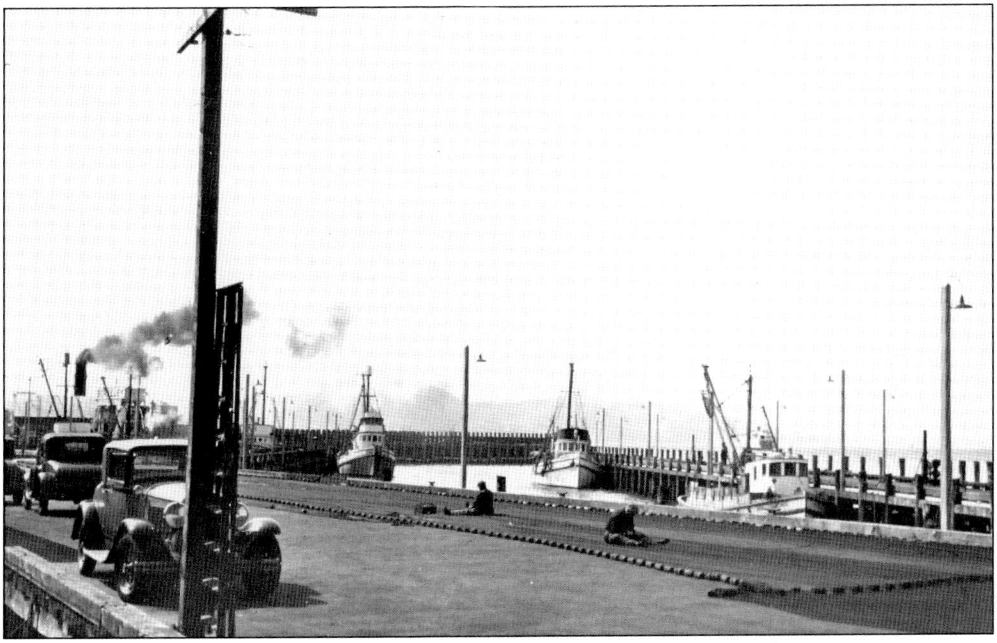

Further down Hyde, on the ferryboat pier, fishermen mend their nets before setting out to sea once again.

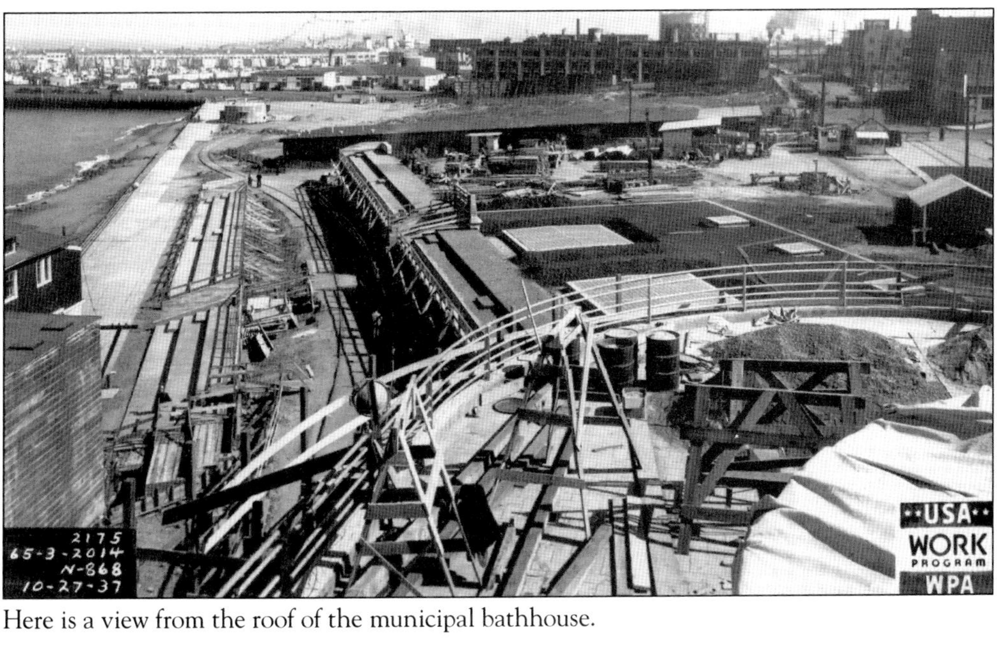

Here is a view from the roof of the municipal bathhouse.

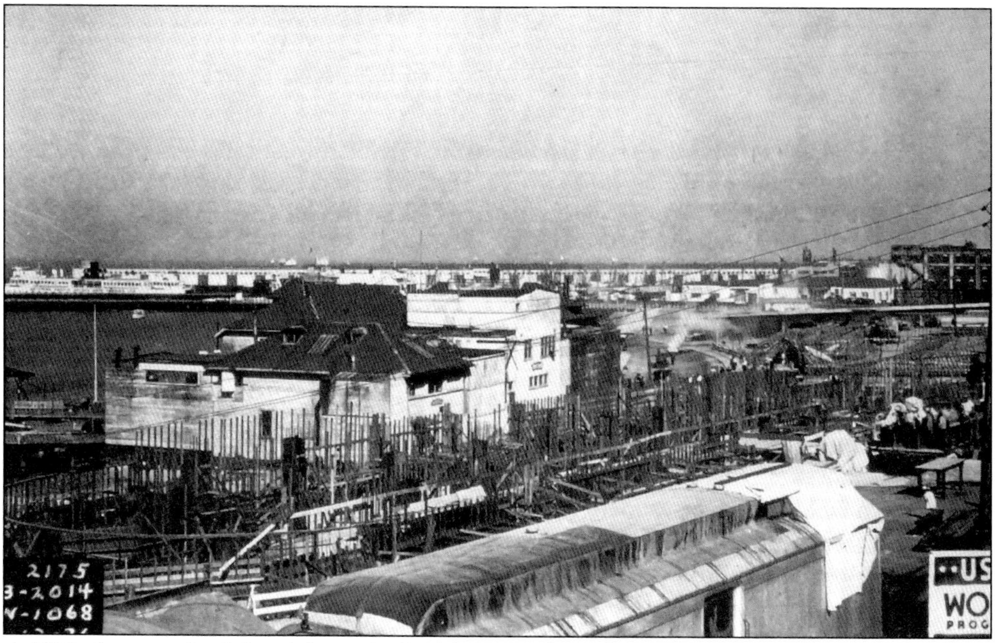

A 1936 photograph of the clubs as the bathhouse is framed out.

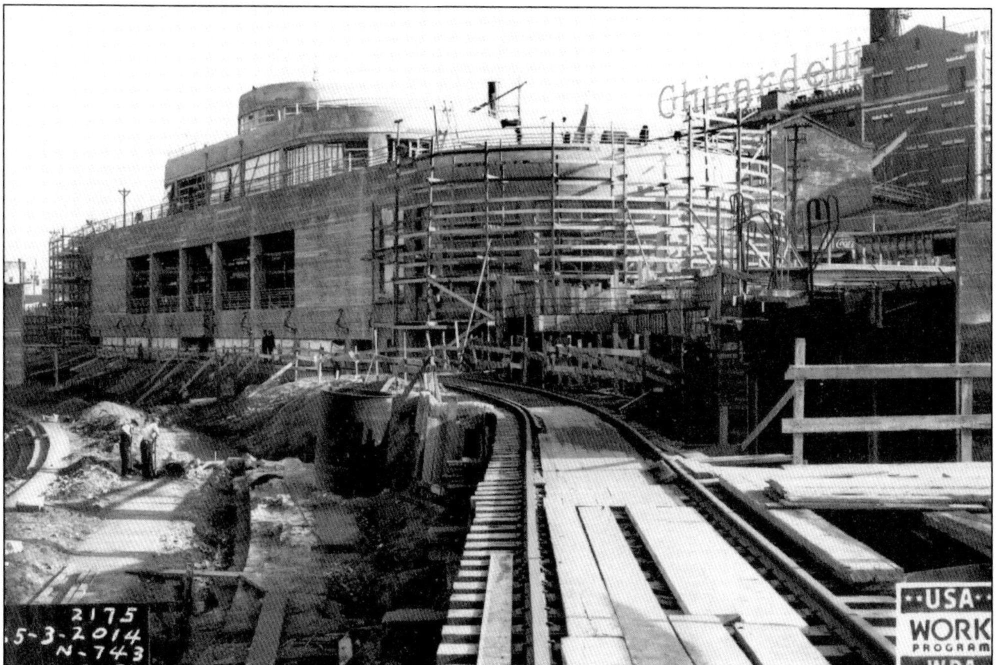

This is another angle of the bathhouse in December 1937.

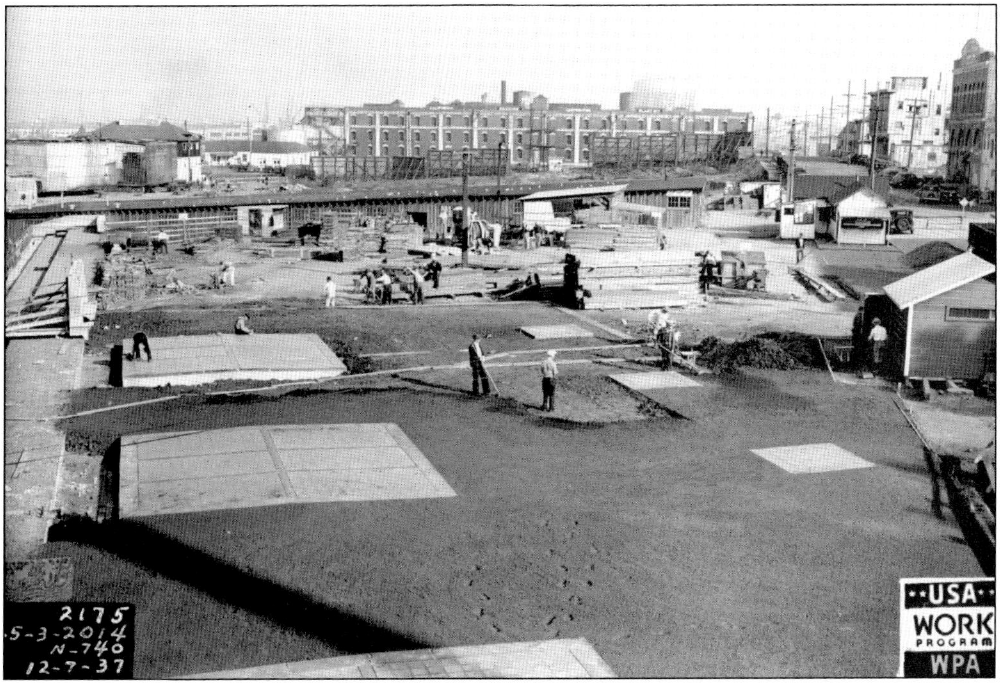

Workmen prepare the ground around the skylights.

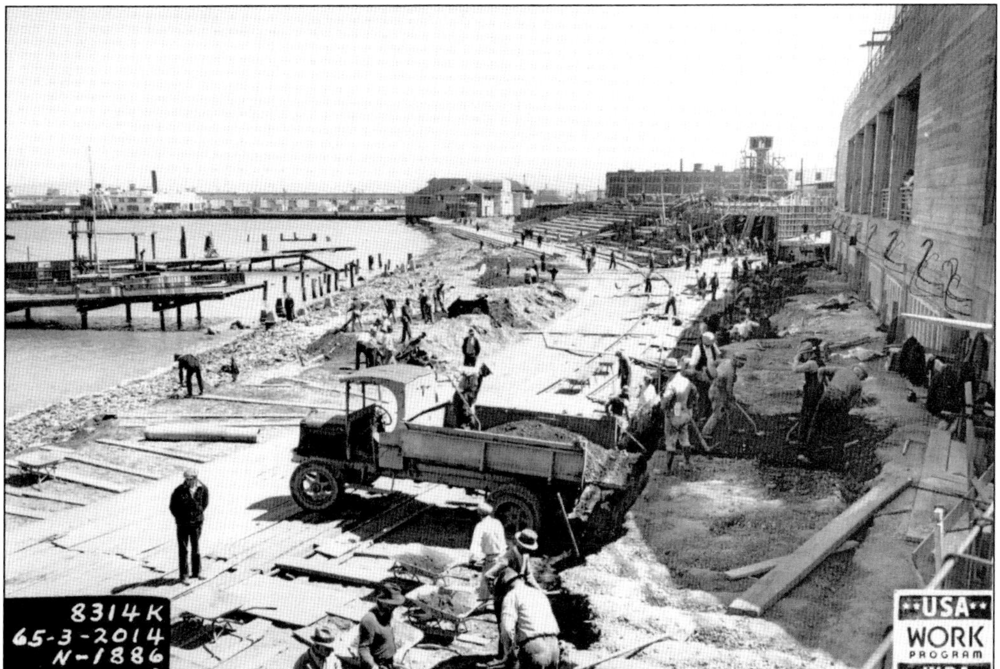

After the clubs have been moved, dirt fills in the area between the bathhouse and sidewalk. The clubs had to be moved before the grandstands could be put up.

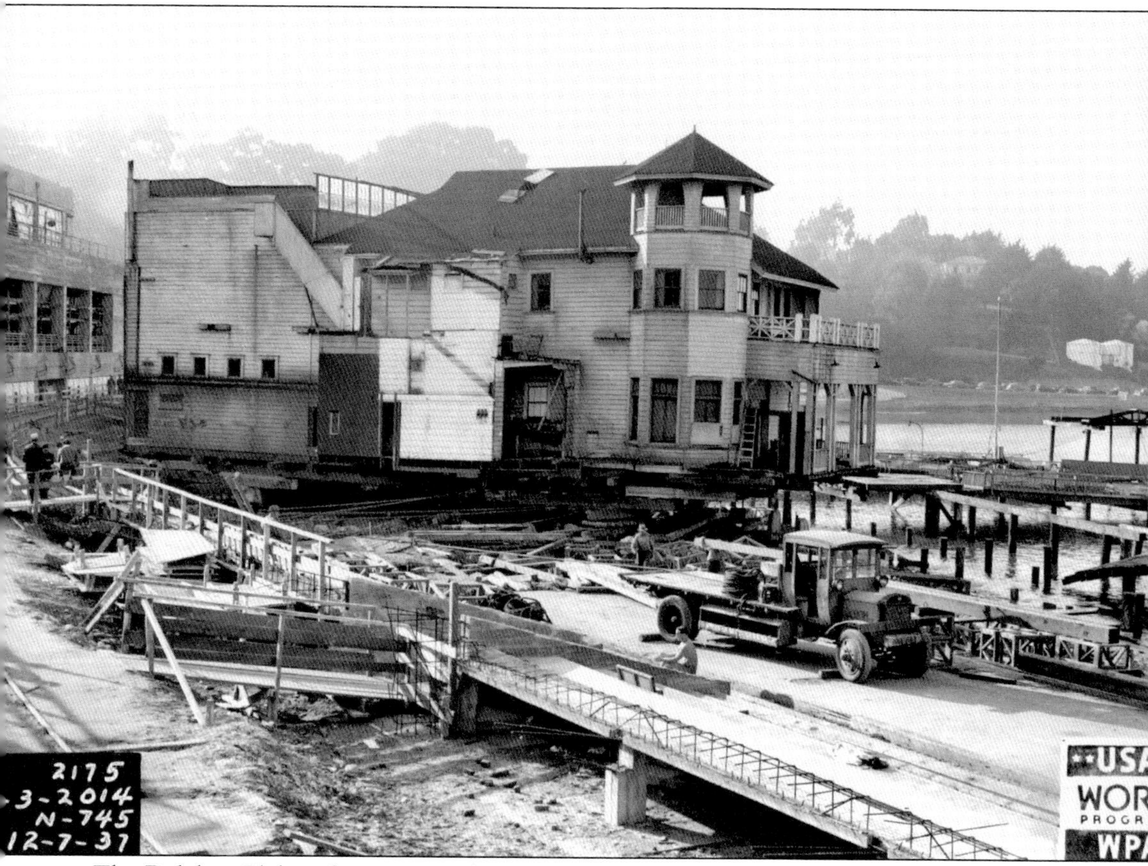

The Dolphin Club makes its second journey. The first was from Van Ness Avenue to Larkin and this was from Larkin to the foot of Hyde Street. It appears a winch on the truck in the foreground slowly pulls the building inch by inch via rollers (note the blocks behind the truck's wheels to hold it in place). The South End was the first club moved, then the Dolphin, and last the Ariel Club.

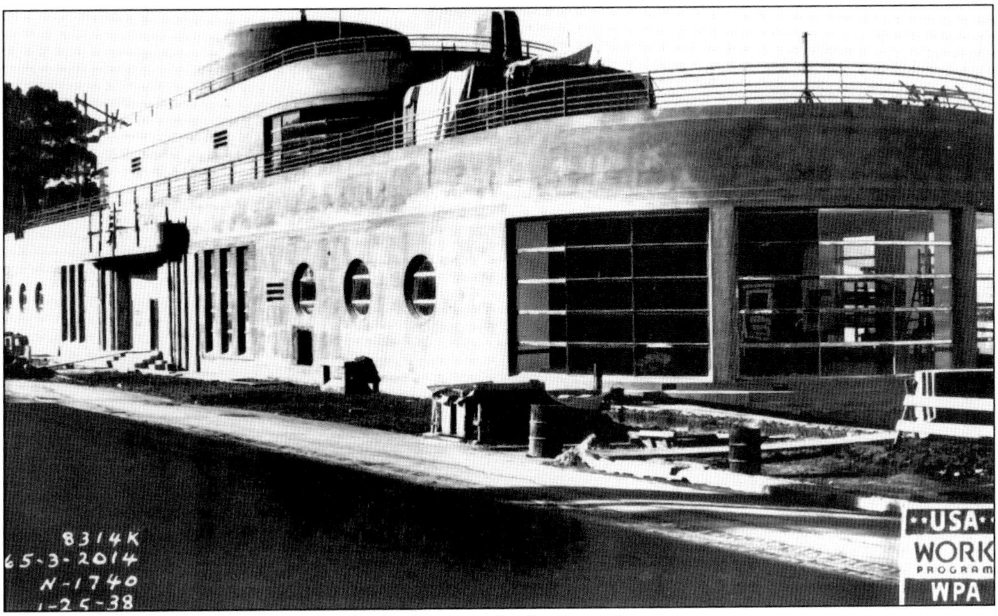

By January 1938, the exterior of the bathhouse had taken shape.

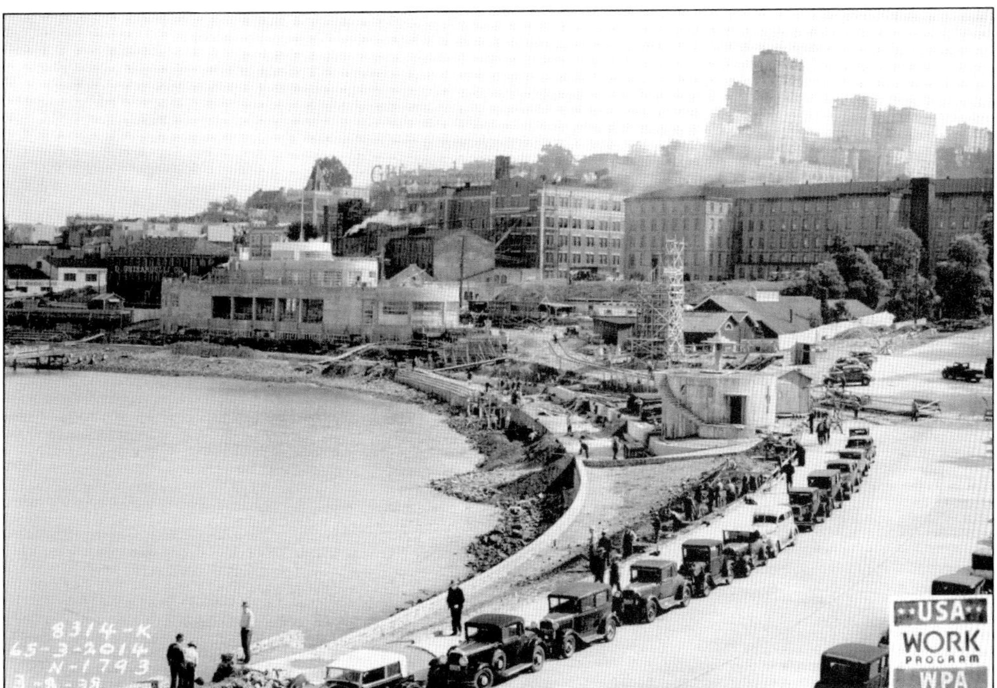

The site is a beehive of activity as the western speaker tower goes up.

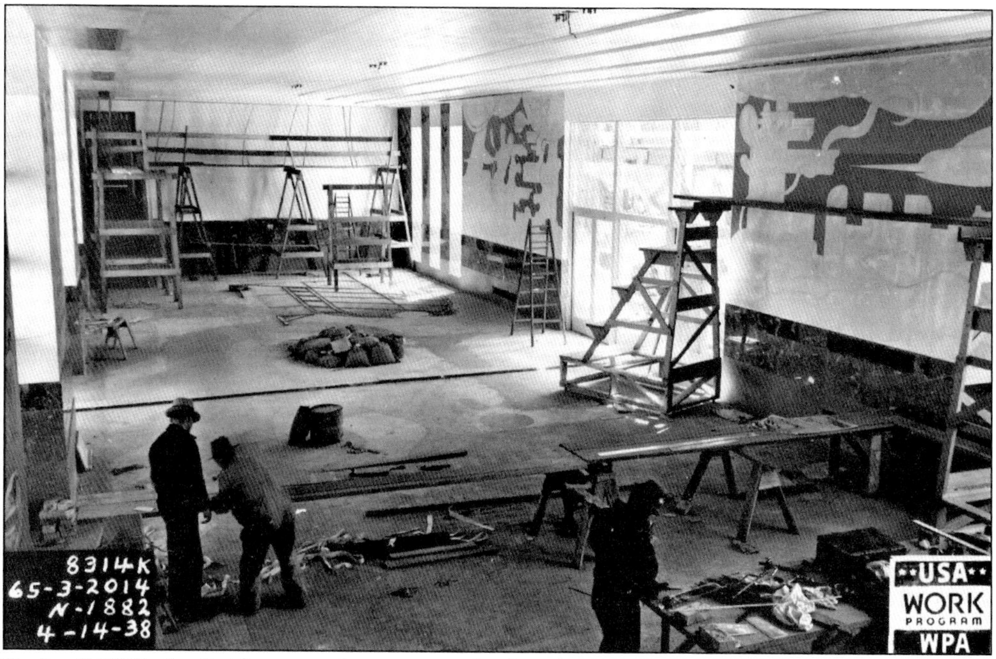

By April 1938, the finishing touches were applied to the interior.

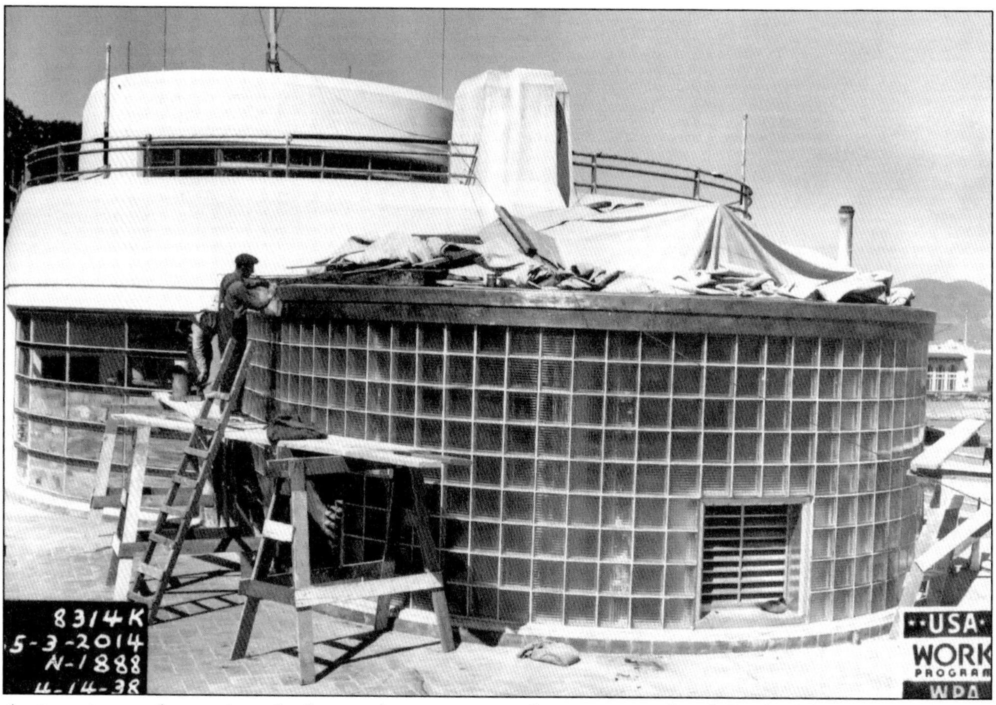

As interior work continued, glasswork went up on the eastern side of the building.

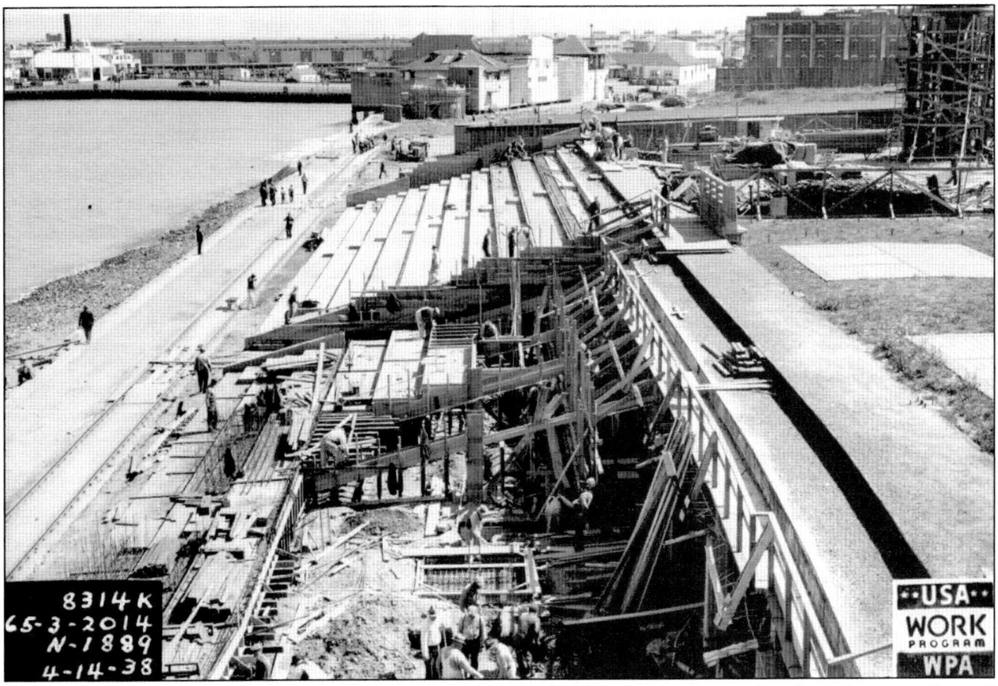

The grandstand was still a work in progress in April. Though little used today, the grandstand held throngs of people in the 1940s and 1950s.

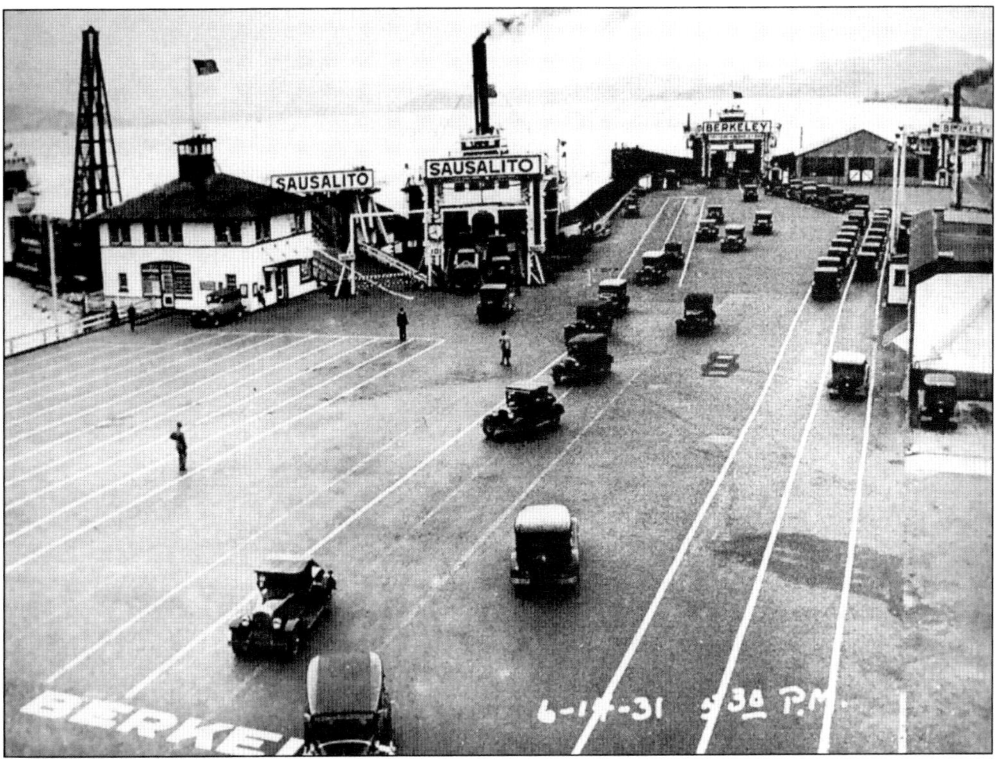

Hyde Street Pier was a very active ferryboat wharf, as this 1935 view attests.

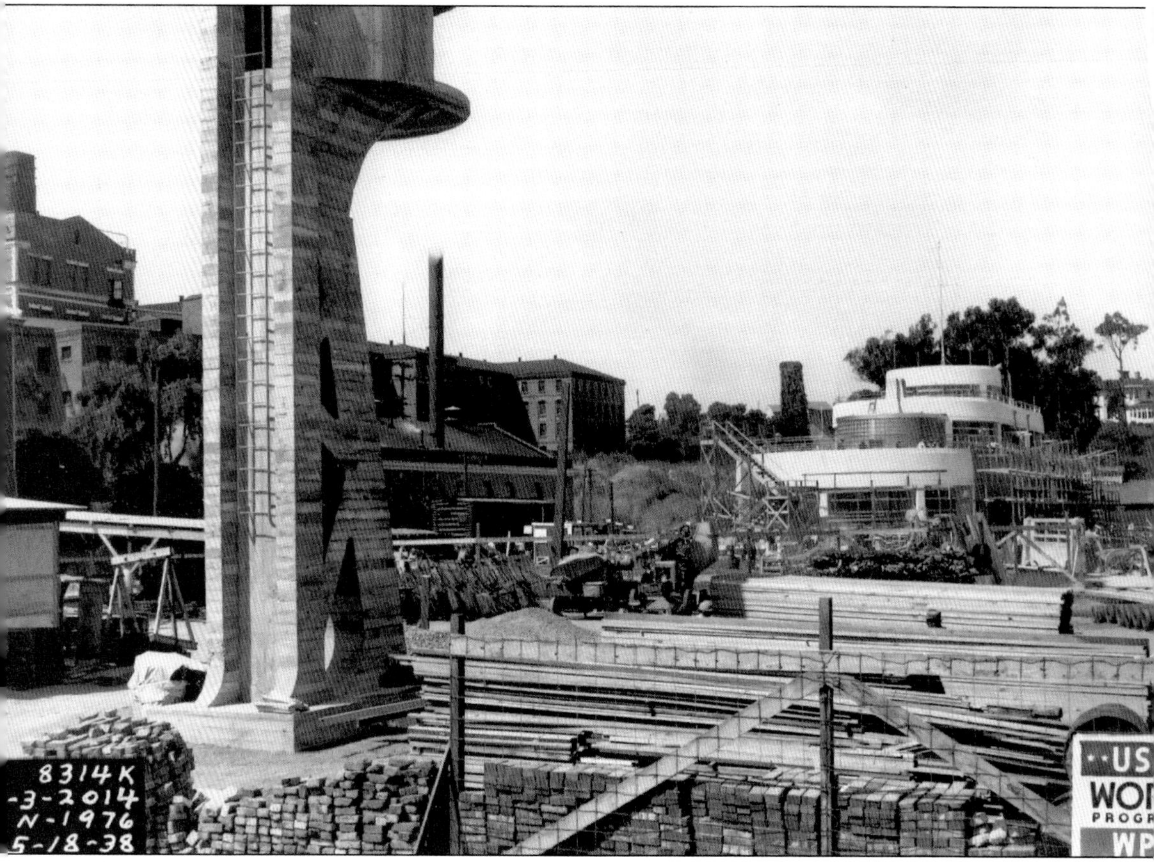

The eastern speaker tower joins its western cousin on the grounds of Aquatic Park.

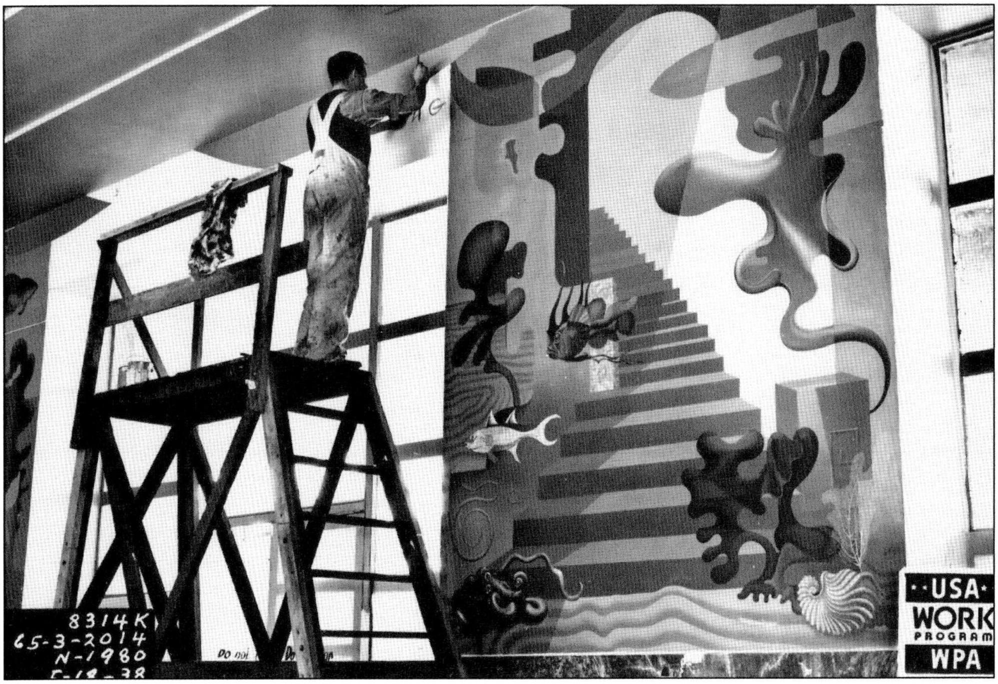

A mural is applied to the bathhouse wall.

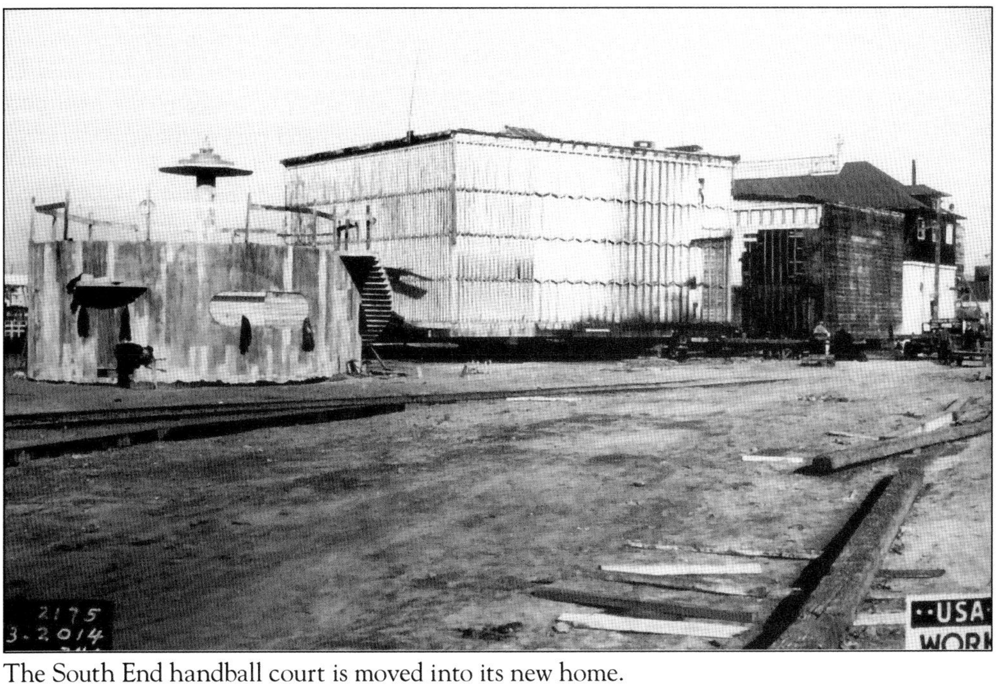

The South End handball court is moved into its new home.

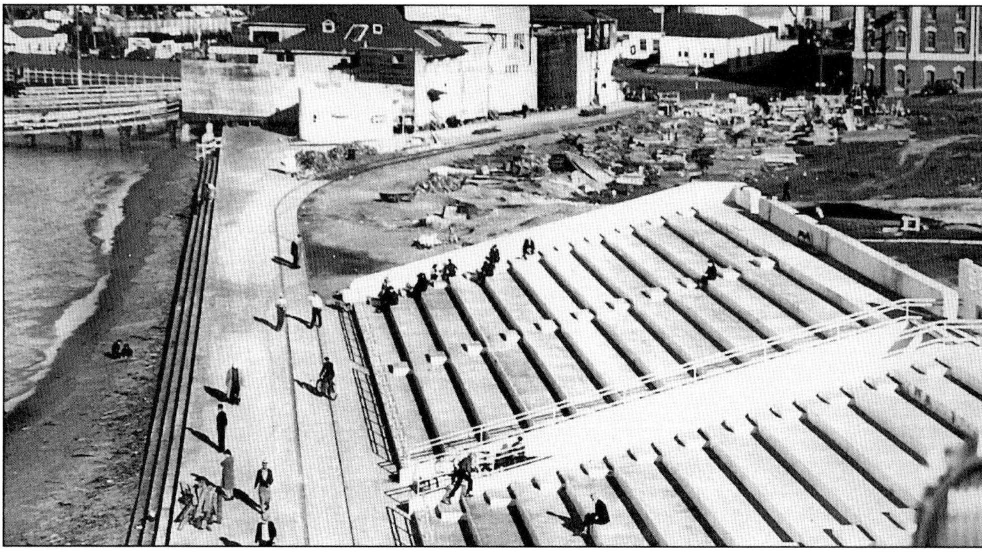

Just before dedication in January 1939, only minimal cleanup remained to be done.

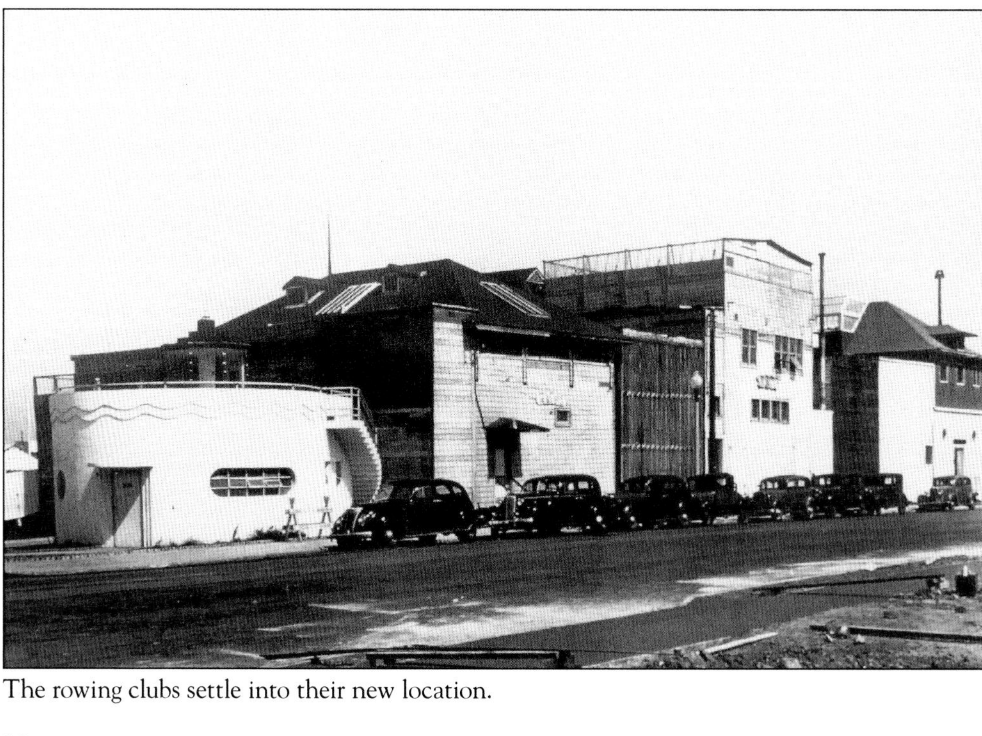

The rowing clubs settle into their new location.

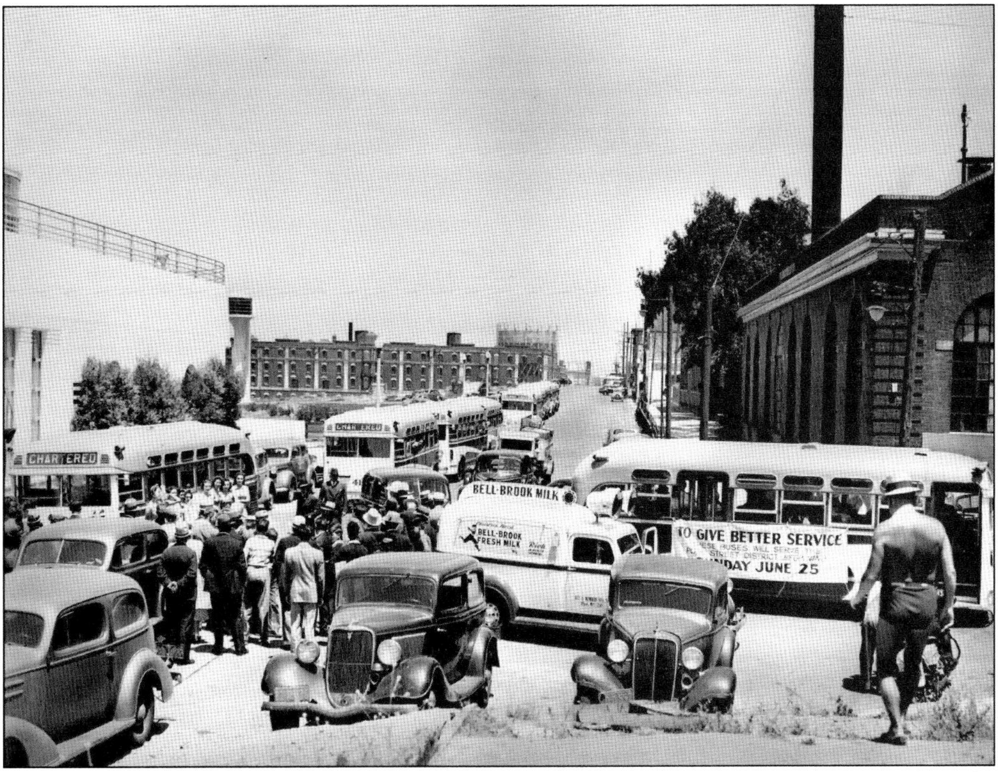

Buses brought the citizens of San Francisco to the new Aquatic Park. The bus on the far right announces that the Polk Street streetcar line will cease operation to make way for bus service.

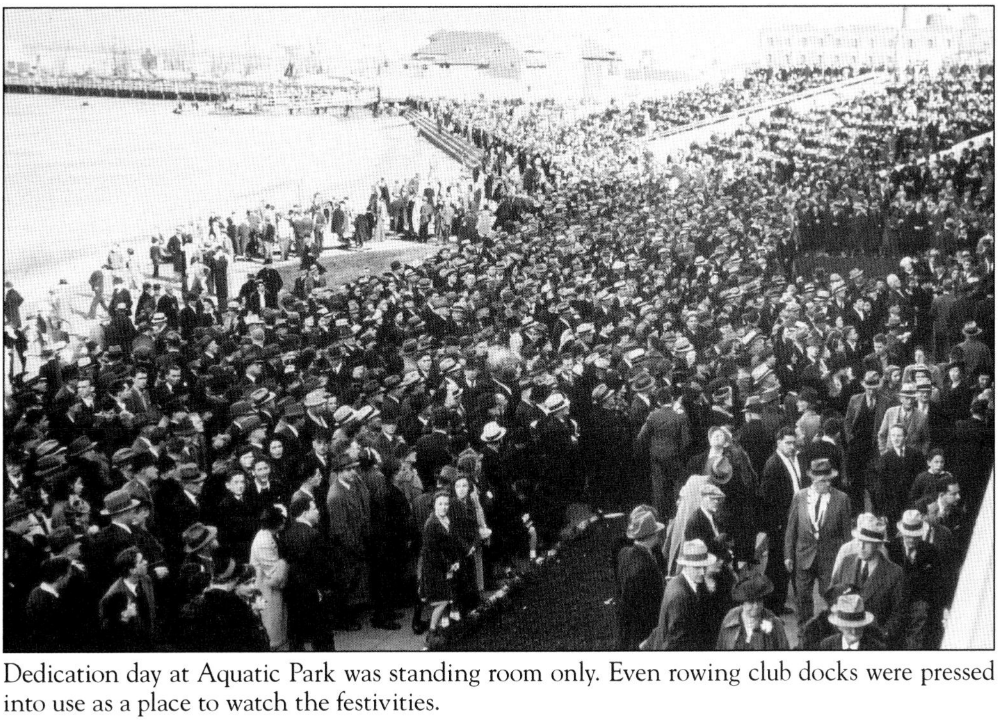

Dedication day at Aquatic Park was standing room only. Even rowing club docks were pressed into use as a place to watch the festivities.

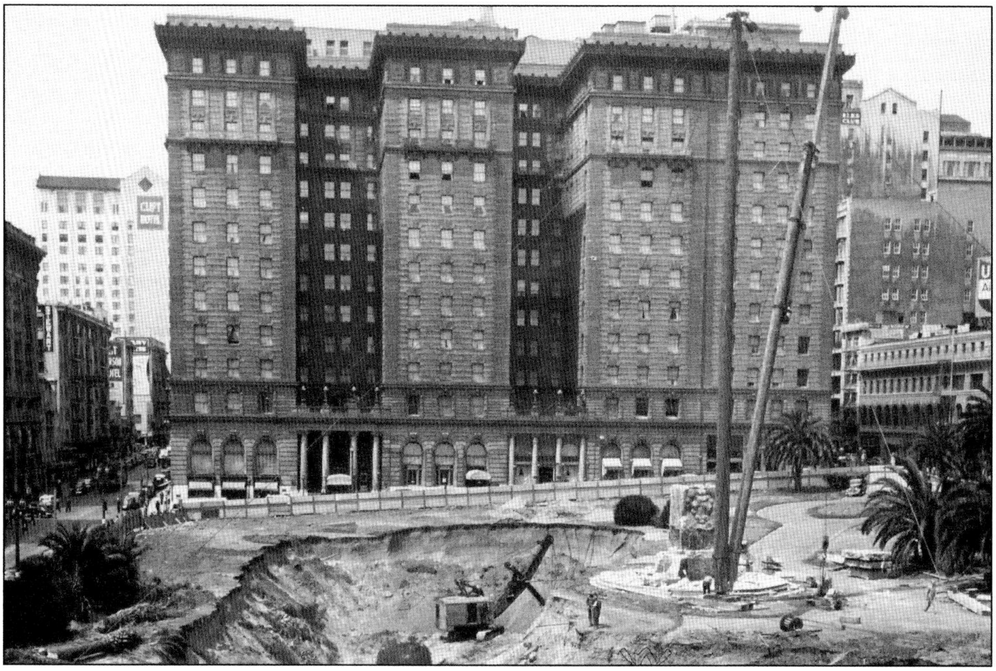

The excavation site of Union Square for an underground garage was the perfect source for sand for the Aquatic Park beach. Tons of sand was shipped to the beach.

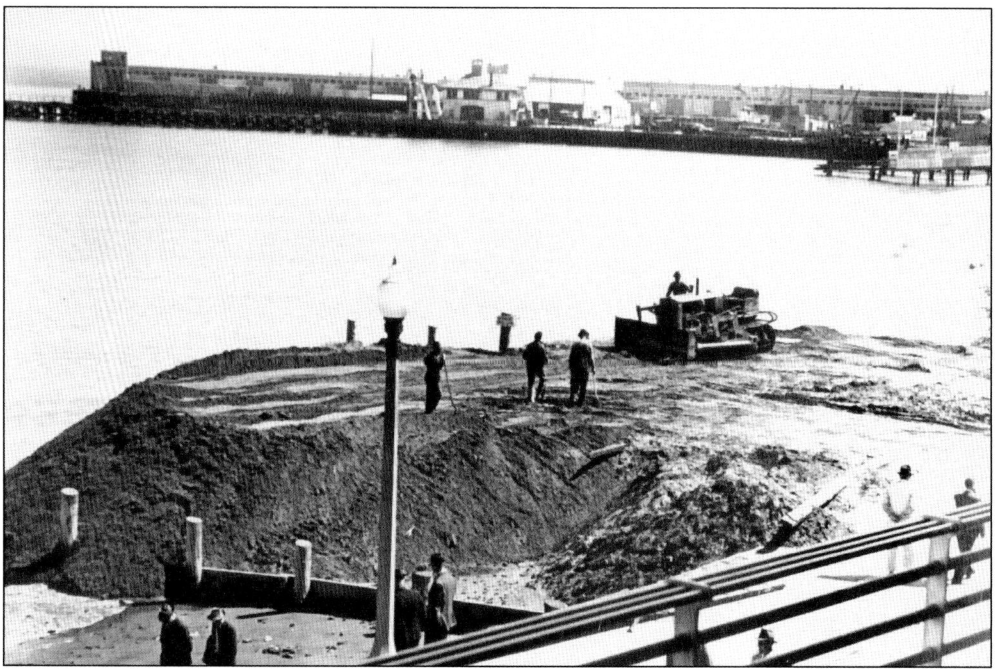

Once the sand was dumped on the beach, it was spread out using bulldozers.

Six

THE MARITIME MUSEUM

During World War II, the U.S. Army took over the municipal bathhouse for use in the war effort. After the war, the city had a building with no tenant. Dozens of groups applied to the city to use the building for events such as veterans' meetings, dances, etc. The administrative work involved in review of these applications was a huge effort, so the city was happy to entertain serious offers for long-term use of the building.

Karl Kortum had the vision for a maritime museum to preserve the city's connection to the sea. With the backing of Alma Spreckels, rowing club members, and others, Kortum made his presentation to the Recreation and Park Department. In September 1950, the board of supervisors approved a lease with the Maritime Museum Association for $1 per year.

Kortum found and had brought to the Hyde Street Pier the following ships: the *Balcultha*, schooner *Thayer*, scow schooner *Alma*, tugboat *Eppleton Hall* and ferryboat *Eureka*, as well as the *Wapama*. The former municipal bathhouse, now the San Francisco Maritime Museum Building, was filled with noteworthy objects and exhibits that told of San Francisco's maritime heritage. Kortum also gathered a marvelous collection of books, photographs, and special collections from around the country and the world for the J. Porter Shaw Library.

Victorian Park was another of Kortum's ideas that became reality. Since the area east of the park grandstands and bounded by Hyde, Jefferson, and Beach Streets was a barren area, the grounds were landscaped and sidewalks put down so the public could take in the beauty of the park and the vessels in the cove.

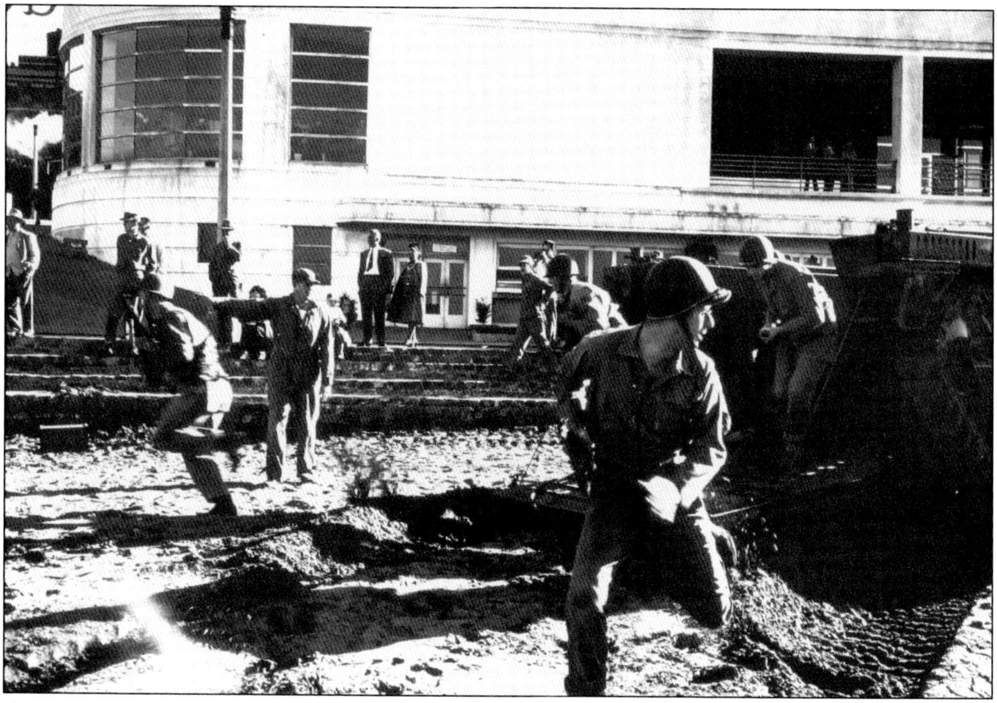

Army troops practice a beach landing during World War II in front of the municipal bathhouse.

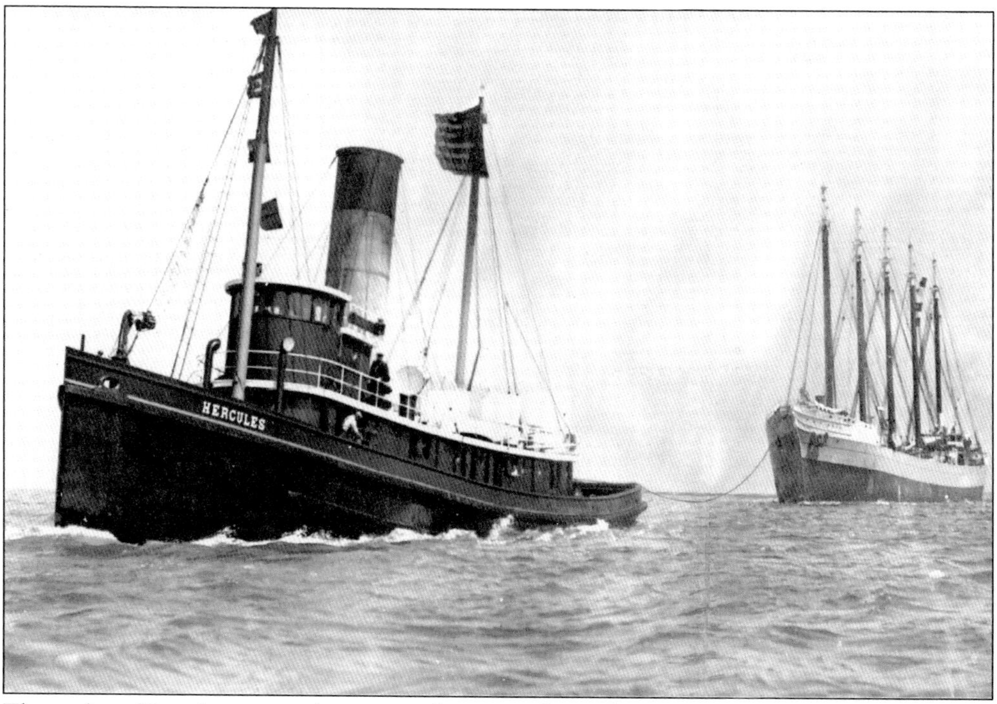

The tugboat *Hercules* is at work towing a five-masted vessel.

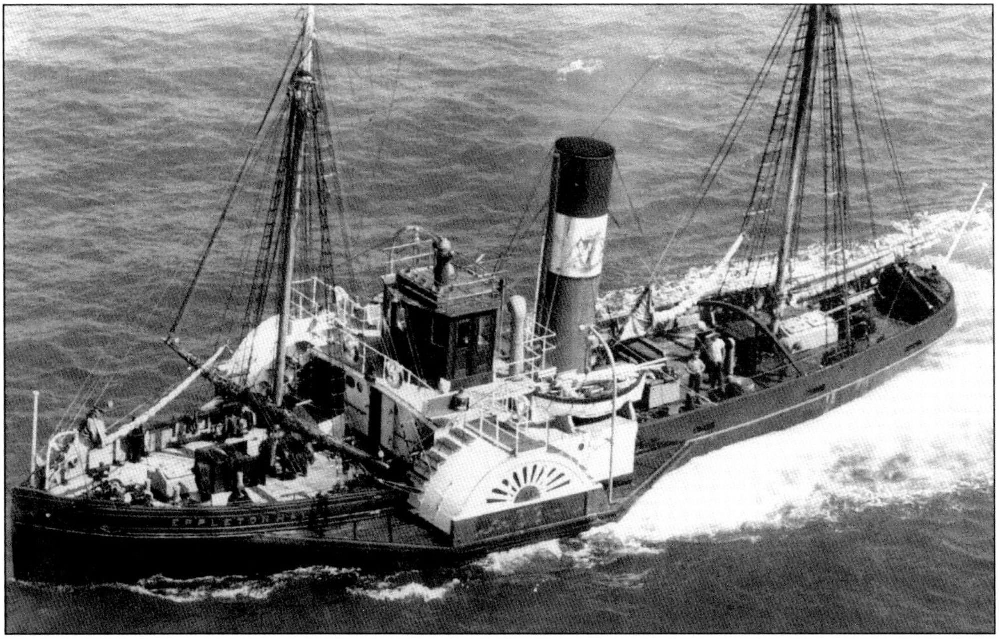

This is the tugboat *Eppleton Hall*.

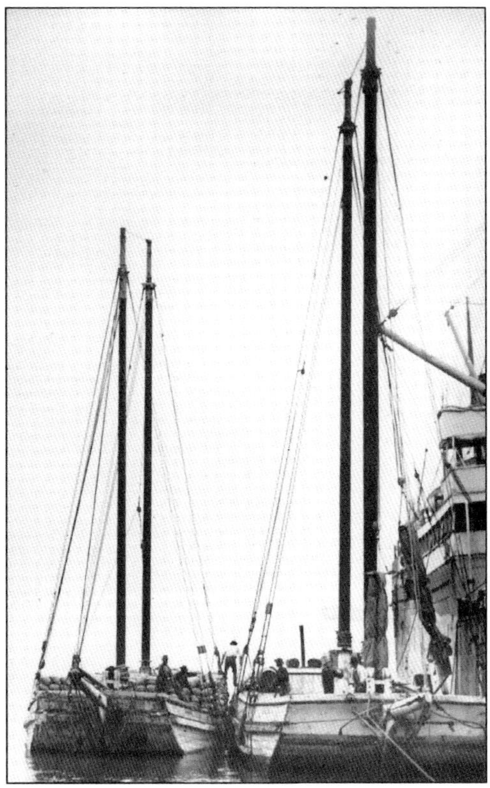

The scow schooner *Alma* is pictured hard at work. Scow schooners moved bulk cargoes like coal, hay, bricks, and wood around San Francisco. For decades, they were the short-haul workhorses of the bay.

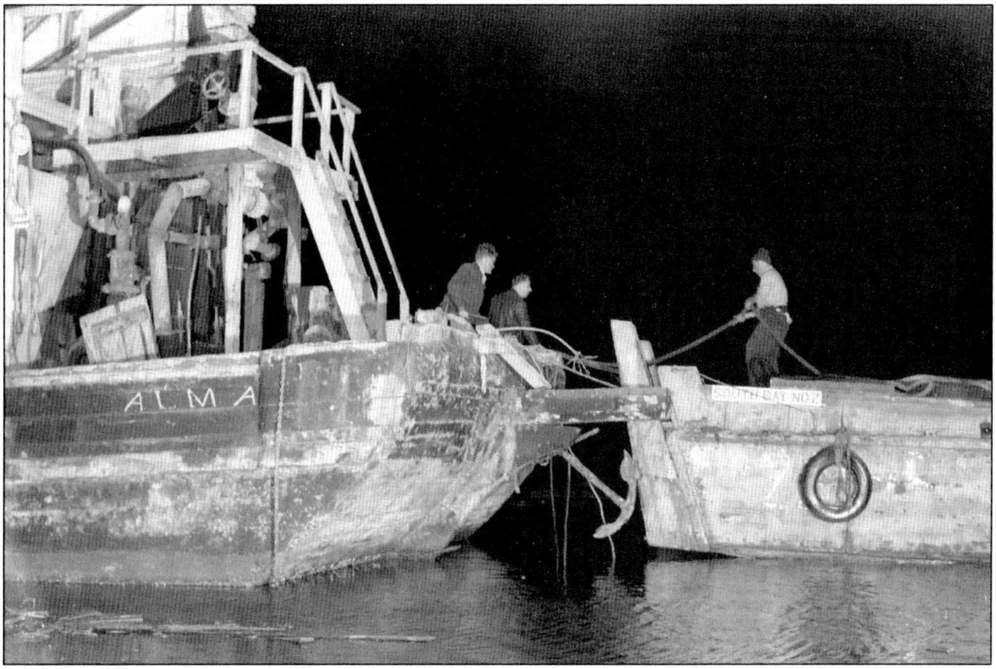

The *Alma*, left, is pictured doing her none-too-glamorous work.

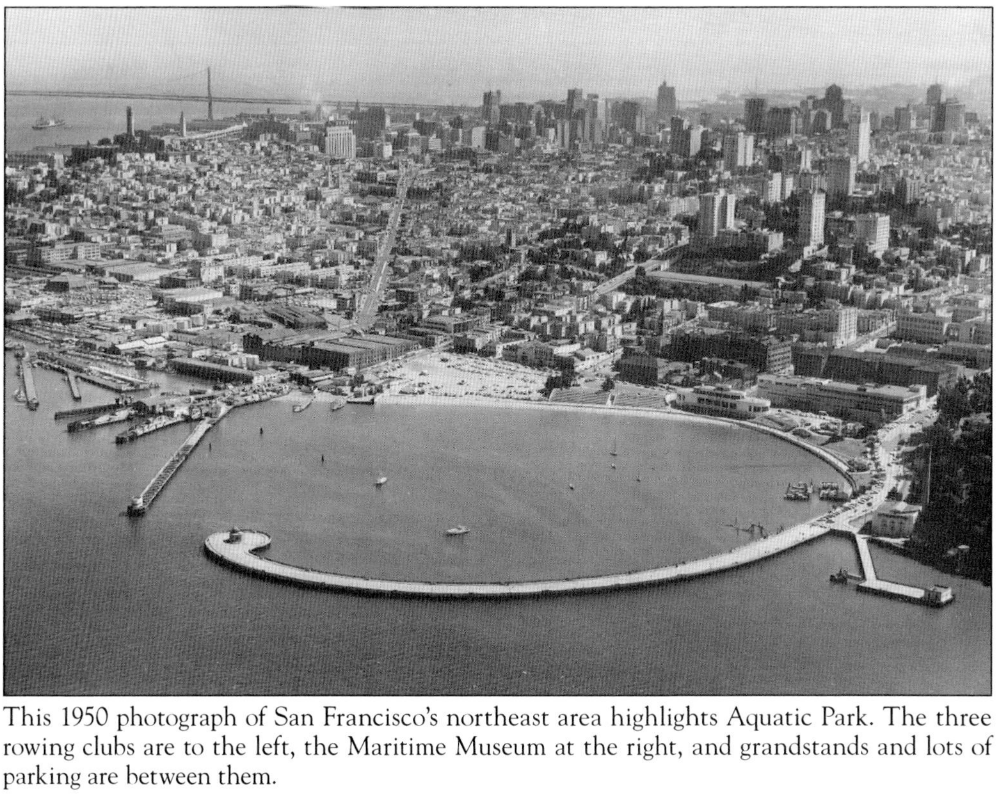

This 1950 photograph of San Francisco's northeast area highlights Aquatic Park. The three rowing clubs are to the left, the Maritime Museum at the right, and grandstands and lots of parking are between them.

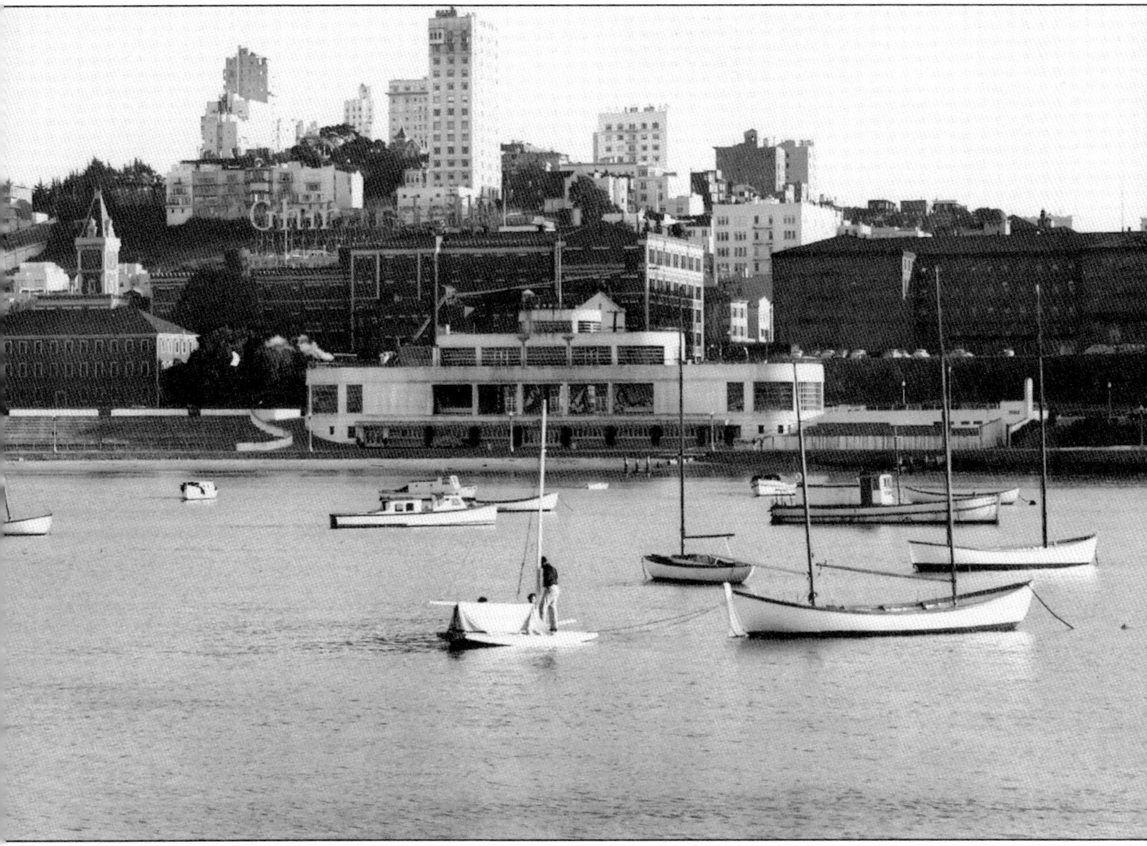

This beautiful 1950 photograph depicts the buildings of Aquatic Park. Small boats have tied up in the cove for over 150 years.

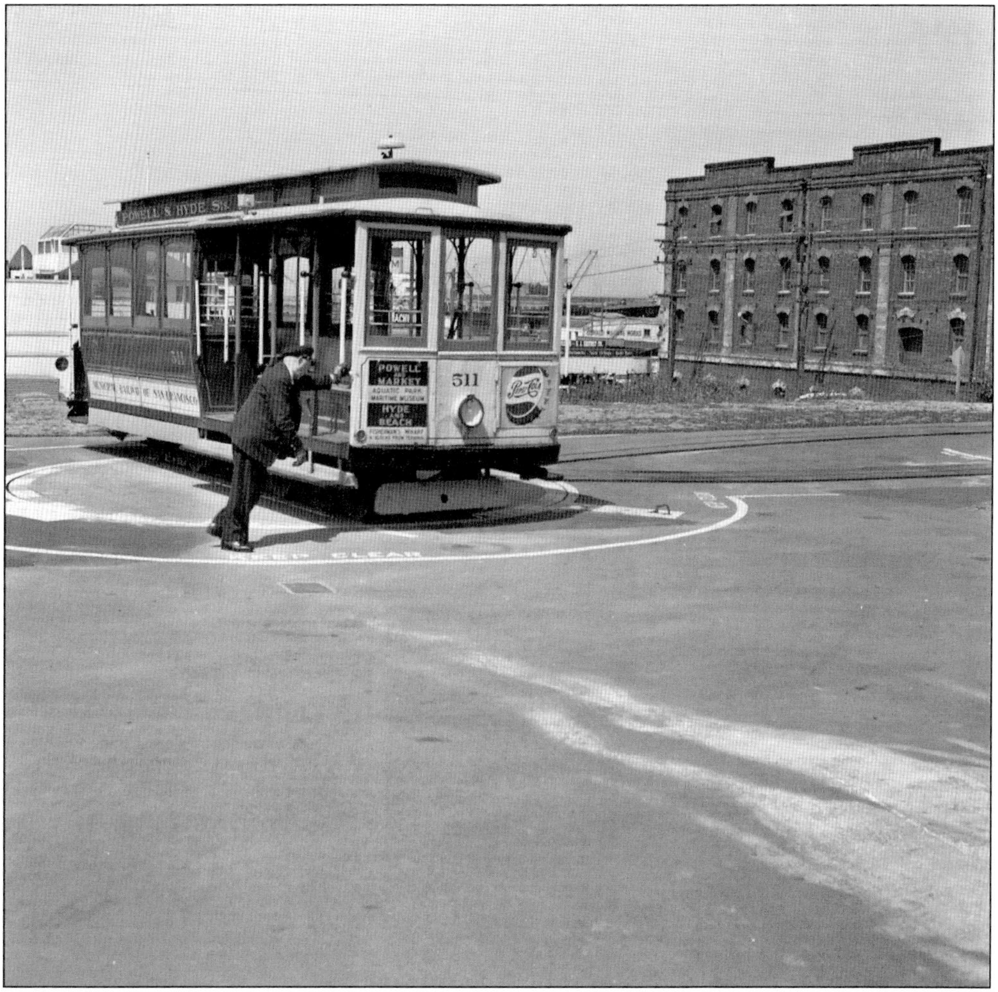

This classic view shows a cable car turning around at Hyde Street. Note the scrubby weeds to the right.

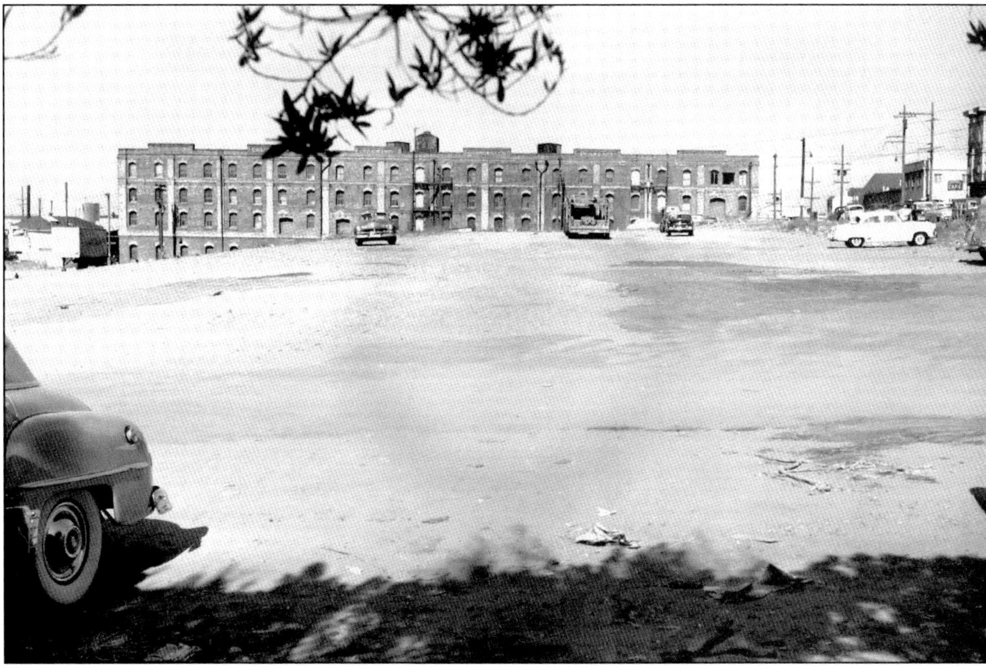

With most windows of the Haslett Warehouse blocked up, the barren ground east of the Maritime Museum was ready for serious improvement.

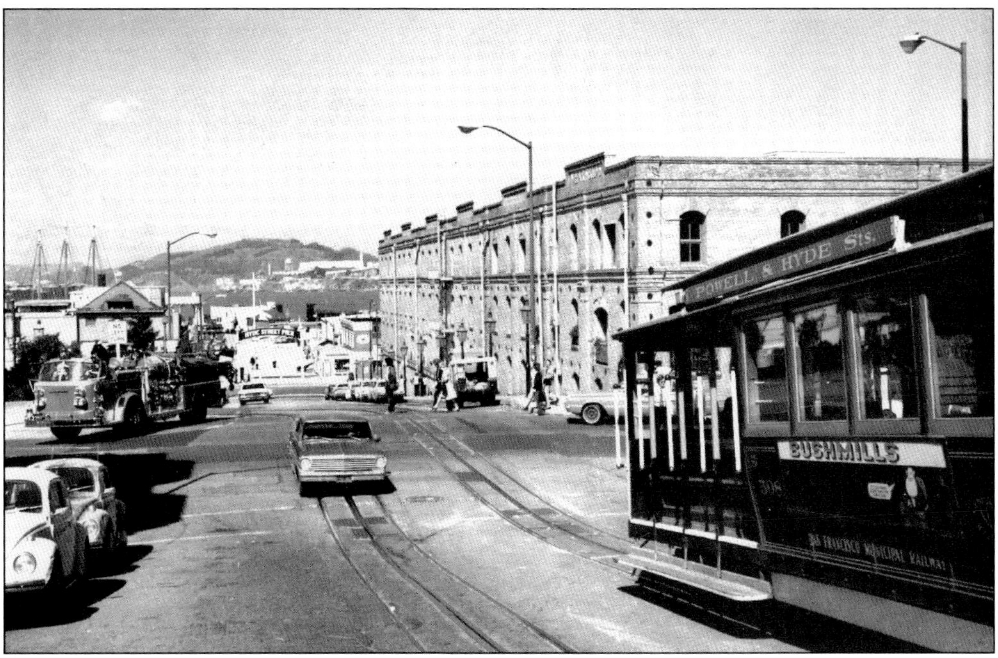

An overhead sign announces the entrance to Hyde Street Pier, center, and Victorian Park greenery is evident just above the fire engine. Even in 1962, the area is bustling.

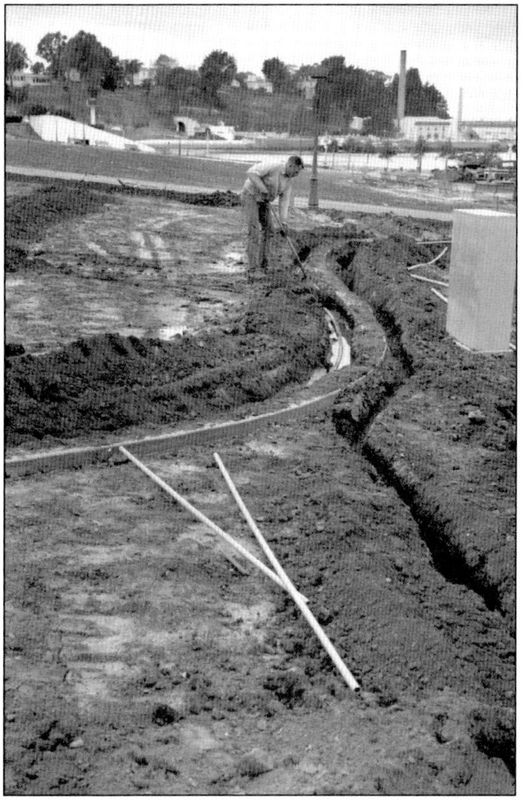

Sprinkler lines are placed in the ground of the soon-to-be Victorian Park.

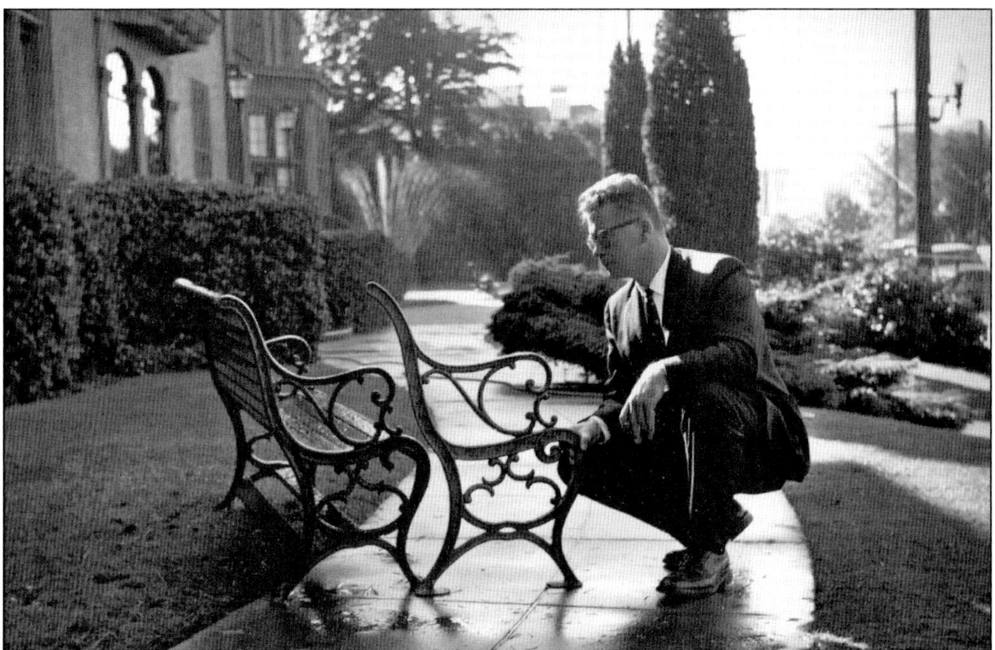

Karl Kortum compares the cast replica in his right hand to an original bench, destined for Victorian Park.

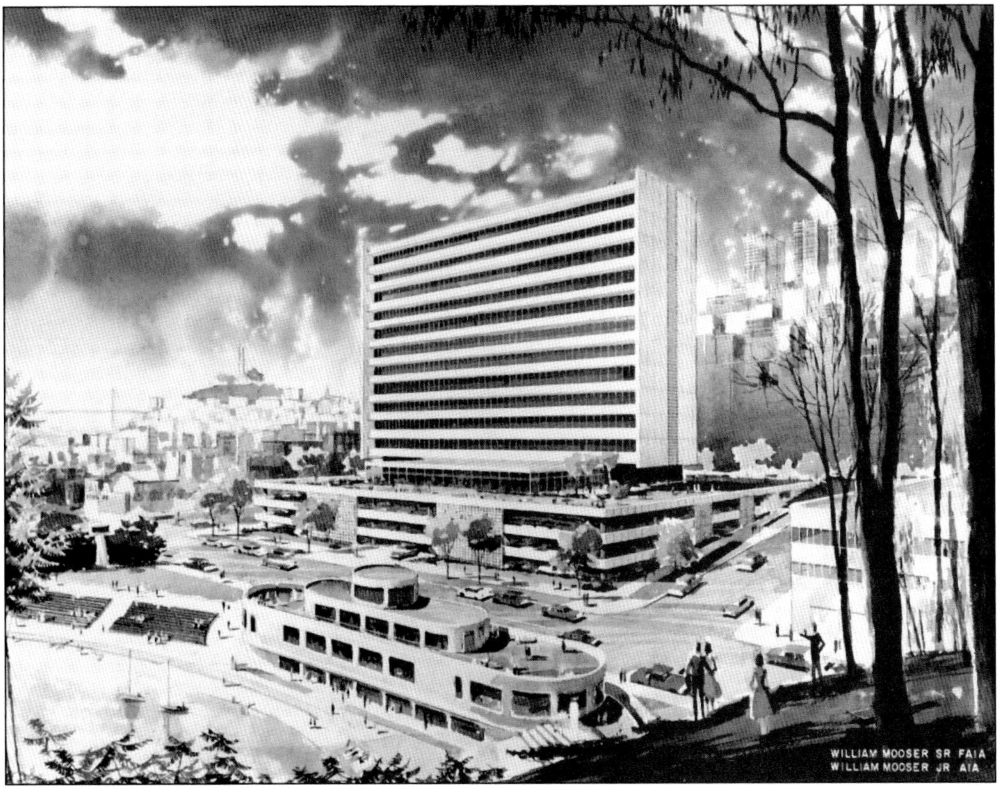

The Fontana Apartments, shown here in an architectural drawing by the Mooser firm, not only meant the destruction of the significant Fontana Warehouse, but also cut off views of the bay and Aquatic Park and ruined the architectural personality of the entire area.

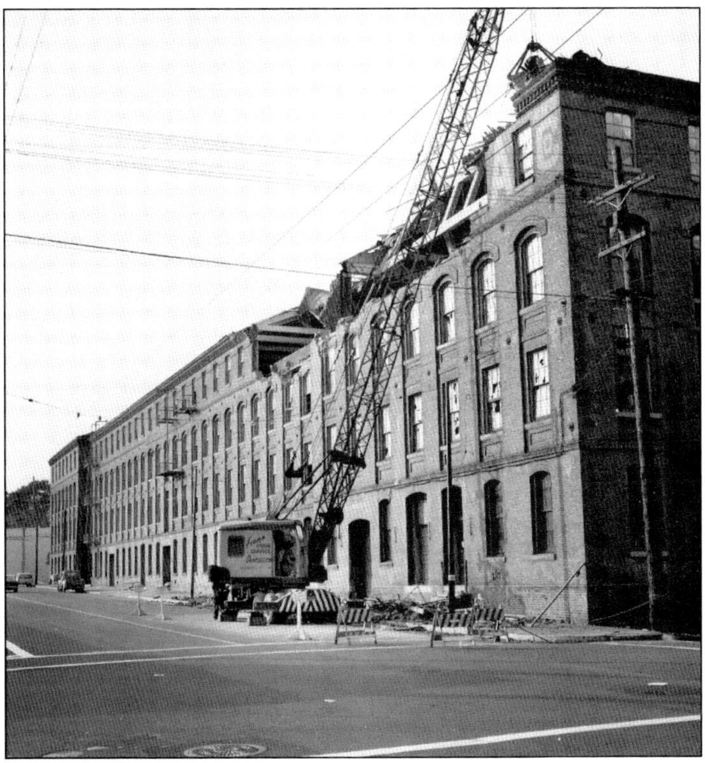

The Fontana Warehouse comes down.

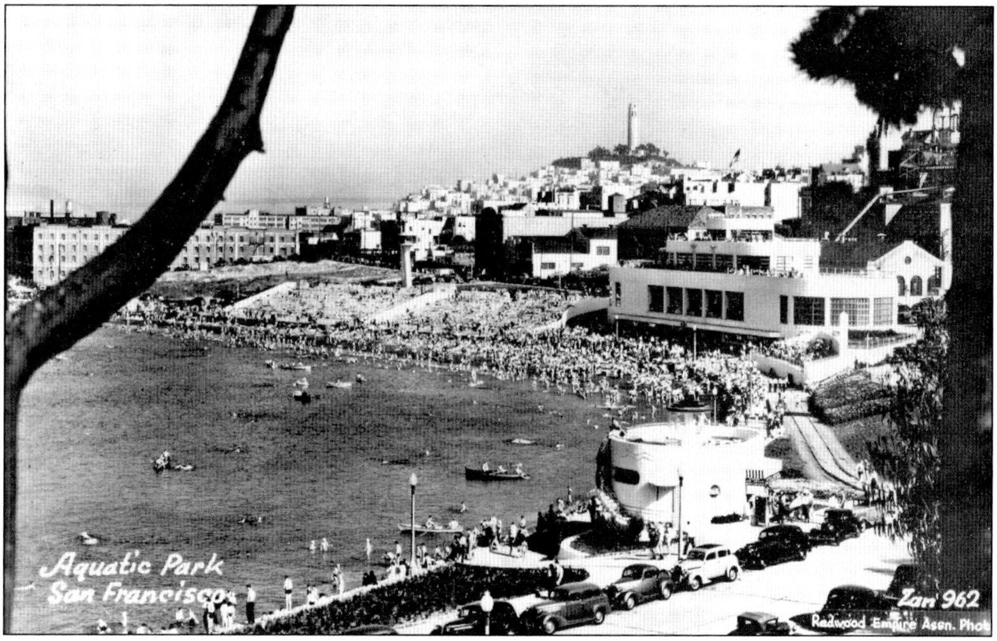

A celebratory day is seen shortly after the park opened.

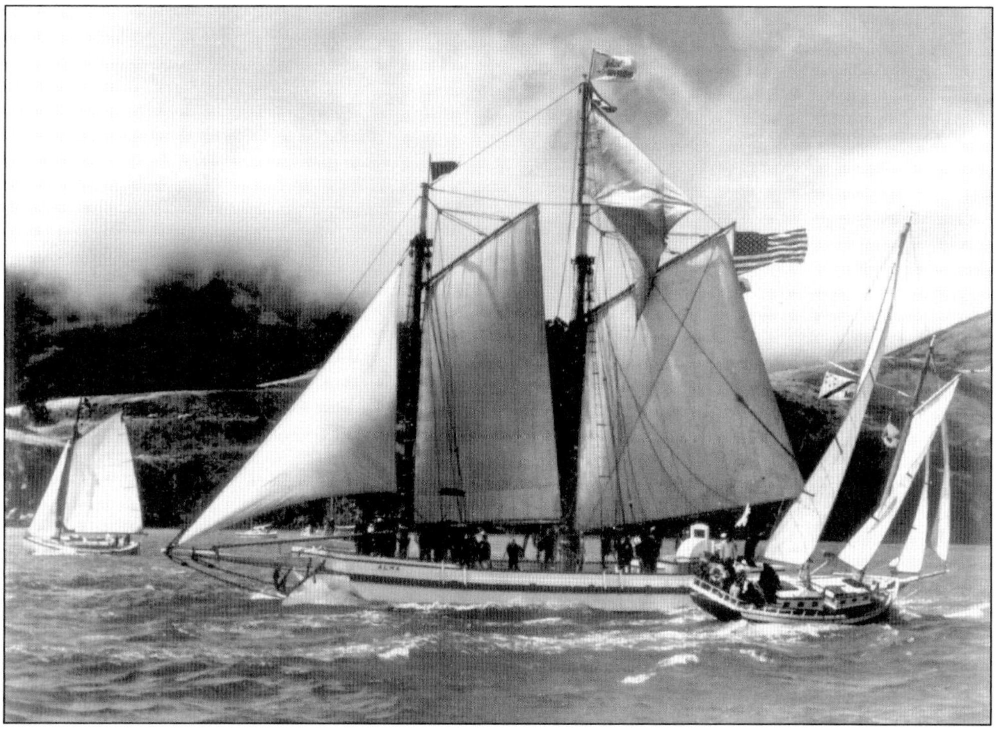
The *Alma* in full sail looks much better than she did in her days as a work boat.

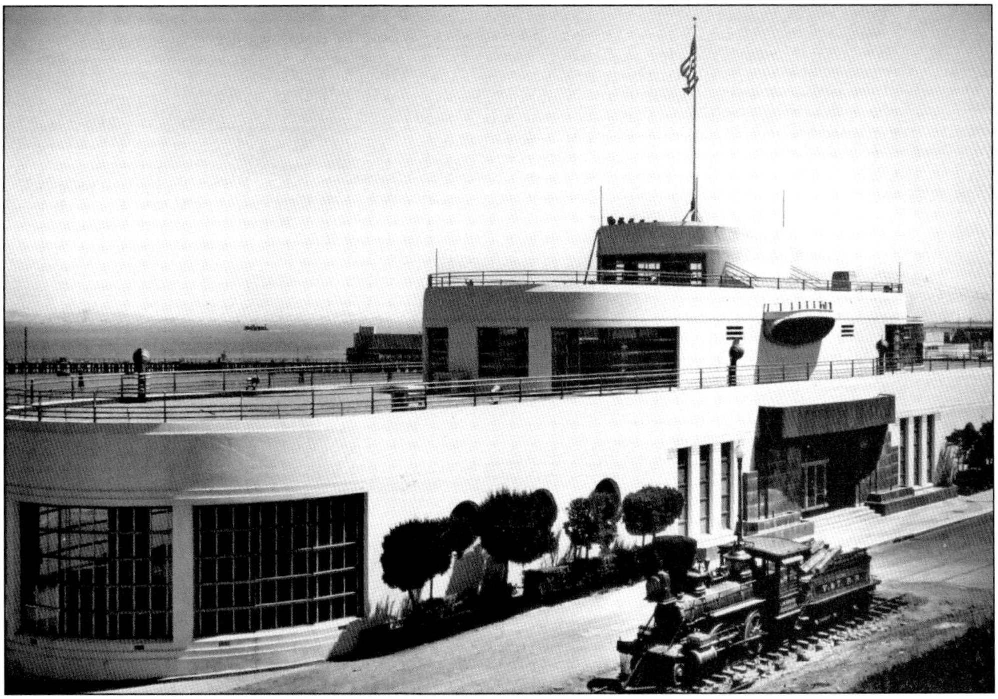

The Maritime Museum Building is pictured about 1964. The locomotive was there to promote a railroad museum, eventually established in Sacramento.

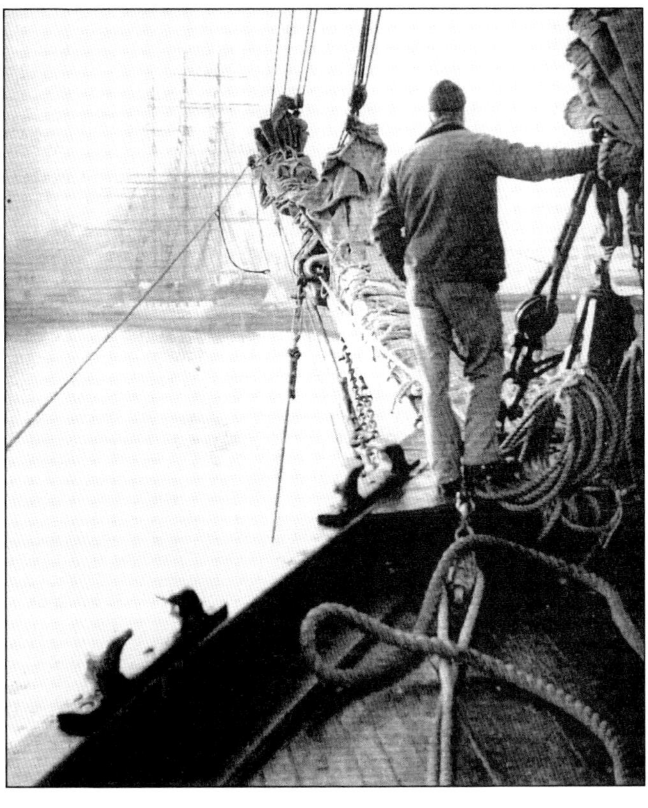

The *Thayer* heads in to the Hyde Street Pier.

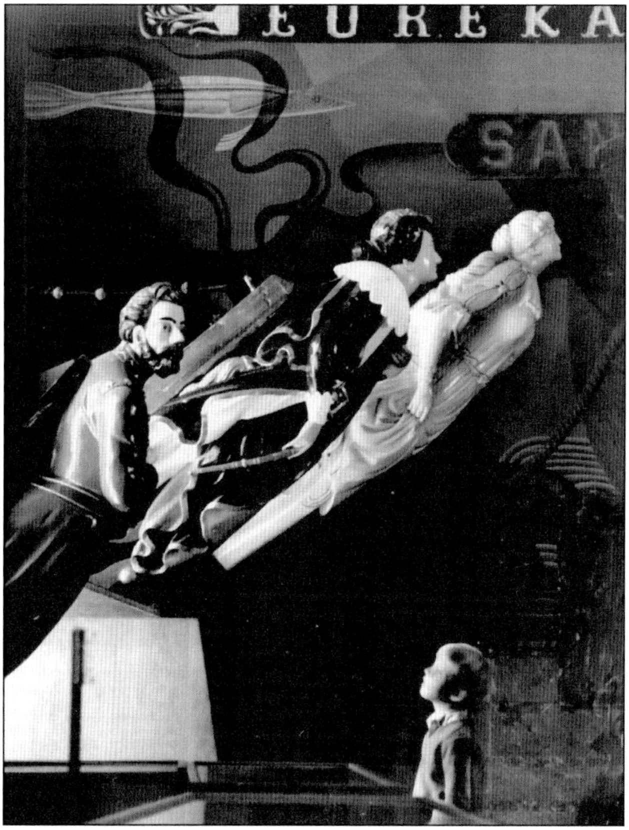

These ships' figureheads captured the imagination of a young visitor to the Maritime Museum.

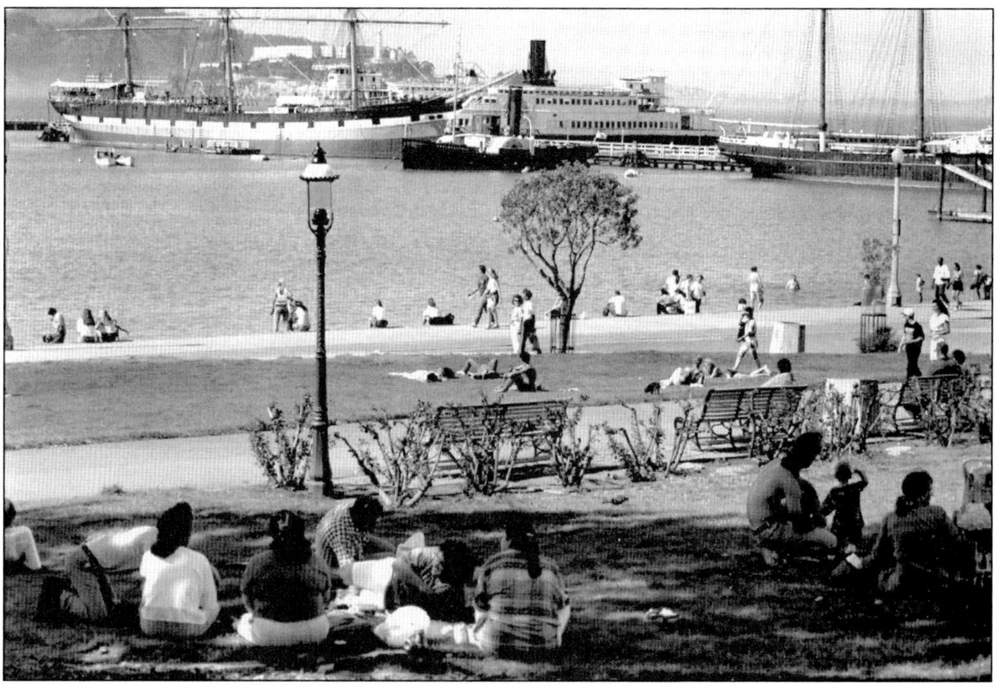

In the 1970s, folks enjoy a lazy day at San Francisco's Aquatic Park.

Seven

The Rowing Clubs

Only two years after the Maritime Museum was created, a big spat broke out between it and the rowing clubs and lasted until the end of the 1950s. Barney Gould, an associate of Karl Kortum, brought the old riverboat hulk *Fort Sutter* into Aquatic Park and ran it aground right next to the clubs. The boat rotted for six years, until torched, allegedly by four South End Rowing Club members.

The clubs continued their traditions of Golden Gate swims—with the addition of an Alcatraz swim after the federal prison on the island closed, played handball, and occasionally rowed. They remained classic examples of the Italian and Irish men's clubs, heavily populated with firemen and policemen. Much to the consternation of their neighbors, they enjoyed a "Garden of Eden," where older men sunbathed nude, which did not always ingratiate them with their neighbors.

The century-old, white male exclusivity was shattered in the mid-1970s when a group of women sued and won the right of admission to the clubs. The San Francisco Rowing Club, which had been known as the Ariel Club, refused to go along, but soon discovered they had made a grave mistake when their boathouse was locked forever. Women are now fully integrated into the two remaining clubs, and many are now life-members (25 or more years membership).

Both the clubs and the Hyde Street Pier Small Boatshop preserve the heritage of small rowboats of San Francisco Bay. Each has its own example, some of which are more than 100 years old. New boats are added to the fleets too, which helps to keep alive the knowledge base of small boat building.

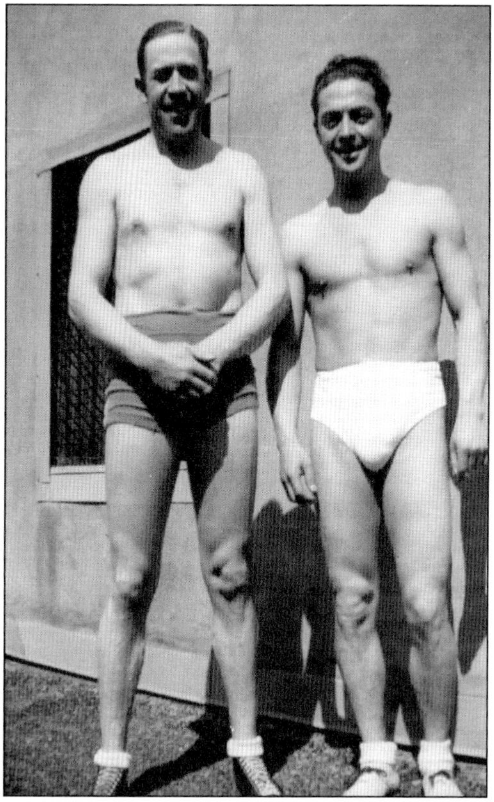

Jack Kent (left) is pictured here with handball great Al Banuet. Kent was a career engineer. He joined South End in the 1920s, was a premier boxing promoter in the 1930s, and ran clubs in the Tenderloin District before it became a seedy area. He was still going strong at 102 years of age.

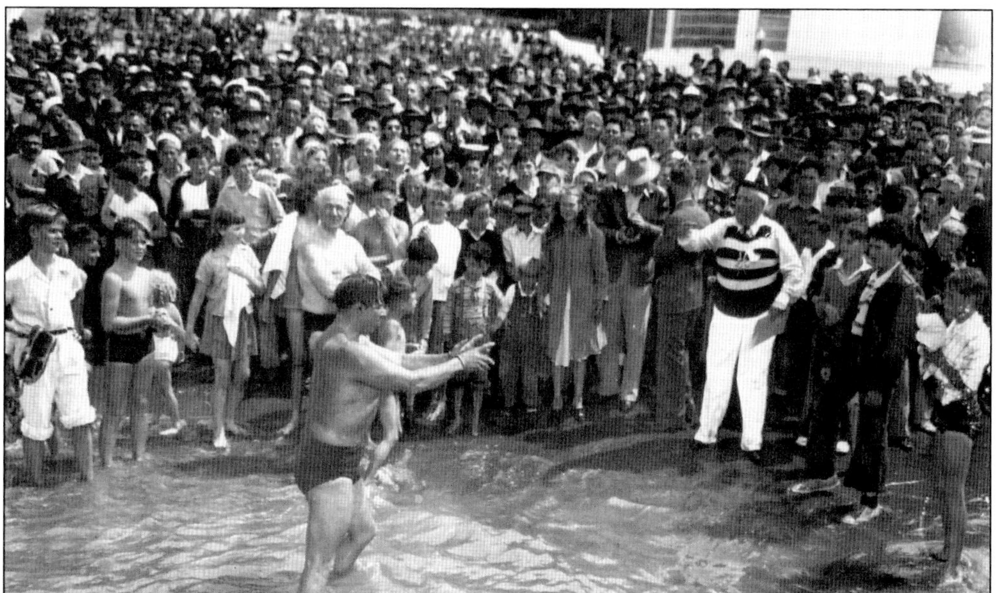

Crowds gather to watch a great stunt—swimming while hands are handcuffed together. Stunts always drew a crowd: Jack La Lanne and Tom Rice towed huge ships with their teeth. The secret was they had the tide at their back.

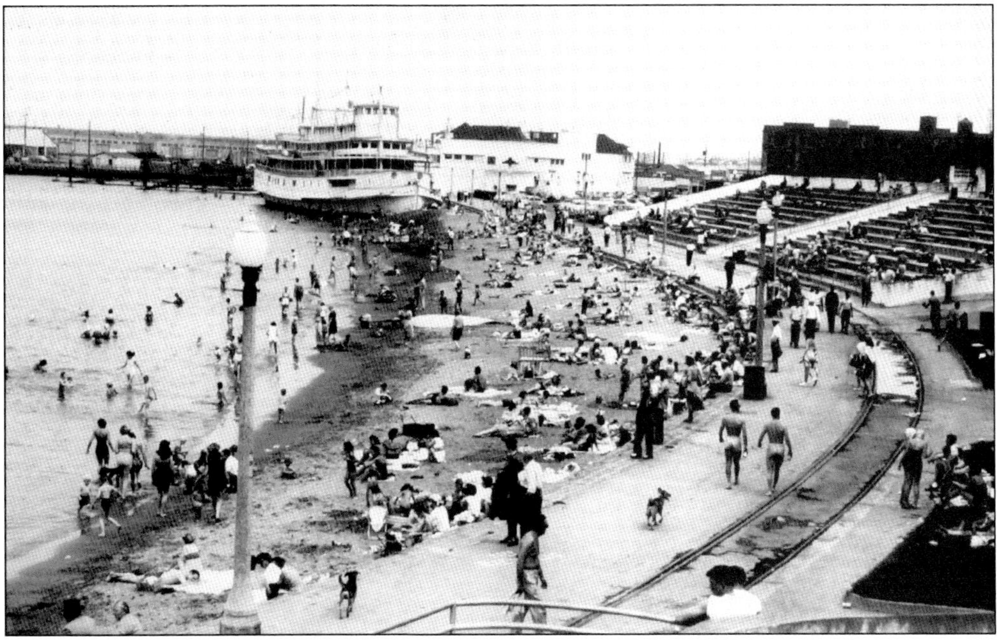

The *Fort Sutter* towered over the rowing clubs and rivaled the Haslett Warehouse in height. It was not in good condition, and the clubs had not been consulted about the boat being "docked" in the park. They were furious.

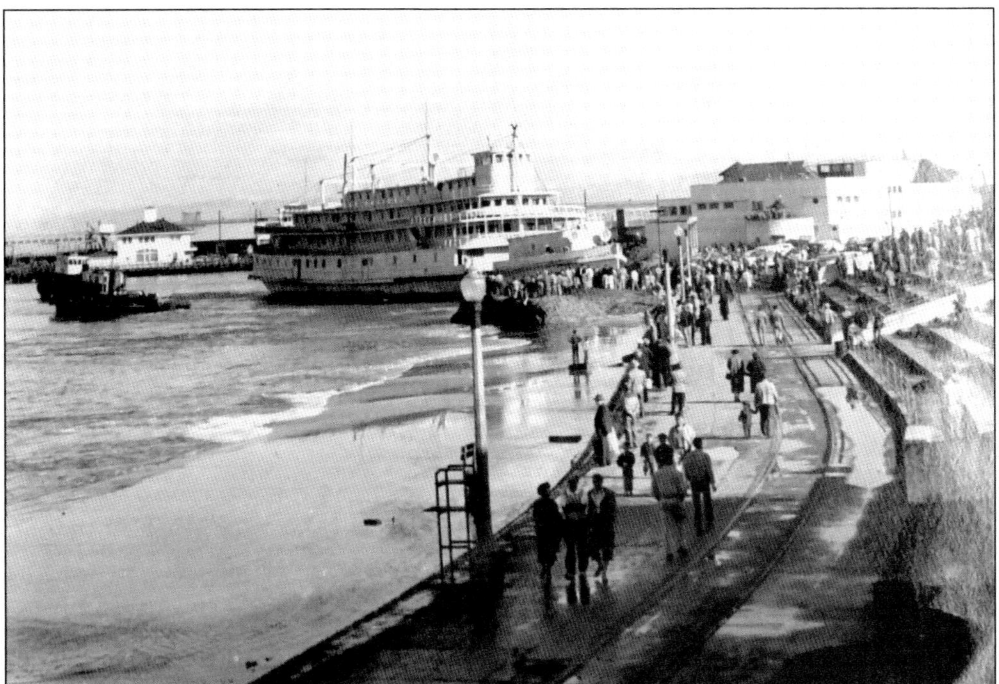

Later in 1953, Gould was ordered to remove the *Fort Sutter* from the park. The tugs badly wrenched the stern, however, and an emergency landing was made at the opposite end of the park.

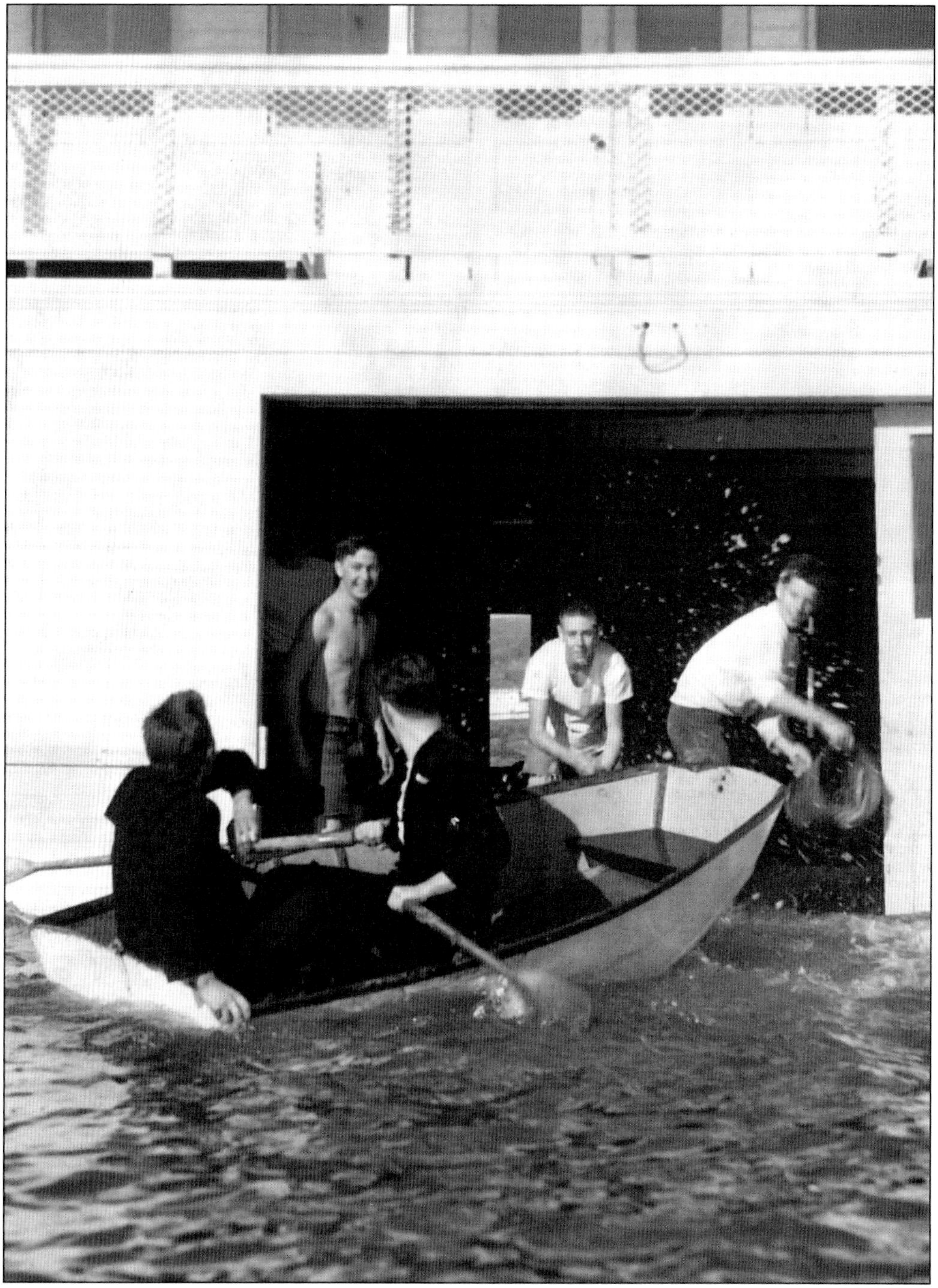

The *Fort Sutter* sat for six years at the west end of Aquatic Park. The condition of the boat grew worse and worse. The necessary financing to restore the formerly opulent riverboat to its old glory could not be arranged, and the future did not look good. The hulk just sat there. Here five young men row a dingy up to an entrance of the boat and throw water on each other.

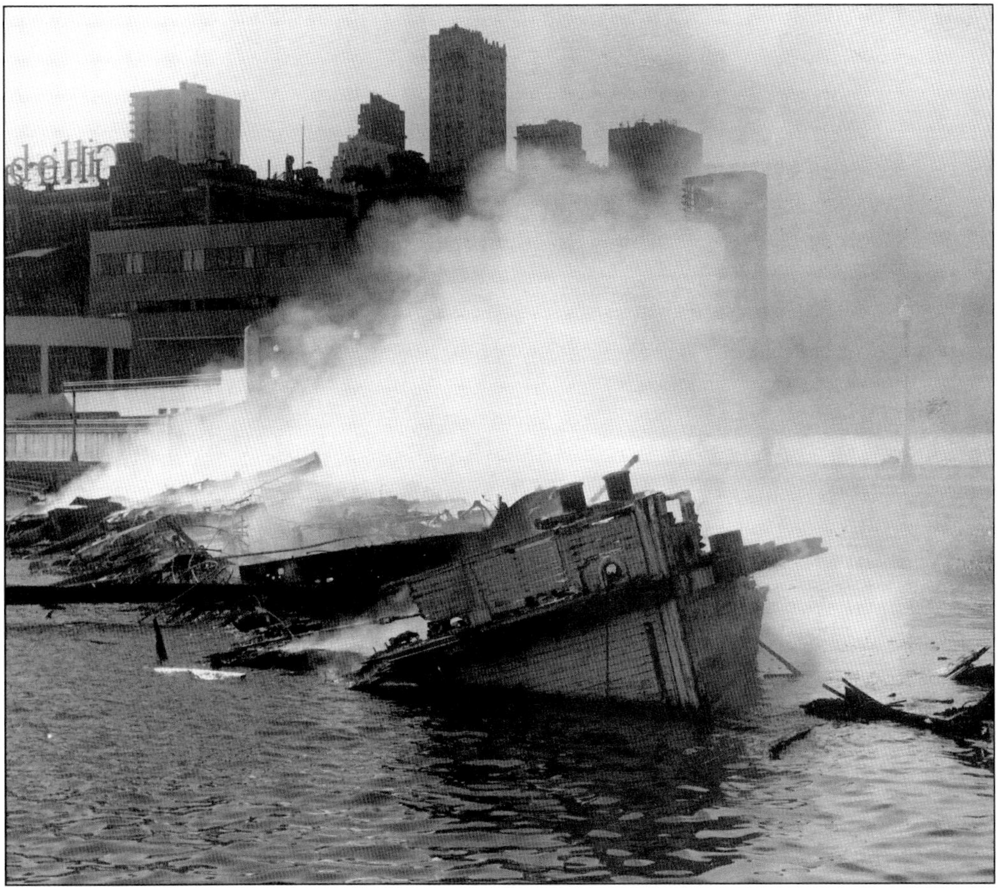

The end of the *Fort Sutter* was far from glorious. It had occupied more than its share of the park for six years, yet the city would not take action. Rats were said to find the rotting wood a welcome shelter. On May 9, 1959, four men raced up the gangway of the *Fort Sutter* with a can of gasoline, dosed the deck, and set a match to it before the two watchmen on board could stop them. In moments, the 240-foot sternwheeler was burning like a "Fourth of July bonfire." After firemen rescued the watchmen, the fire chief said, "Let her burn. We'll save money on it." The arsonists were never arrested and the *Fort Sutter* sat no more in Aquatic Park.

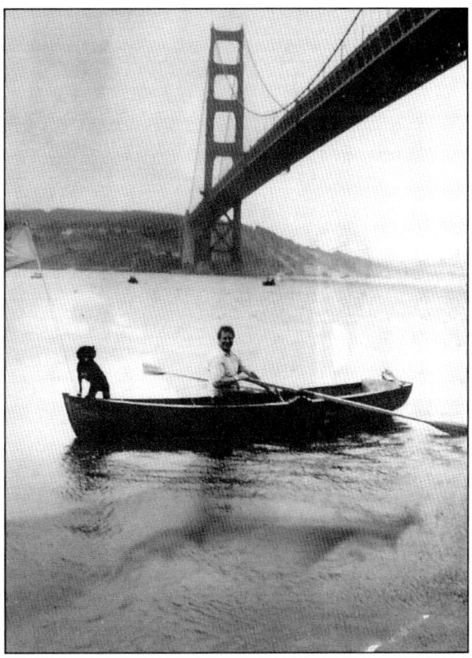

Around 1965, Norm Peterson poses with his dog Blackie at the Golden Gate Bridge. Peterson is still a very active South End member at age 80.

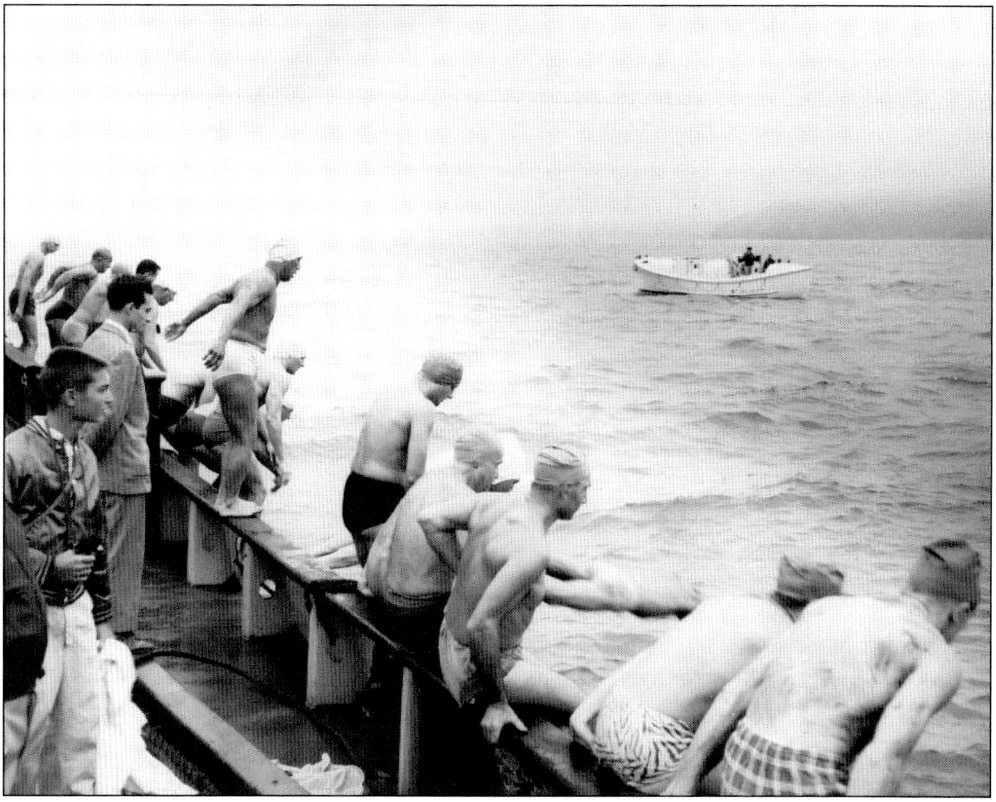

The moment of truth arrives as it is time to jump in San Francisco Bay to swim the Golden Gate. Not only is the water very chilly, but the tides can pose as much danger as the cold, even when they are carefully studied. Contrary to the old Alcatraz myth, sharks are not a problem in the bay, at least not man-eaters. Sand sharks are common, but not a risk.

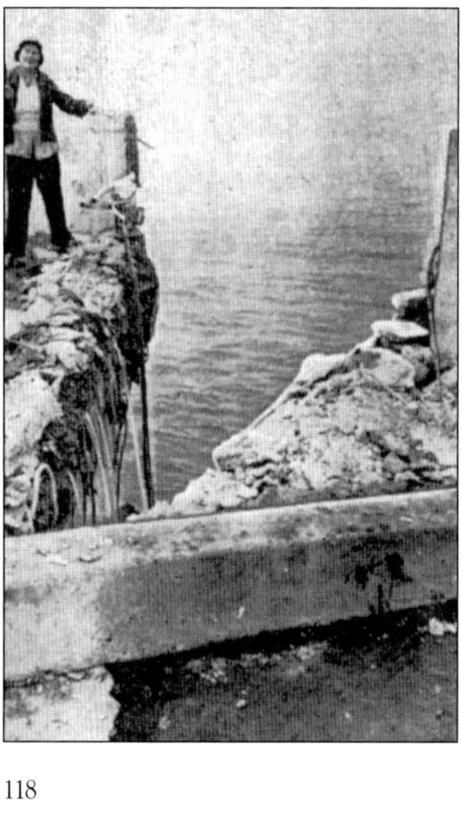

One evening in 1953, a very heavy fog shrouded San Francisco Bay. A ship crept along Muni Pier, hoping to find its way, and then boom! The ship slammed into Muni Pier, forcing the fishermen nearby to scramble for safety. This woman points out where she was when the freighter struck.

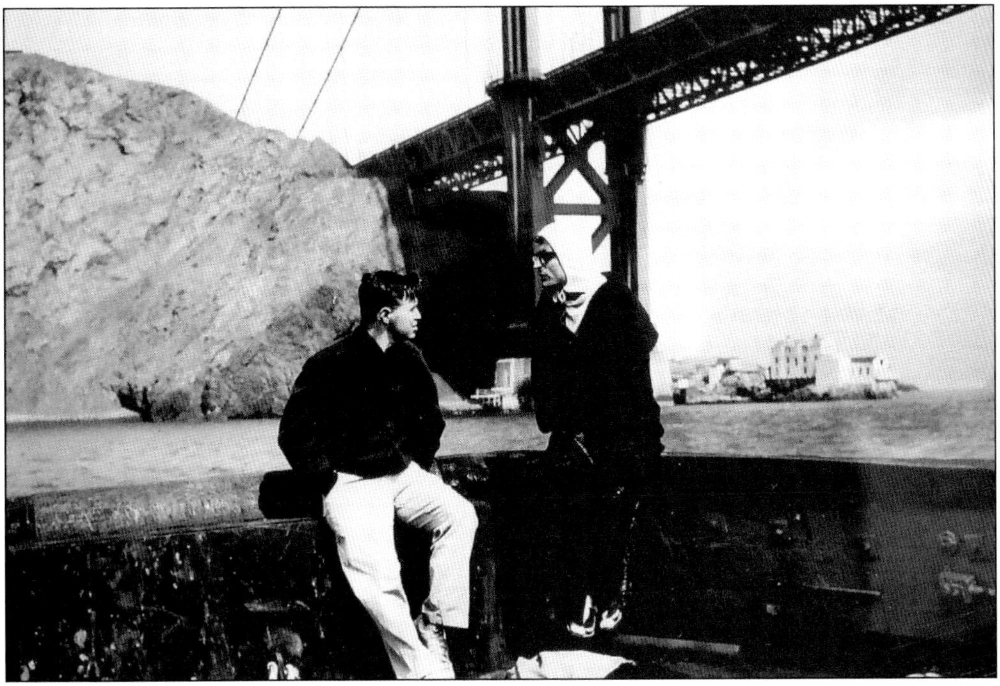

Bob Cunningham, left, and Joe Flahaven talk about strategy and the bay after Flahaven had just edged out Cunningham to win the 1962 Golden Gate swim. The boat the men are on is outside the gate, as the view is toward the rocky Marin Headlands, Lime Point, and the north tower of the Golden Gate.

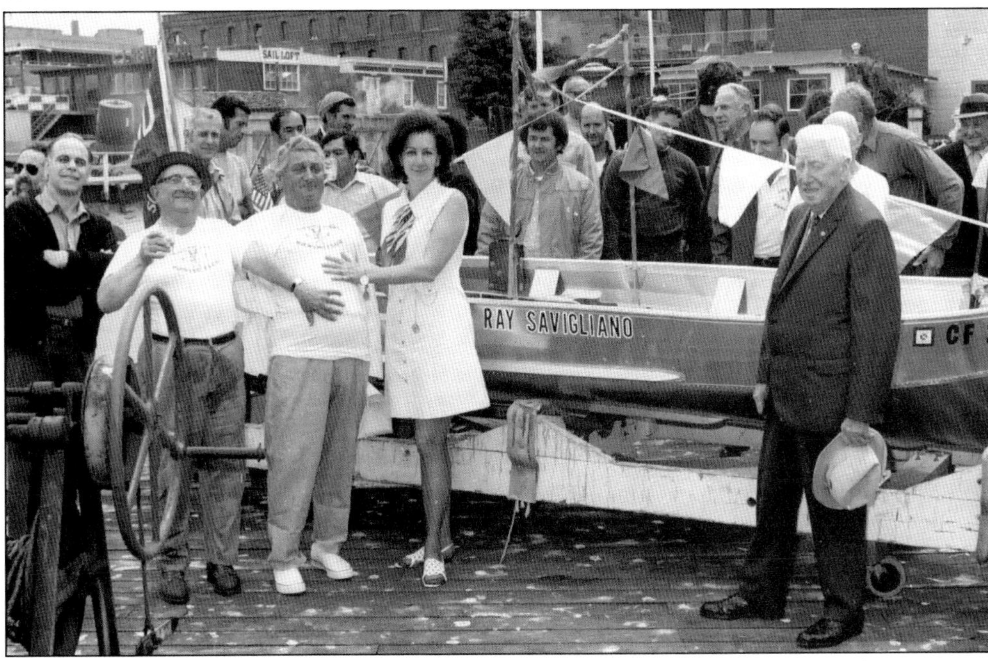

Ray Savigliano is pictured at the christening of a boat named for him. Ray was known as an eating and drinking machine, but he had loads of friends at the South End and did a good deal to preserve the club fleet of wooden boats over the years.

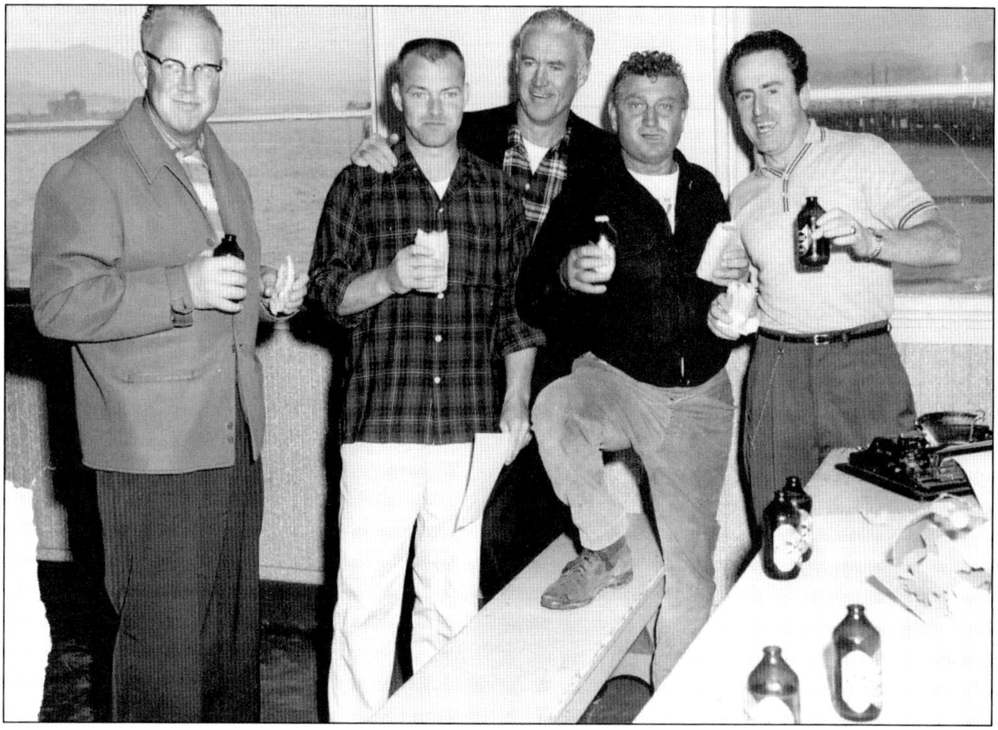

The most popular pastime at the clubs was drinking beer and talking. Pictured, from left to right, are Fred Herms, unidentified, Dan O'Neill, Ray Savigiliano, and George Farnsworth (also known as Furlong). For years, Farnsworth was the spiritual force of the South End.

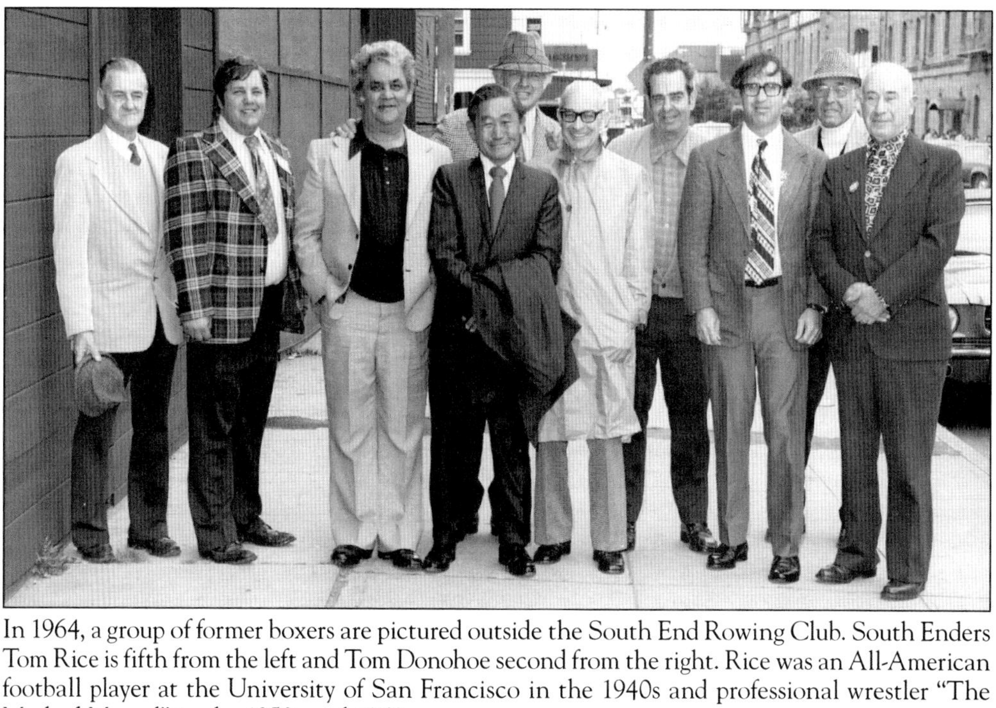

In 1964, a group of former boxers are pictured outside the South End Rowing Club. South Enders Tom Rice is fifth from the left and Tom Donohoe second from the right. Rice was an All-American football player at the University of San Francisco in the 1940s and professional wrestler "The Masked Marvel" in the 1950s and 1960s.

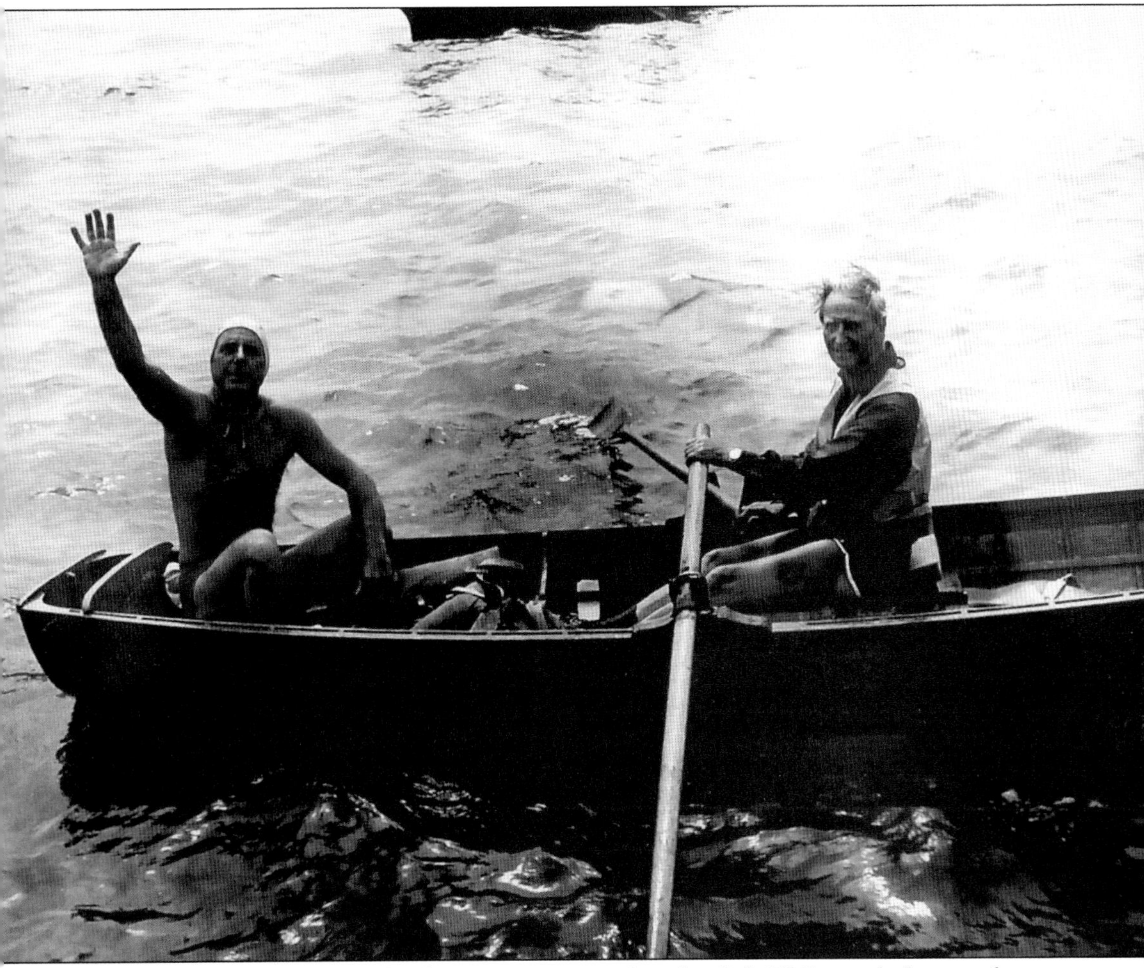

South Enders John Lynch and Sal Reina are pictured in the *Col. Ed Penaat* before or after an early 1970s swim of the gate. Lynch was a longtime policeman, and Reina ran the Venice Drug Store for decades. Sal continued to row even after his 90th birthday. The pulling boat *Sal Reina* was named in his honor.

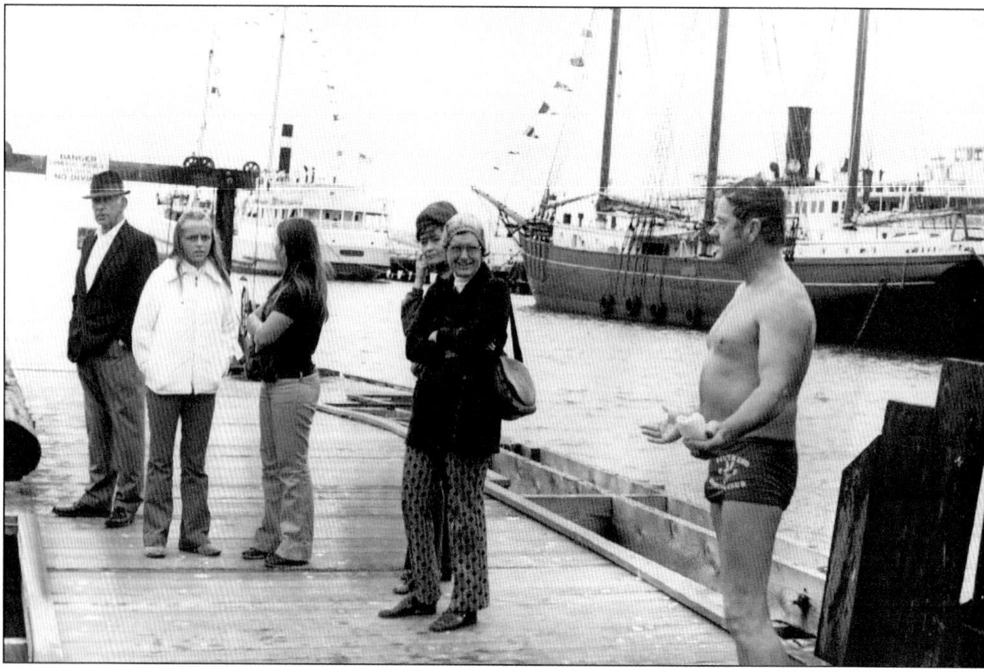

South Ender Norm Peterson, pictured at right, explains how he almost won the swim in 1973. Norm is still active at 80 years of age—he swims Alcatraz and rows in regattas around the Bay Area.

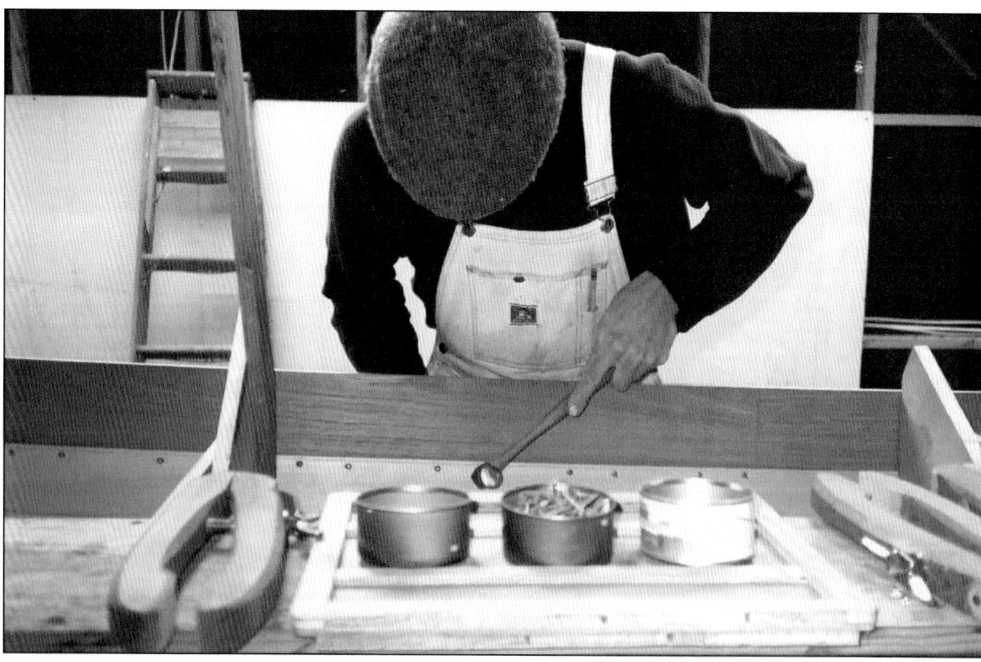

Jeremy Fisher-Smith hammers a rivet into place on the *Sal Reina*.

The author, left, is pictured with old-timer Leonard Riportella. Leonard was a great gentleman who knew how to have a good time. He loved to regale listeners with stories of old-time San Francisco. The author's personal favorites were tales of his adventures when the Tenderloin District was a fun, safe place. Drinking and gambling would figure in the stories, but always in a fun-loving way.

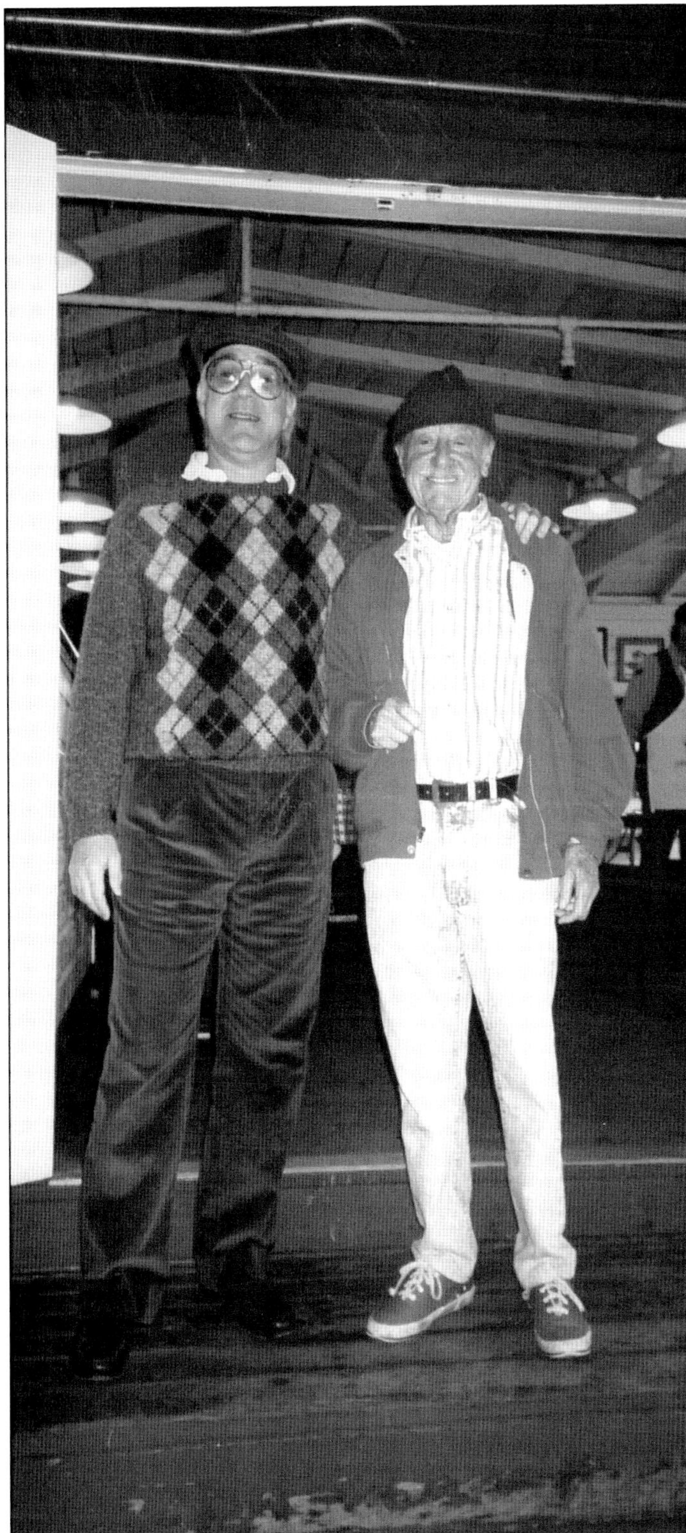

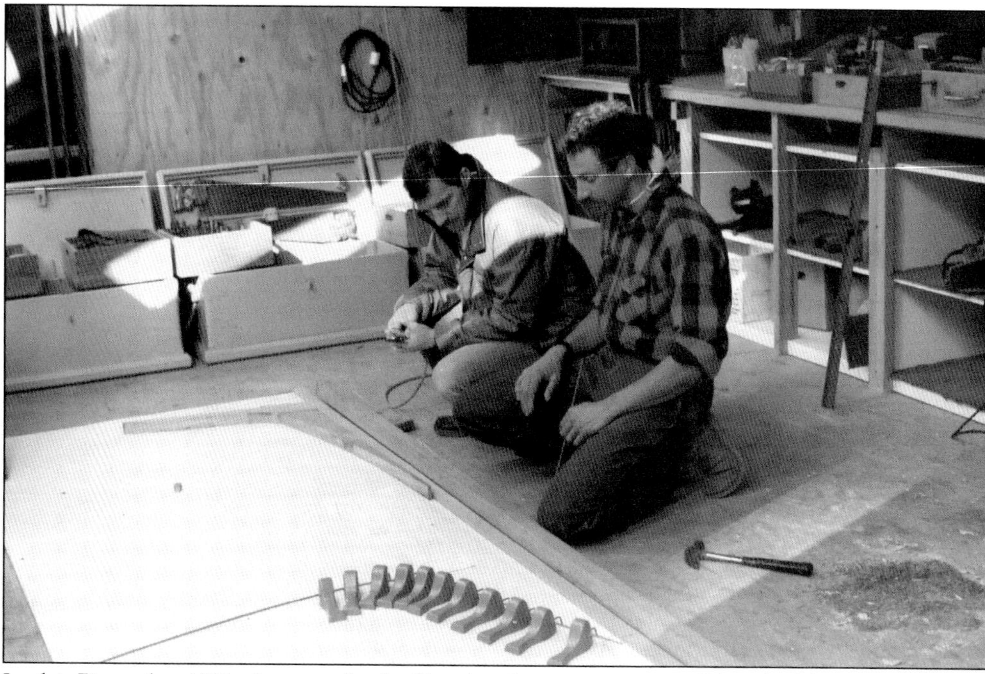

In this December 1991 photograph, the Bay Area's preeminent small boatbuilder, Jeremy Fisher-Smith (right), explains to South End rowing commissioner Tom Busby how to lay the lines for the new boat *Sal Reina* with splines.

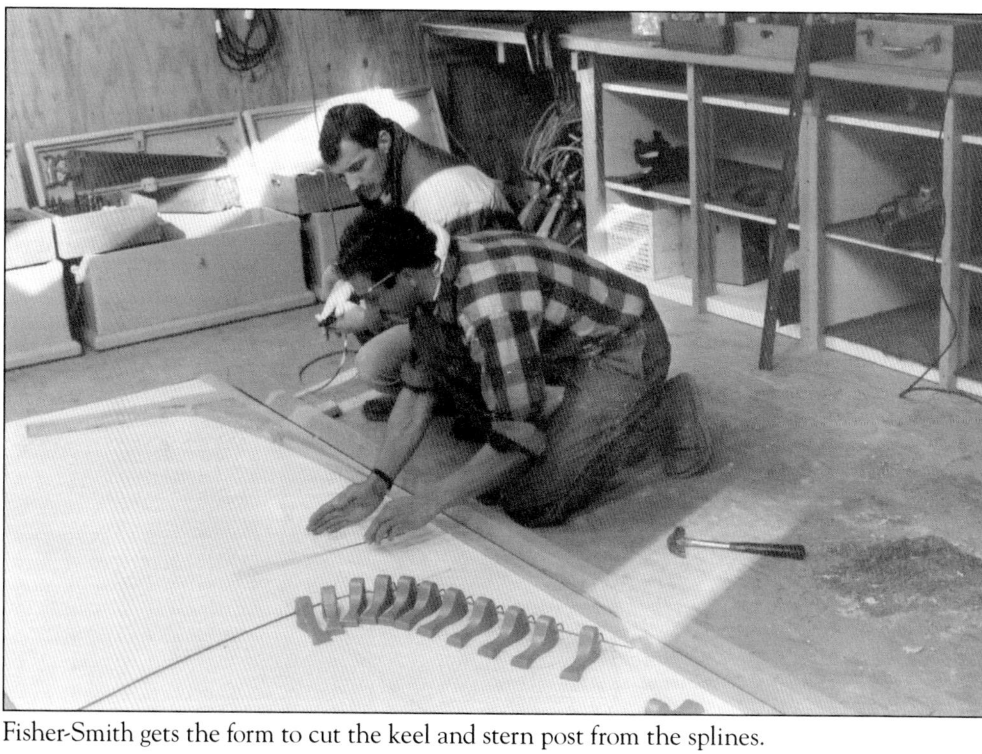

Fisher-Smith gets the form to cut the keel and stern post from the splines.

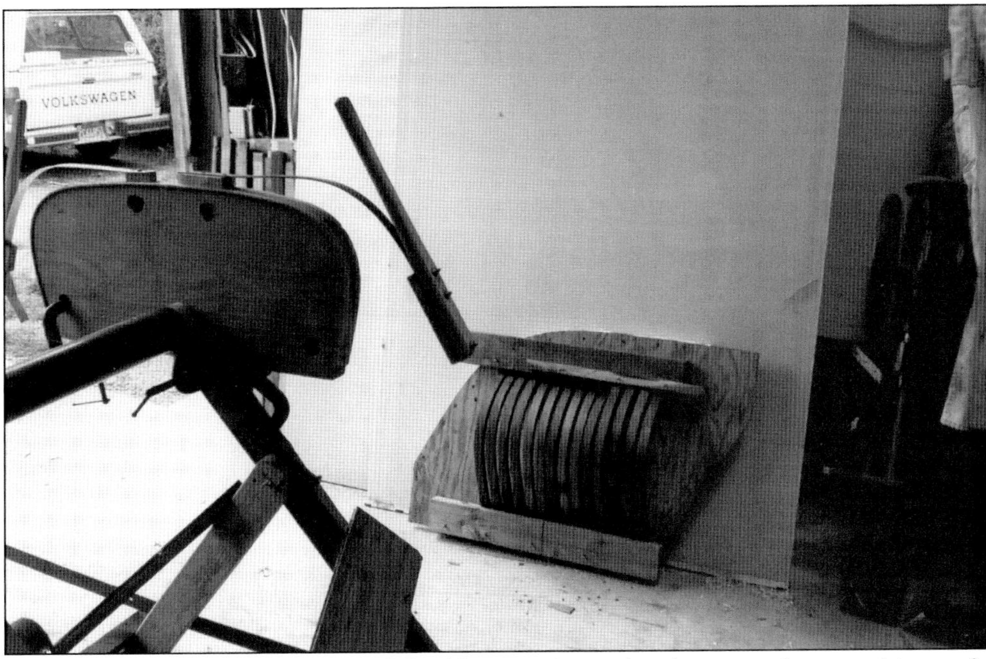

Wood is steamed in a steam box until flexible as spaghetti, then bent into shape, in this case for the ribs of the boat. Fourteen ribs are held in place on the boatshop floor.

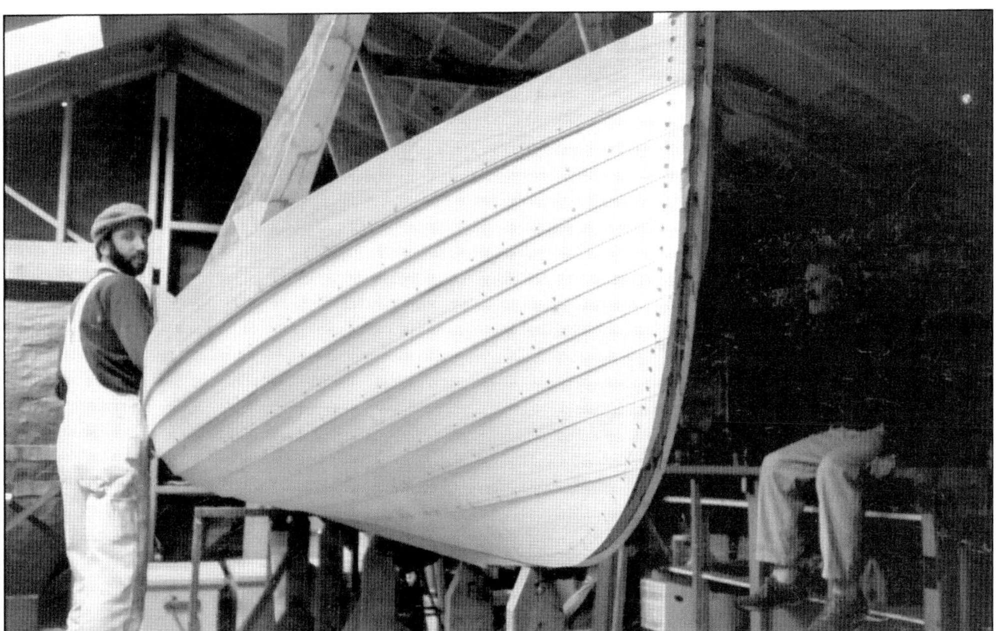
Five months later, the hull is nearly complete.

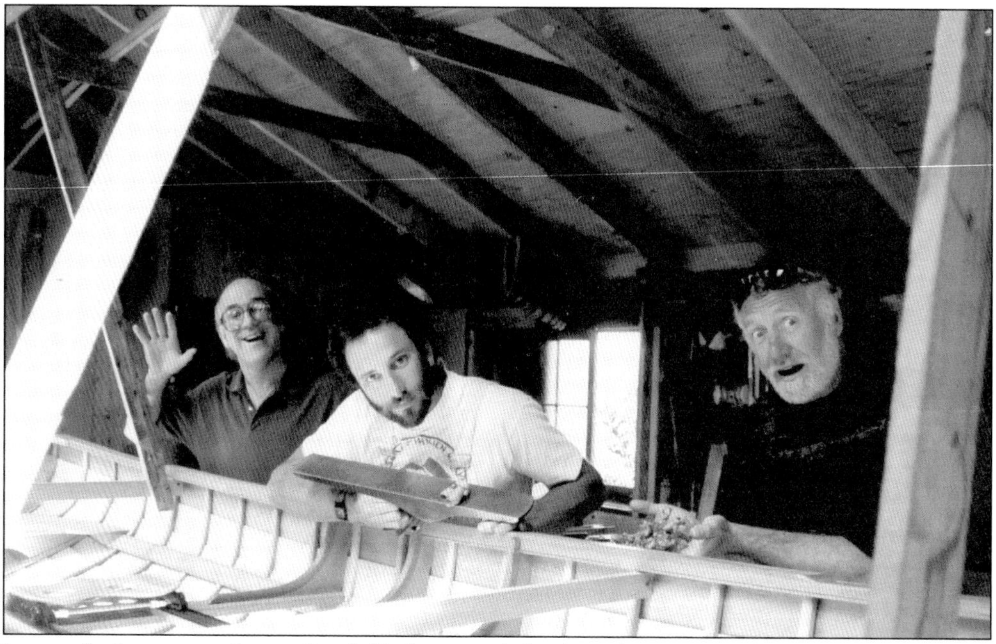

Jeremy finds progress slow as South Enders invade his boatshop. Pictured, from left to right, are Bill Pickelhaupt, Jeremy Fisher-Smith, and Dave Kennedy.

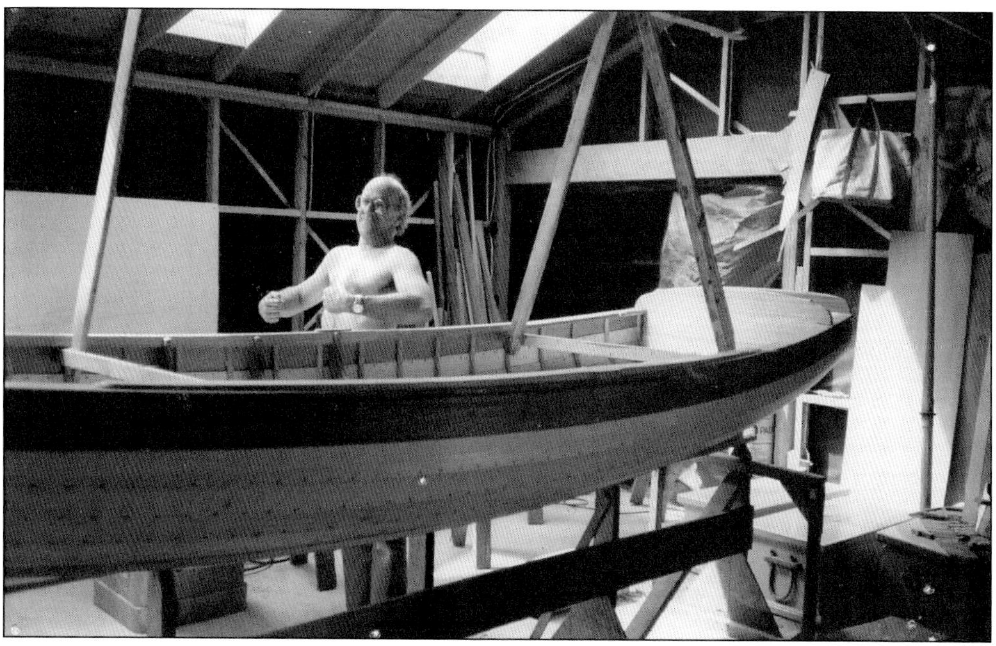

Pickelhaupt shows the proper technique to get the most out of a stroke.

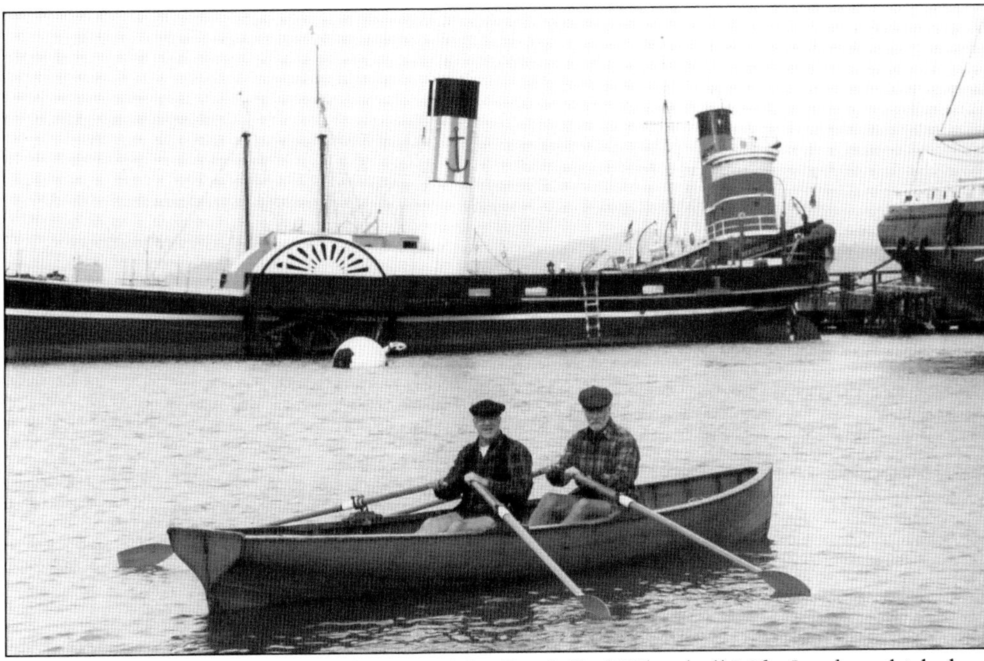

Pickelhaupt and Kennedy are at the oars of the South End Whitehall *Mike Lawley*, which dates from no later than 1923. The pair glides up to the *Thayer*, with the side-wheel tugboat *Eppleton Hall* and bow of the *Hercules* to the rear. Excellent coordination of effort is the most important basic skill for good oarsmanship in any rowing boat with more than one person. The Whitehall will travel swiftly, is rugged enough to handle most San Francisco Bay storms, and is very stable—the necessary characteristics for any good port craft.

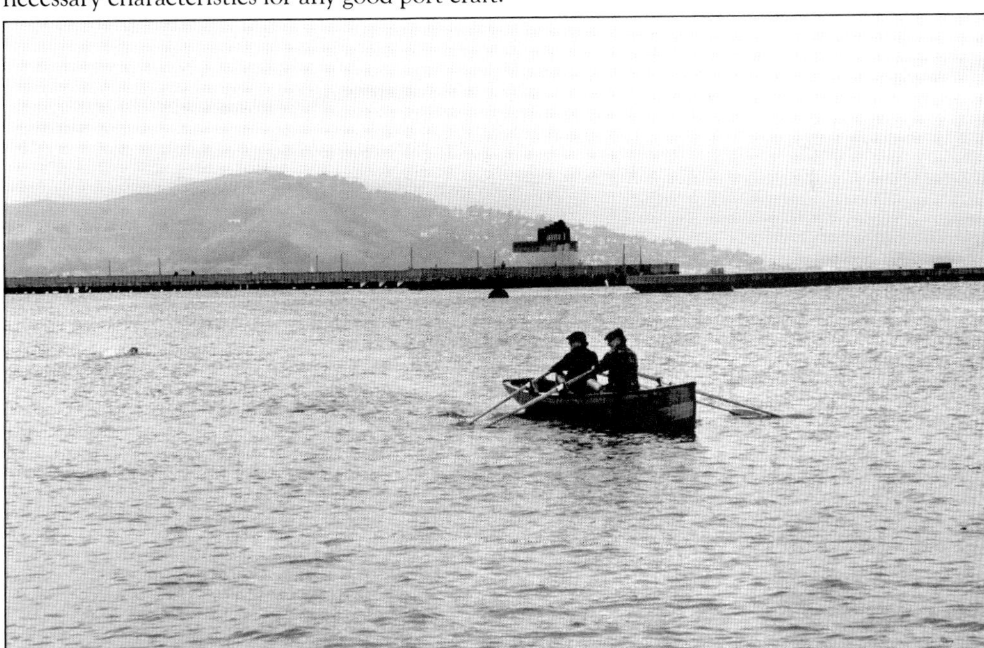

This is a typical view of Aquatic Park from a rower's perspective. Rowers must always be careful of swimmers in the cove. Note the half-visible head in the left part of the picture.

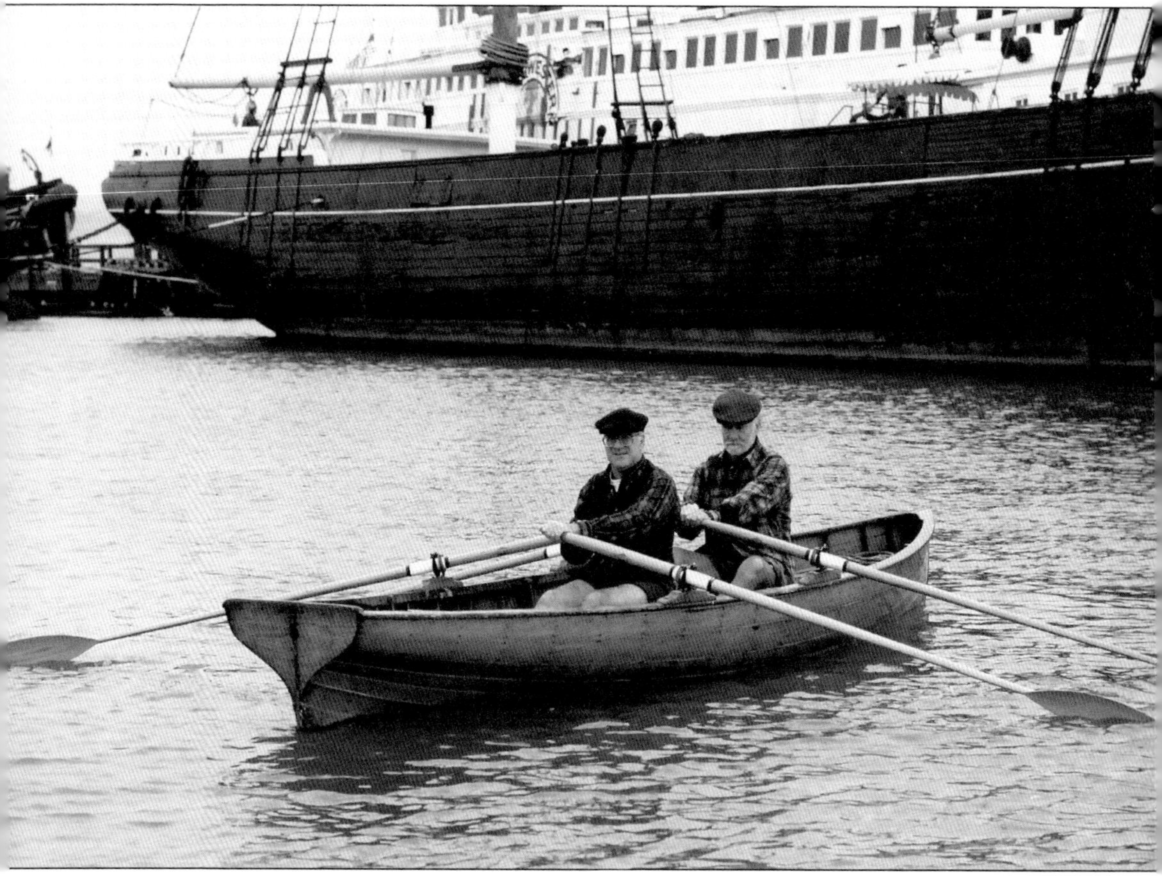

It's time to bring the *Mike Lawley* ashore, rinse her down, and stow the oars for another day.